KEYSTONE CORRUPTION CONTINUES

CASH PAYOFFS, PORNGATE AND THE KATHLEEN KANE SCANDAL

BRAD BUMSTED

AUTHOR OF *KEYSTONE CORRUPTION*

Mechanicsburg, Pennsylvania USA

Published by Sunbury Press, Inc.
105 South Market Street
Mechanicsburg, Pennsylvania 17055

www.sunburypress.com

For information about special discounts for bulk purchases, please contact Sunbury Press Orders Dept. at (855) 338-8359 or orders@sunburypress.com.

To request one of our authors for speaking engagements or book signings, please contact Sunbury Press Publicity Dept. at publicity@sunburypress.com.

ISBN: 978-1-62006-693-5 (Trade Paperback)
ISBN: 978-1-62006-694-2 (Mobipocket)

Library of Congress Control Number: 2015958506

FIRST SUNBURY PRESS EDITION: August 2016

Product of the United States of America
0 1 1 2 3 5 8 13 21 34 55

Set in Bookman Old Style
Designed by Crystal Devine
Cover by Amber Rendon
Edited by Jennifer Cappello

Continue the Enlightenment!

Dedicated to the professional prosecutors and agents of the attorney general's office, past and present.

CONTENTS

FOREWORD

Journalism is at its best when it's expository, thorough and fully in context.

Brad Bumsted offered a sample of that in his 2013 book, *Keystone Corruption*, a history of the shortcomings, failures and crimes of Pennsylvania's public servants.

It covers everything from construction of the Capitol in Harrisburg in the very early 1900s (and the criminal convictions of those who jacked up its costs for personal gain) to the jailing of modern-day legislative leaders who used their offices for political gain.

When I reviewed the book in a Philadelphia Daily News column, I noted if I was in charge there'd be a copy on the desk of each state lawmaker on opening day of every new session.

Why?

To remind them of the state's history in hopes they might want to change it.

Brad and I have written about Pennsylvania politics and America's largest "full-time" legislature for decades; the penchant for corruption is a constant.

This sequel, *Keystone Corruption Continues: Cash Payoffs, Porngate and the Downfall of Kathleen Kane*, updating his 2013 book proves that.

And it's a good thing he's still at it, however depressing that might be for taxpayers and anyone interested in public service in the Keystone State.

For maybe the telling, retelling, expanding and updating of all that's wrong in Pennsylvania can finally force someone with political power to say, "You know what? Enough is enough."

Maybe one legislative leader one day soon will take to the House or Senate floor, or some other public forum, and call for multiple, sustained efforts to bring confidence and respect to the institution of the legislature.

He or she, I don't care of what party, can start with an apology: for the stolen and wasted millions of dollars; for the violations of public trust; for creating a culture that's made our state one of the nation's most corrupt.

Then he or she can outline measures to make our politics more about serving the public and less about self-serving politicians.

Like what? How about redistricting reforms to allow actual rather than just partisan representation? Or campaign-finance reforms to level political playing fields. Or voting reforms to encourage rather than discourage public participation.

Citizens deserve leadership that's willing to trust the democratic process rather than cling to a gerrymandered, jury-rigged system built to protect incumbents.

Journalism, as practiced by Bumsted, can help. It holds up a mirror to our state. It reminds us that ongoing failure to enact reforms means continuation of what's gone before.

There's value in knowing our history. There's value in knowing, when it comes to corruption, our history is largely static. But a greater value rests in the possibility that telling, retelling and updating that history can lead to actual change.

That's the value of journalism offered by Bumsted herein.

—**John Baer,** columnist for the *Philadelphia Daily News*, and author of *On the Front Line of Pennsylvania Politics, Twenty-Five Years of Keystone Reporting*

January 2015

ACKNOWLEDGMENTS

Thanks to my wife Gail, and daughter Lindsey, for their continued support. Paula Knudsen Burke Esq. was a proficient copy editor with key changes in many chapters and great advice. Thanks also to others who edited chapters: Sandy Tolliver, former deputy managing editor of the Pittsburgh Tribune-Review, and my Trib colleague, Kari Andren.

Robert Gentzel, a former press secretary for four state agencies, did a masterful job of proofreading the manuscript. He pushed through and completed it in roughly one week. Gentzel was press secretary for the Attorney General's office, Auditor General's office, Treasurer's office and the State Employees Retirement System (SERS.)

Gentzel was dying at the time he helped me. He passed away in March 2016 about three weeks after sending me his edits. Because of his health, I had been concerned about asking him to do the entire book. I first asked him to edit a new chapter. He did it in a day. I then asked about the book. He did it in a week. He found several errors and typos. His family members told me at his memorial service that editing gave him something he truly loved to do. He loved words, writing and reading. He was an excellent editor. He'll be missed, not only by his family, but by his friends and former colleagues at the state Capitol. I didn't know until reading his obituary that he had a journalism degree from Penn State and spent the early part of his career as a reporter for the Harrisburg Patriot-News. I did know firsthand he ran the best press operations on Capitol Hill when he was press secretary for Attorneys General LeRoy Zimmerman and Ernie Preate.

Special thanks to Frank Craig, Tribune-Review editor, who gave permission to use words and photos from Trib stories.

All opinions and mistakes herein are mine alone.

INTRODUCTION

It was 5:58 a.m. The text message cut through the quiet with a staccato de-di-Ding, de-di-Ding. A rapid cadence. It's normally a light, sort of pleasing sound, but this morning it sounded like a jackhammer on Angela Couloumbis' iPhone. She didn't know it immediately but she had a bad case of food poisoning. She just knew she felt like hell. She and Craig McCoy, both Philadelphia Inquirer reporters, had shut down a bar at 2 a.m. where she consumed a considerable amount of fried food and some beers. The text message less than four hours later popped up on her iPhone in her room in the Marriott, Philadelphia.

The sender seemed as angry as the text message's sound. It was Adrian King, first deputy for Attorney General Kathleen Kane.

Intending to stay no more than a year with Kane, King left a position at Philly's prestigious Ballard Spahr law firm to head Kane's staff when she first took office in 2013. King was texting Couloumbis on March 16, 2014—already three months past his planned departure date. The lawyer knew his way around Harrisburg. He had been a deputy chief of staff and Cabinet member under former Democratic Gov. Ed Rendell, the former Philadelphia mayor once called "America's Mayor" by Al Gore. King was a top-notch staffer and attorney. Kane was a political novice whose highest position in public office had been assistant district attorney in Lackawanna County. She was lucky that King, her former Temple Law School friend whom she had dated as a student, had agreed to help her. She needed his advice but soon would ignore it.

Kane was swept into office in November, 2012 defeating Cumberland County District Attorney David Freed, the favorite of Republican Gov. Tom Corbett, the former attorney general. She was well financed with a $2 million campaign fund established in large part by her then-husband, Chris, whose family owned a successful trucking company, Kane is Able. Corbett, unpopular with voters two years after his election, indirectly was the target of Kane's campaign more than Freed. Kane became the first woman and first Democrat elected attorney general.

By almost all accounts, Kane had a very positive year in 2013. By the end of that first year, she was being talked about for U.S. Senate and perhaps governor. And on the heels of the 2012 campaign, she believed her own press clippings (even though she claimed she never read stories about herself.) A top adviser told her she was spoiled by the fawning media coverage and it would end, perhaps rudely. She didn't hear it or didn't believe it. She asked the adviser: what he was talking about? It was almost beyond her comprehension that her glowing press coverage would end. She just didn't get it.

Kane would crash faster and harder than any public official in recent history.

* * *

Couloumbis' rude awakening occurred after the Inquirer story hit the streets on Kane declining to prosecute four legislators taking cash payments and an ex-traffic court judge accepting a $2,000 Tiffany bracelet, events videotaped by an undercover informant posing as a lobbyist. The undercover operative for OAG was Tyron Ali, a street wise and smooth talking man who poses as a lobbyist in meetings with state legislators. The piece hit like a category-five political hurricane. The long-term reverberations of the story would impact state politics for at least two years.

A cold front had moved into southeastern Pennsylvania. A winter storm warning was forecast for St. Patrick's Day morning, less than 24 hours away.

The frigid weather was appropriate for the sting story's immediate aftermath.

Couloumbis felt woozy. She told King in a text she needed coffee and that she'd get back to him. She found a Starbucks, but could barely hold down the coffee. King's primary gripe was about the font size used for the article. In truth, he felt the reporters made every effort to be fair. But at that time, he was Kane's lead guy on rebutting the Inquirer's story. As first deputy, King was part spin doctor, legal advisor, office manager for almost 800 people and uber-press spokesman on occasion. He was a bulldog for Kane on the sting story. It was impossible to imagine one day he would be an adversary, a witness against her in a grand jury.

But how do you argue with videotape that the Inquirer reporters either had reviewed or were told about in intimate detail?

"KANE SHUT DOWN STING THAT SNARED CITY POLS," the above-the-fold headline screamed on page one. King suggested to Couloumbis that the Inquirer went down to the newspaper's morgue to find the font used for the bombing of Pearl Harbor.

Couloumbis gave King the reporter's standard and truthful line to those who think headlines are over the top: those writing the story have no control over the content or size of a headline.

As headlines go, it was huge. As stories go, it was just as big.

The story was about Case File No. 36-622.

As J. Wesley Leckrone, a political science professor at Widener University would later say, the sting case was distinguishable from other rampant criminal cases involving Pennsylvania pols because it was "naked corruption"—cash payoffs for alleged promises of official action.

It was also an amazing piece of journalism because the Inquirer named the state legislators taking cash bribes, based on sources and the reporters' knowledge of the case file. Ballsy, I thought at the time. Couloumbis and McCoy, through very solid reporting and fair writing, had unleashed a political time bomb.

It was the beginning of the end for Kathleen Kane.

* * *

On the 16th floor of Strawberry Square, Kane and her top staff were in crisis mode through the weekend and on the night of March 16, 2014. When a newspaper breaks a story like this, there's not a lot you can do as a one-person bureau to come back. My only hope that Sunday night was to try to reach King on his cell phone and maybe speak to Kane. He answered after a few rings. I asked if Kane would be available. He told me to come to the office. I'd have to call from the outside door and he'd have to come down and let me in. Mark Scolforo of the Associated Press beat me there and had already cleared out to do a story.

An hour or so after of the call, I entered the bunker. King had stubble that looked like at least three days' growth. Mostly empty pizza boxes sat on file cabinets outside the conference room.

I entered the inner sanctum.

Kane's conference room offered a panoramic view of the Capitol complex. Wearing a sweater and jeans, she sat at the end of a conference table. She had make-up—lipstick, a compact, mascara—beside her on the table. One of her aides, Erik Anderson, would stay for the interview, I was told. Anderson was a staff lawyer and he sat to her right at the conference table with a legal pad. I was never bothered by a pol having someone sit in as a witness. I was taping anyway.

Oh wait, Kane was not a pol. She was a prosecutor, not a politician, as her campaign slogan from 2012 stated.

Kane seemed relaxed. She was above all confident. One thing I would learn about her over the next year is that outwardly she came off looking composed under pressure at least for the longest part of her ordeal. What happened behind the doors of the attorney general's office was a different story. She'd flip out, blame aides, and demand firings of employees she thought crossed her or did not serve her well, numerous insiders told me. She wasn't adverse to four-letter expletives to make a point, staffers said. She was extremely stubborn and would obsess over perceived slights. Her confidence—some even called it courage for taking on an office way above her political and governmental experience—would ultimately be viewed as arrogance.

The firing of a top deputy under a court's protective order in 2015 "shows utter arrogance and there's no other word for it—stupidity," said a June 2015 Philadelphia Magazine article.

Don't take this the wrong way. I genuinely liked Kathleen Kane at first and kept an open mind about her for a long time—well into 2015. She was different and promised a new approach to an office held by Republicans since it was established as an "independent" row office in 1980, separate from the governor's office. Kane, a Democrat, was also the first woman elected as attorney general.

Kane and Eugene DePasquale, a York Democrat as auditor general, promised to be the only public officials who potentially might hold accountable a Republican-controlled legislature and GOP Gov. Tom Corbett, who was elected governor in 2010.

I thought Tom Corbett, the only attorney general since the office became elected in 1980, earlier did an outstanding job going after political corruption. Former Chief Deputy Frank Fina was Corbett's go-to guy on corruption. He directed the sting case. Fina is a key name in the Kane saga.

Kane and Fina would publicly spar on the sting case. There was no love lost even before but it would become a full-fledged battle. Kane upped the ante and charged racism was an undercurrent of the sting case that Fina supervised. Fina would eventually become Kane's obsession. Absent that latter fact, it might have ended differently.

It's shocking but by May 2015, the Pennsylvania political community was waiting to see if Kane, who held so much promise in 2012, would be facing the possibility of criminal charges herself.

Montgomery County District Attorney Risa Vetri Ferman was deciding whether to file criminal charges against the state's top law enforcement officer. She was conducting her own investigation based on a statewide grand jury report that alleged Kane committed several crimes stemming from the leak of separate 2009 grand jury information to the Philadelphia Daily News in an alleged effort to embarrass Fina. With a reputation for thoroughness, Ferman was redoing the investigation sent to her by Judge William Carpenter, who supervised the statewide grand jury. His appointment of special prosecutor Thomas Carluccio to investigate the case initially had been challenged as illegal by Kane but was upheld by the Pennsylvania Supreme Court in March 2015.

The statewide grand jury report made public by Carpenter with consent of Carluccio and Kane's lawyers recommended Kane be charged for allegedly lying to the grand jury, a bizarre cover up, and official oppression. If Ferman filed charges, Kane would become the second attorney general in 20 years to potentially face prison time.

But first let's back up. Political corruption cases ran rampant in Pennsylvania from 2008-2011. But in 2012 and entering 2013, it appeared that things had calmed down. It looked like we might be in for a respite.

It began to change quickly. In fact, Kane was the state prosecutor who filed charges in a major corruption case a few months after taking office, taking on a holdover investigation of the Pennsylvania Turnpike that Corbett initiated as attorney general in 2009.

Little did anyone realize then that Kane herself might become a defendant a year-and-a-half later depending on Ferman's decision.

To get the full picture, one must start with Tom Corbett's swearing in as governor in January 2011.

* * *

(Sources: as cited, the Philadelphia Inquirer's sting story in March 2014; a Philadelphia Magazine story on Kane by Robert Huber in June 2015. Much of it comes from Tribune-Review stories on Kane and public documents including the statewide grand jury report against Kane and my own first-hand observations in Montgomery County court. It also references letters Kane, Fina and Fina's new boss, Philadelphia District Attorney Seth Williams, publicly exchanged after the sting story was published; other material comes from my own interviews, and background provided to me by people involved in the case. It includes Trib stories from the 2012 election. Rendell referenced as "America's mayor" by Gore in a May 1994 *New York Times* magazine article. Other background comes from my earlier book *Keystone Corruption: An Insider's View of a State Gone Wrong* published by Camino Books.)

* * *

Next: A new round of corruption explodes in 2013.

1

LOST OPPORTUNITY

Jan. 18, 2011

Just when you think it's over.

It's not.

A run of corruption prosecutions resulted in an unprecedented situation by mid-2012 with eight state legislative leaders serving in state and federal prisons at the same time. By the dawn of 2013, however, it looked like things had finally calmed down in the Keystone state.

Corruption has been cyclical in Pennsylvania since the Civil War. And perhaps, we were ready for a respite. From 2007 to 2012, thirty-eight officials with ties to the state Capitol were charged by state, federal and local prosecutors.

Instead of stopping, this latest cycle seemed unending.

Eighteen more state officials were charged with crimes after I finished my last book *Keystone Corruption: A Pennsylvania Insider's View of a State Gone Wrong* (Camino Books Inc.) in the fall of 2012. Most resulted in convictions. Many walked on lesser charges. Still, that increased the total number of state officials charged to 56 since 2010 when the so-called Bonusgate case against House Democrats unfolded.

The state officials charged were most often accused of using state tax money for campaigns and for personal use. In the federal cases, bribery was typically a central element. A state Supreme Court Justice, who made a reputation as a reformer, went down for using her Superior Court seat resources to campaign for the high court.

In this avalanche of corruption, two ex-House Speakers Bill DeWeese, D-Greene County, and John Perzel,

R-Philadelphia, even briefly shared a prison cell at the Camp Hill state prison.

Separately, local elected and appointed officials—judges, contractors, county and school district employees—were charged by the feds in various corruption and pay-off schemes in northeastern Pennsylvania including the Kids for Cash case. In the nation's worst case of judicial corruption, two Luzerne County judges took bribes from a contractor to send juveniles to private detention homes.

In the Bonusgate case, Democratic leaders authorized the use of taxpayers' money as secret bonuses to encourage legislative staffers to work on campaigns. In short, taxpayers paid $1.4 million for "boots on the ground" to help House Democrats win elections.

In the Computergate case, so-named by a Dauphin County judge, Perzel authorized illegal use of multi-million dollar state equipment and databases in an effort to give Republicans an edge in campaigns.

Former Attorney General Tom Corbett's office prosecuted both. He reaped enormous publicity from those cases in the 2010 race for governor as the Bonusgate case was heading to trial.

Corbett portrayed himself as a reformer. His campaign hit on the excesses in the legislature. He said that his first step as governor would be releasing a legislative reform plan. "I'm ready to go to work," he said in a TV commercial. "Day One: I'm handing Harrisburg my reform plan. It ends the perks and special privileges."

Riding the wave of his corruption prosecutions, Corbett handily won the 2010 contest.

After Corbett's inaugural in January 2011, I waited for the reform plan. I kept calling Kevin Harley, his press secretary, asking where was his reform plan? OK, he was busy the first day, understandable. Still, I was a bit disappointed. I had believed Corbett would actually move forward regardless of the political consequences. What about the second day? Nothing. Third? No. A week went by before Corbett announced a superficial plan that looked like it was mainly to assuage the media and not anger lawmakers.

It was far from a sweeping reform plan and relied largely on the legislature to reform itself, much of which was already underway because of the Republican governor's election, Harley explained. In other words, the suggestion? Corbett was the reform.

Corbett told the Tribune-Review it would be an ongoing dialogue with legislative leaders and lawmakers. Translation: he wanted to cool it and not rile fellow Republicans controlling the House and Senate.

The plan? Eliminating or reducing lawmakers' "walking around money," or discretionary grants; paring down the $188 million legislative surplus as a legislative contribution to reducing the deficit; requiring documentation for the $157 flat payments, or per diems, that lawmakers can collect for overnight stays in the state capital, without receipts; requiring House members to contribute toward their health care costs as senators already did; and creating a user-friendly online database to enable taxpayers to search for state spending.

This was hardly the stuff of a former corruption-busting prosecutor. Corbett did keep old-style WAMs out of budgets, for the most part, but per diem reform never really unfolded. House members had already agreed to pay more for health care, and the database became a reality. It was far short of badly needed transparency. You can look up a salary but you can't use it for comparative purposes like an actual database. The governor never got agreement on a substantial surplus reduction.

In fairness, Corbett paid a steep political price for ending WAMs. If he had those grants to dole out, he might have secured more of his legislative agenda, programs such as school choice and state liquor privatization.

It's not all on Corbett. Legislative leaders never stepped up in the aftermath of the worst legislative corruption scandal in modern history.

Still, Corbett squandered the most meaningful opportunity for major reform in decades.

Corbett's own grand jury, dubbed the "mad as hell" Bonusgate grand jury, issued a call in May 2010 for sweeping changes—fundamental structural changes in the legislature's structure and operations. It was shelved by the legislature and Corbett acted as if it didn't exist. From term limits to ending the partisan legislative caucuses that cost taxpayers millions in duplication and delays, the grand jury recommendations created more resentment among lawmakers than reform. It was written by a prosecutor "who knew nothing about the legislature and despised it," a top House Republican staffer told me.

The ability of legislative leaders to filibuster reform by going through the motions of the arcane bill-passing process frustrates both citizens and activists. They even formed a well-meaning legislative reform commission that produced some meager changes in the rules but never attacked the root of the problem.

All hell broke loose again in early 2013.

I'm pretty cynical but even I was stunned.

State Rep. J.P. Miranda, D-Philadelphia, was charged with conflict of interest, perjury and criminal conspiracy for allegedly forking over state money to a no-show employee who was accused of kicking back a share to Miranda's sister. It was 1970's-style "ghost payroll" corruption charged by Philly prosecutors. Ironically, the investigators behind it: former state attorney general's office prosecutors responsible for 25 convictions in the Democratic Bonusgate and Republican Computergate scandals who departed the state prosecutors' offices because of the 2012 election of Attorney General Kathleen Kane, whom they saw as inexperienced and political.

Former Chief Deputy Attorney General Frank Fina led the way out the door.

Kane defeated the more experienced Cumberland County District Attorney David Freed, who was Corbett's handpicked candidate.

When Kane took office she had holdover cases from the Corbett era, one an extensive investigation of alleged corruption at the Pennsylvania Turnpike Commission.

On March 13, 2013, Kane and State Police Commissioner Frank Noonan announced a grand jury presentment against eight ex-turnpike officials who served during the Democratic administration of former Gov. Ed Rendell. It was a "pay to play" case, Kane said: officials took gifts, expensive dinners, trips, lavish accommodations, limo rides to Manhattan and tickets to professional sporting events. The implication was that in return, they allegedly fixed professional services contracts and raised campaign money for selected lawmakers and gubernatorial candidates.

"The grand jury found that these men were using the Turnpike to line their pockets and to influence elections," said Kane.

It appeared on the surface to be non-partisan: here was Kane, a Democrat, filing charges against other Democrats in a holdover case from Republican Corbett's tenure. Kane was still riding high as the new superstar of the Democratic Party. Governor or U.S. Senate did not seem out of reach for her, after leading the ticket in 2012 outpolling even President Barack Obama.

She was the "it" girl of Pennsylvania Democrats.

* * *

Noonan, a former old-school FBI agent, had been Corbett's chief investigator in the attorney general's office. The guy had actually worked under J. Edgar Hoover. That's how old-school he was. Noonan was however widely respected.

The turnpike investigation was launched by Corbett in 2009. It was actually Fina's case. Fina was the senior state prosecutor under Corbett who directed the corruption cases against Democrat and Republican legislative officials, namely Bonusgate and Computergate. He supervised the turnpike case with Laurel Brandstetter doing the hands-on work. Some of the investigations wrapped up under Corbett's appointed successor, Linda Kelly.

Many defendants and defense attorneys despised Fina. They claimed under-handed, hardball tactics along the lines of a philosophy that "you're either a witness (for the prosecution) or a defendant." Fina gave no quarter. He knew how to put together cases and how to win. He was arguably the best investigative/prosecutor in Pennsylvania state courts. He seemed driven by his disdain for politicians and what they do.

Sitting in the Capitol Media Center at Kane's news conference, I remember thinking how much innuendo mingled with some fact there had been about the extent of turnpike corruption over the past few decades. Historically, there's no question there'd been heavy layers of sleaze—blatant patronage and favoritism.

Noonan said Pennsylvanians "have all heard rumors about the turnpike for years. It was fairly well known or thought, but there's a big difference between that and having evidence and this is what we have." He was talking about criminal activity. One must go back to 1956 and a $9.5 million scandal involving turnpike officials and a contractor scheming to fraudulently fill mine "voids" on the Northeast Extension to approach turnpike corruption of the level alleged in the 2013 indictment, according to the book *Pennsylvania Politics Today and Yesterday* by the late Paul Beers.

Defense attorneys insisted there was no evidence that the defendants, ex-turnpike officials, vendors, and a state Senate leader, took action in return for gratuities. Rendell was not implicated but his CEO, Joe Brimmeier, a longtime Pittsburgh politico, was charged with crimes in the bid-rigging and influence peddling case.

Brandstetter's departure three months before a slated trial for remaining defendants foreshadowed problems with the case. Was the turnpike case crumbling?

Brandstetter, a tall attractive brunette with a resemblance in stature to Kane, worked for Fina, who supervised the public corruption unit.

Fina, a career prosecutor, wanted no part of serving under Kane. Brandstetter hung on for 1½ more years while Fina was persona non grata in the Kane regime.

First, an older case was wrapping up in the western part of the state—with a different prosecutor.

THE THREE ORIES

The Orie sisters' saga was coming to a bitter end. The highly unusual case of three sisters in public office facing corruption charges took what appeared to be the last turn.

Former Supreme Court Justice Joan Orie Melvin, who championed judicial reform as a candidate in 2009, was convicted of felonies; people throughout the North Hills still believed she and her sisters, ex-Senate Majority Whip Jane Orie and Joan's aide, Janine, had been political targets of Allegheny County DA Stephen Zappala, a Democrat and son of former Supreme Court Chief Justice Stephen Zappala Sr. The DA denied it. I was told authoritatively by a pol with sterling local connections that even after Jane was released from prison she theoretically could have been re-elected—the Ories were that popular and viewed as Zappala victims by loyalists in the North Hills, a sprawling suburb of Pittsburgh. Joan and Jane were convicted of using state-paid staff to work on their campaigns. Jane added the insult of forging documents to help her case, or so a jury decided. She continued to maintain her innocence. The Ories' convictions, which included theft and conflict of interest charges, were upheld on appeal. No evidence surfaced of Zappala engineering it. Felons are barred from running for state office.

Jane Orie lost the sympathy of many supporters for the forgeries, which she continued to deny after her conviction.

Jane served 20 months in prison. She told WTAE TV it was "Hell on earth." Joan was sentenced to three years house arrest. Sister Janine, a court aide of Joan's, was sentenced to one year of house arrest.

The cases against Jane Orie and former House Speaker DeWeese were dubbed "Pettygate," by their lawyer William C. Costopoulos, of Lemoyne. That was certainly the case compared to the monumental explosion that was about to take place on Pennsylvania's corruption front.

Melvin's appeals were painful to watch. The outcome was predictable. The odds seemed stacked against her. Part of her sentence, public shaming, was wiped out on appeal. That was the photo of her in handcuffs to be sent to every judge in the state along with a letter of apology.

"I DO WHAT THE FUCK I WANT"

First came another case on the scale of the Ories'. Kane's office charged Sen. LeAnna Washington, D-Philadelphia/ Montgomery, with forcing her staff to organize a birthday fundraiser that served as her largest annual source of campaign revenue. It was a case reminiscent of those from the Corbett era—misuse of public resources.

The most memorable thing about the Washington case was her comment to an aide who questioned legislative work on campaign tasks. "I am the fucking senator, I do what the fuck I want, and ain't nobody going to change me." To me, it was symbolic of the arrogance in Harrisburg.

The timing was suspect to some because of what happened next. Washington was charged March 12, 2014, by the attorney general's office. On March 16, 2014, the Philadelphia Inquirer broke the hardest hitting piece in Pennsylvania I've seen in decades: the sting case. Bombshell is a cliché but it is still apt. The story by Angela Couloumbis and Craig McCoy reported that Kane decided not to prosecute a case in which four Philadelphia Democratic legislators took cash gifts for the attorney general's office from an undercover informant wearing a hidden video camera and recorder. A fifth official, an ex-traffic court judge in Philadelphia, was given a bracelet, the story said. It was largely based on sources. But the story incredibly named names.

There is no overstating the impact of this case on government and statewide politics.

The year's events were a blend of old-style corruption—cash payoffs and ghost payroll allegations—with the relatively newer type prosecutions: using state resources for campaigns and pay to play.

I kept thinking it was surreal. Cash and jewelry handed out by a man that legislators still believed was an active lobbyist seeking support on issues.

As events unfolded, the implication was that Kane had tanked the case against black lawmakers because it was lousy politics in Philadelphia. Kane, however, rattled off numerous reasons why she believed the case was legally flawed and she implied the prosecution was racist.

Kane's defenders suggested Seth Williams envisioned running statewide for attorney general in 2016. A former spokeswoman denied it.

According to political observers, it's supposedly bad politics for a Democratic prosecutor likely to seek statewide election to go after black leaders in a majority black city where Democratic voters outnumber Republicans by more than a 6-1 margin. Personally, I think corruption crosses all color lines: citizens of all races abhor corrupt state politics. Sure, it may be tolerated a bit more in places with a history of corruption like Philadelphia. But that is not a racial issue. It is cultural. The district attorney of Philadelphia, Seth Williams, is black. He puts white and black defendants away.

Was the timing of the Washington indictment an attempt at political inoculation for Kane as Inquirer reporters were gearing up for a major story about declining to prosecute a corruption case backed up by video? Or was it a coincidence? Here was a corruption case filed against a black senator that grabbed headlines just prior to the sting case. It was already in the pipeline. They can't do cases that quickly. But prosecutors do have discretion on wrapping up the grand jury and getting a judge to approve release.

"PENNSYLVANIA HUSTLE"

We'll never know the ultimate reach that the sting investigation, unfettered, could have had. I believe Fina had envisioned a state-based version of Abscam, the 1970s and 1980s sting case that snared seven federal lawmakers. Fina had plans to expand the undercover operation to include a fictitious business in Harrisburg with an office and staff that would make offers to Democrat and Republican legislators and target non-profits some were using as piggy banks. The plan was to examine relationships "between legislators and certain lobbyists," according to a July 2012 internal memo from Fina to former Attorney General Linda Kelly, Corbett's appointee who served the remainder of his term after he was elected governor in 2010.

It was well in advance of the movie *American Hustle*, based loosely on Abscam, but the theme was the same.

But clearly resources were an issue. Fina wrote the memo to Kelly after the conviction of serial predator Jerry Sandusky in June 2012. Fina had been one of the two prosecutors in Sandusky's trial along with Joe McGettigan. Office resources had also been exhausted on recent corruption cases against DeWeese, D-Greene; a second trial on separate charges for convicted felon Mike Veon, the former Democratic whip; former Rep. Stephen Stetler, D-York; and former Republican whip and House GOP Chief Counsel Brett Feese, of Lycoming County.

Fina's memo included a footnote that stated several state troopers and agents assigned to assist with the sting had been transferred to the Sandusky case and it was time to make a decision on moving forward with the sting case or file charges based on evidence gathered at that point. Kane, who was running for office in 2012, would later say she never saw the memo.

The Fina memo might have been CYA. It might have been the real deal. In any case, I regret that it did not come to fruition. I've often thought a large scale sting operation like the FBI's "Tennessee Waltz" against the Tennessee legislature would be the only way to ignite action, by the public and by lawmakers, to once and for all clean up the Pennsylvania state legislature and some agencies. The FBI sting in Tennessee from 2003-2005 resulted in lobbyists from a fictitious company said to be recycling surplus electronic equipment paying $150,000 in bribes to lawmakers. It led to the conviction of a dozen state and local officials.

No Tennessee Waltz. Hardly a Pennsylvania Polka.

Despite Fina's best efforts, it's arguable that state attorney general's investigators are ill-equipped—compared to the FBI—in taking on undercover sting operations.

Only in the final stages of writing this book in May 2016 would I learn there had in fact been an FBI sting on the Pennsylvania legislature. The scope was still unknown. But FBI agents had managed to convince lawmakers a phony company needed legislation passed and they managed a unanimous Senate vote on a bill sponsored by a soon-to-be accused felon (from an unrelated case).

What would have happened with an even wider Abscam-type net?

Many folks I know are repulsed by the idea of actively seeking out crimes through sting investigations: offering the opportunity for public officials to take bribes. I have no problem with it. If a guy is honest, like state Rep. Curtis Thomas, D-Philadelphia, he'll do what Thomas did: he threw the undercover agent out of his office, prosecutors said.

A pornography scandal would also rock the Corbett-era Bonusgate and Sandusky prosecutors in 2014 and 2015 with Kathleen Kane using it as a political tool and eventually part of a criminal defense.

THE SHOCKER OF 2015

There was yet another major case to unfold suddenly in 2015, one that would shock the political establishment. That was state Treasurer Rob McCord, a Democrat, who resigned and admitted to shaking down contractors for campaign money.

Before the current run was over—and experience suggests it probably isn't—the ex-mayor of the state's capital city would be charged by Kane in a bizarre case whereby Stephen Reed was secretly buying and storing Western artifacts for a museum that was never launched. The finances of the capital meanwhile were in shambles.

The purpose of this book is to take you behind the scenes of some of these events, give you personal insights and observations about some players, add commentary and analysis from knowledgeable sources and explore why the first round of corrupt activity essentially over a decade (2000 through 2010) didn't smack the legislature and top state policyholders in the face. It will also provide the reader with a summary in one document of the corruption scene in Pennsylvania through most of 2015. Finally, as reviewed in my previous book, *Keystone Corruption*, what can be done about it?

It is not a history book. It won't cite chapter and verse on all of Kane's legal battles or all of her missteps. I will attempt to give you a snapshot of what it was like on the frontlines of covering her case and those that proceeded it.

It is a saga about elected officials betraying the public and about the seeming jinx of Jerry Sandusky, as he sits with that goofy smile in virtual solitary confinement for the remainder of his life with his loyal wife Dottie continuing to proclaim his innocence. Sandusky's political voodoo spell seems to snare any elected official who touches his case.

Corbett won in huge fashion in 2010. Kane was the top vote getter in 2012, outpolling President Barack Obama. She rode the Sandusky issue—the length of time (33 months) it took Corbett to arrest Sandusky—and it played a significant role in her victory. There were a lot of doubts among voters in retrospect about Corbett's effort. But he and successor Linda Kelly did put Sandusky behind bars. One can argue Kane's repeated pounding on that issue set the stage for Corbett's historic defeat in 2014. Many voters believed he cut massive amounts of education funding.

What did voters get from the promise of Corbett and Kane, and all the trust they placed in them?

And, still, the corruption continued like a festering sore with spin-offs of the McCord case continuing with FBI investigations of public officials.

* * *

Note on sources throughout the book:

As with *Keystone Corruption* much of the sourcing is from events I experienced firsthand or was involved in after the story broke. In some cases it is from original documents in my possession. I am fortunate to be the state Capitol reporter for the Pittsburgh Tribune-Review assigned to cover the state Capitol where, unavoidably, corruption has been part of my beat.

Primary sources used throughout this book: my earlier book *Keystone Corruption*, Pittsburgh Tribune-Review stories, turnpike and court records, and public statements at news conferences by Philadelphia District Attorney Seth Williams.

* * *

(Sources: The Philadelphia Inquirer, primarily stories by Couloumbis and McCoy but also Tom Fitzgerald and Jeremy Roebuck on the sting case; Philadelphia Daily News articles by Chris Brennan; Associated Press stories by Mark Scolforo; Pennlive.com stories by Charles Thompson; Salena Zito's December 2013 Trib column; *Kids for Cash* by William Ecenbarger; the FBI's website, FBI.gov.; state websites for legislators; a piece by WITF's Scott Detrow appearing on NewsWorks about Corbett's reform promises; Couloumbis' story with Jessica Parks on former Senator Washington; Tony Romeo's KYW Radio story on Washington being charged; WTAE TV in Pittsburgh on Melvin's initial sentencing and the interview with Jane Orie; ex-Trib reporters Bobby Kerlik and Adam Brandolph's stories on the Orie case; Beers' book *Pennsylvania Politics Today and Yesterday* as cited; Tracie Mauriello of the Pittsburgh Post-Gazette on Corbett's reform effort; copies of federal search warrants obtained from Reading and Allentown city halls; and several Morning Call stories as background on the McCord spin-off investigations.)

Note: Jane Orie's appeal to federal court was pending several Morning Call stories.

* * *

Next: The Pennsylvania Turnpike scandal unfolds.

2

TURNPIKE SCANDAL

March 13, 2013

HARRISBURG—The Pennsylvania Turnpike, carved through the Allegheny Mountains, opened shortly after midnight on Oct. 1, 1940 as "America's Dream Highway." At that time, the nation's first superhighway ran from Carlisle to Irwin. Grants from the Roosevelt administration got it rolling. When it opened, drivers went joy riding. At least four motorists got so caught up in the experience they ran out of gas. In Irwin, the first driver on the turnpike was Carl A. Boe, 43, of McKeesport. Toll collector Morris Neiberg welcomed him. The first driver in Carlisle was Homer D. Romberger, a feed and tallow dealer, who took a 47-minute drive to Fort Littleton, according to *The Pennsylvania Turnpike: A History* by Dan Cupper. The toll highway was this state's version of the Autobahn (though there's no actual fair comparison) because there was no speed limit initially. It was celebrated in a 1970s country song "Pennsylvania Turnpike, I Love You" by Vaughn Horton.

How did I miss that one?

Sure it evokes nostalgic memories. Stopping for dinners at Howard Johnson's—a rare treat in the 1950s. And flat tires, misplacing toll tickets, operating by old-fashioned map when there were no GPS or directions via cell phones. Speed traps. Long lines of traffic. You name it.

Fairly or unfairly, the turnpike has had a reputation for two things: providing your safest route in winter with dry roads—even after a major storm—and as a place where a nephew or cousin who knew the right pols landed a toll taker job or a summer paving job. Management jobs were available to really well-connected folks.

But it was costly and inefficient. In his landmark 1993 book on turnpike corruption, *When the Levee Breaks: The Patronage Crisis at the Pennsylvania Turnpike, the General Assembly & the State Supreme Court*, author William Keisling wrote of "outright lawbreaking, waste, two-party privilege and politics at the Turnpike."

"Girlfriends, brothers, husbands, sons-in-law and other close relations and associates were still being hired left and right into well-paying Turnpike jobs. Two patronage chiefs, one for each party, were still employed by the Turnpike," Keisling said he was told in an anonymous letter apparently from a "mid-level employee of the Pennsylvania Turnpike Commission"—a device used to open the book. Critics complain of Keisling's exaggerations as a writer, but several lawmakers in the mid-1990s told me about his book and they said it was spot on. In the book, he gives names and calls into question the legality of hiring practices based on a 1990 U.S. Supreme Court ruling. In a 1990s series for Gannett newspapers, I was able to confirm many of Keisling's assertions.

The practices continued unabated. "The politicians weren't about to merrily give up any piece of this pie," Keisling wrote. He noted the unusual degree of cooperation between the two major parties to share the spoils.

According to Keisling, here's how it worked at the agency: New hires were "rubber stamped" by a personnel committee, comprised of friends and relatives of the pols. They in turn appointed more friends and relatives, he suggests. On paper it looked good.

What Keisling unearthed was more than doling out toll-taker entry level jobs. He also showed the complex web between the Senate, the agency and then the Supreme Court. He revealed widespread "pinstripe patronage" where big law firms that donated thousands of campaign dollars to the party in power—and the party out of power at the Capitol—landed turnpike contracts with lucrative fees often for boilerplate legal work on bonds.

Today, the Peter J. Camiel Services Plaza remains as a monument to the bond between pols and turnpike officials.

Camiel was a former Democratic senator and former chairman of the Philadelphia Democratic City Committee. He was charged and convicted along with Sen. Vincent Fumo, of Philadelphia and former Senate Majority Leader Tom Nolan, of Allegheny and Westmoreland counties, in a "ghost" payroll scandal. In 1981, a federal judge overturned a jury's guilty verdicts on mail fraud charges and acquitted all three men.

Maybe it takes an acquittal to get a service plaza named after you.

* * *

Scandals and corruption had persisted at the turnpike for decades.

In 1957, five people including two turnpike commissioners were convicted in a make-work scheme under a $19 million contract. Mine voids were needlessly being filled and bills inflated in the Manu Mine scandal. Former Gov. George Leader called it "literally highway robbery." The president of the construction company was the nephew of one of the commissioners. The nephew was also convicted in the nine-week conspiracy trial in Dauphin County Court.

A turnpike commissioner appointed following the '56 scandal was charged with bribery, extortion and conspiracy in 1963. Six years later, the FBI arrested the agency's general counsel for taking cash to steer a company to a builder. Then in 1978, former Turnpike Commissioner Egidio Cerelli, whose case was mentioned in *Keystone Corruption* and which I covered in federal court in Pittsburgh, was convicted for extorting money from contractors for contributions to the Democratic Party when he worked as a PennDOT supervisor. Cerelli was a good-natured pol who stood trial after an earlier mistrial. He was a friend of then-Gov. Milton Shapp and a power in Westmoreland County politics. He drew a three-year prison term. At his death, he predicted the practice of politicians demanding money from contractors, often known as macing, would continue in one form or another.

Another scandal I saw—well, fortunately I didn't literally see it—unfolded in 1999 after nude pictures of former Senate President Pro Tempore Robert Jubelirer's wife were discovered on turnpike computers. His wife resigned from her

$65,500 a year job as assistant deputy executive director. Jubelirer filed for divorce. A male turnpike worker who took the photos was fired. Earlier, a female turnpike employee won a $250,000 court settlement on grounds she had been passed over for the post given to Jubelirer's wife, saying his wife lacked credentials. By 2013, the romance of the grand opening was long gone.

LICENSE TO BORROW

Republicans controlling the state House were moving to abolish the Turnpike Commission and fold all operations into the Pennsylvania Department of Transportation. Rep. Donna Oberlander, a Republican representing Clarion and Armstrong Counties, said she considered it an "outdated" and "corruption-infested" commission running an "antiquated and mismanaged" agency.

The bill didn't get traction. The commission's $9 billion debt proved problematic.

Kudos to Oberlander and previously Rep. Mike Vereb, R-Montgomery County, for trying. But even if they won House passage, the Senate represented a steel barrier against such foolishness. Why? Because for decades, Senate leaders controlled it.

As designed, the five-member commission running the state's toll road and major east-west highway was an independent state agency. If the Turnpike Commission became part of PennDOT, the debt wouldn't disappear. Taxpayers would be responsible for it. That's a bitter pill for most lawmakers to swallow.

Staying in debt, oddly enough, assures the agency's survival.

"The Turnpike itself remains in existence only so long as it remains in debt," said a presentment by the 33rd Statewide Investigating Grand Jury. "When all bonds, notes or other obligations and the interest thereon have been paid . . . the Turnpike and the connecting road, tunnels, and bridges shall become a part of the system of State Highways and shall be maintained by the Department of Highways free of tolls; and thereupon, the Commission shall be dissolved," the Grand Jury said quoting an incorporating document of the agency. "The Grand Jury finds this to be of particular note given the practices of the Pennsylvania Turnpike Commission regarding the expenditure of state dollars discovered during the course of this investigation."

Note the free tolls never happened. Never will.

The original planning called for the turnpike retiring its debt in 1954 and becoming part of PennDOT, according to *The Pennsylvania Turnpike: A History*, by Cupper.

The agency was in effect given a free license to spend—and borrow.

And spend they did.

PennDOT manages 41,000 miles of roadway. It's run by seven executives or one for every 5,857 miles of state roadway. According to Oberlander, the turnpike had nine executives at that time for 545 miles of roadway. That effectively is one executive for 60 miles of highway.

There are different ways to calculate it but the comparison is apt. The turnpike is an extremely costly operation given the relatively small share of roadway it operates. Drivers pay a premium to ride on it.

By 2014 after opening a section of the Mon-Fayette Expressway in western Pennsylvania, the road mileage crept up to 550. The agency employed about 2,100 people, about the same as 10 years ago despite the advent of electronic tolling and less need for toll takers.

The debt and tolls have been increasing steadily since the enactment of a 2007 transportation law. That law used expanded turnpike debt to pump $450 million a year into highways, repair, transit and bridges throughout the state. The turnpike has forked over $4.5 billion for other state uses. Under a 2014 law effectively raising the gas tax and motorists' fees, the bulk of the $450 million will be spent on mass transit.

In 2016, for a cash-paying customer, it cost $46.10 to ride from the Delaware River Bridge in Philadelphia to the Gateway Toll Plaza. Essentially that's from the New Jersey to Ohio state lines. The E-Z Pass electronic toll was discounted to $32.95. The cross-state distance is almost 357 miles.

From 1956 to 2013, cross-state tolls increased from $3.90 and 1.1 cents per mile to $9.15 and 10.9 cents per mile in 2013, Turnpike records show. (The E-Z pass rate was $30.77 or 8.6 cents per mile.)

* * *

Few knew the outrageous spending by commissioners and other agency officials over the years. Tolls, a share of the state gas tax and vehicle registration fees, pay for the highway and its maintenance. The part-time commissioners, who are political appointees, traveled and entertained like medieval barons. They doled out jobs to friends and relatives.

TURNPIKE EXCESSES

A series of articles by the Tribune-Review in 2005 showed:

- Audits from 1987 through 1997 found weaknesses in hiring procedures but those audits were repeatedly ignored. Patronage and nepotism flourished.
- Former Turnpike Commissioner Jim Dodaro helped his son, Daniel, get a job as an operations auditor for $55,795 in 2003. Ex-CEO Joe Brimmeier hired his cousin, Ed Schauer, as a plumber for about $34,000. He also hired the son of former Turnpike Commissioner Robert Brady, the Philadelphia Democratic Chairman and now a U.S. congressman. Brady's son got a $74,637 job as assistant director of operations in the east. Dodaro stated he was proud of helping people get jobs, including the guy who cut his grass. "Hell yeah I'm proud of it," Dodaro told the Trib. "I've helped a lot of people." The problem with patronage: no one else has a shot at the jobs and we can't be sure the best qualified folks got the jobs. Brimmeier insisted he first made sure people could do the work.
- The influence of former Senate Democratic powerbroker Vincent Fumo and former Senate President Pro Tem Robert Jubelirer, an Altoona Republican, on internal agency decisions. Fumo was of counsel with a law firm that landed turnpike work. But it was "going too far to say they controlled the commission," said Mike Long, then Jubelirer's top aide. He called that "patently false" and said the commission ran the agency. However Long admitted "we weighed in" for a turnpike equipment operator whose wife worked in Jubelirer's district office to ensure a promotion and

more than $5,000 a year raise. Long is now one of the most powerful lobbyists in Harrisburg. Jubelirer was defeated in 2006 after engineering the 2005 legislative pay raise.

- Mitchell Rubin, the former chairman, racked up $72,000 in meals and travel over five years. His expenses included $6,268 for trips to Paris and Madrid, according to a sidebar to the series by former Trib reporter Chris Osher. A $1,869 bill at Topper's at the Wauwinet Inn in Nantuckett included $125 for Beluga caviar, $76 for four quail salads and sirloin steaks for $46 each. He also dined at two four star restaurants in New York at public expense. Rubin didn't reveal who it was he treated. They were listed as unspecified legislators. On four occasions, Rubin billed the public for his trips to Manhattan for an annual political event called the Pennsylvania Society. One expense: a $3,277.36 dinner at Alain Ducasse. A former turnpike auditor told the Trib he flagged Rubin's expenses but no one did anything about them.

It was later revealed in a federal indictment of Fumo that Rubin was a "ghost employee" of the Senate collecting $150,000 from taxpayers over five years. Rubin's wife, Ruth Arnao, had been Fumo's top staffer and co-defendant.

THE TURNPIKE INDICTMENT

All of this was the backdrop for the searing indictment Attorney General Kane and State Police Commissioner Noonan would deliver at the March 13, 2013, news conference.

The hype surrounding Pennsylvania's Turnpike Corruption case was incredible.

The Grand Jury's findings "open the window to the operation of the Pennsylvania Turnpike commission and many of their associates in the private sector," said Noonan. "It shows a culture of greed, corruption and political influence that is beyond imagination. The people of Pennsylvania deserve better."

Kane, at that joint news conference with Noonan, called what happened at the agency "stealing from the public pure and simple." The indictment alleged a sweeping pattern of influence peddling and bid-rigging.

Finally, I thought, someone was going to get to the bottom of the patronage pit and scandalous agency that was an anachronism and was on the table for elimination by the legislature. But getting any turnpike abolishment bill through the Senate faced an uphill battle, aside from the issue of dealing with agency debt. There's the treasure trove of political goodies that historically existed for a few select Senate leaders: jobs and steering contracts to donors. For decades, it had been the playground of Senate leaders of both parties. The Senate caucuses kept their influence because two-thirds support was required for confirmation of gubernatorial appointments to the commission. One party couldn't do it alone so deals on nominees were necessary.

In fact, the grand jury presentment alleged a 60-40 split of the political spoils with the party holding the governor's office getting the majority.

When Corbett, the former hard-charging attorney general, became governor he named Roger Nutt, the father of his campaign manager, Brian Nutt, as the turnpike's executive director. Roger Nutt had highway experience, but it smelled bad coming from the would-be reformer. Remember, it was Republican Corbett who launched a turnpike investigation in 2009 so he knew a lot about the inside dealings there under Rendell.

"No bid contracts and pinstripe patronage have been common practices at the Turnpike Commission, but no serious reform has taken root since the institution serves up favors, jobs and projects to Democrats and Republicans," said Eric Epstein, co-founder of Rock the Capital, a political reform group.

Eight former turnpike staffers were charged a little more than two months after Kane, a Democrat, took office in January 2013. The so-called "pay to play" case from the outset sounded like a winner. For one, any jury comprised of reasonably aware Pennsylvanians would know how much more they pay each year to ride on the turnpike. Politicians have been milking it since 2007 to pay for road improvements in other parts of the state. The average prospective juror might also be aware of longstanding rumors of corruption.

So showing that some turnpike officials were showered with contractor-provided gifts, many of which were not reported as required on disclosure statements—from gift certificates at plush resort Nemacolin Woodlands to tickets for sporting events, limos, expensive dinners and travel—would be relatively easy. So the theory went. There'd be no question those vendors obtained or maintained their contracts with the agency. So what if each gift could not be linked to a specific contract or sponsored fundraiser for a favored politician? The grand jury investigating the case didn't make those specific connections. An insightful lawyer-legislator at the Capitol told me he had no doubt a Dauphin County jury still would make the connections on its own and convict all or many of the six defendants technically part of the "pay to play" case. Two other defendants, it later became clear, were a minor part of the case.

Some of the principals were charged with commercial bribery, a statute that includes a subsection not requiring a quid pro quo.

The big players: Mitchell Rubin, former turnpike chairman and former Democratic Senator Vincent Fumo's go-to guy at the agency; longtime Pittsburgh pol Joe Brimmeier, the agency's CEO and an appointee of Gov. Ed Rendell; former Senate Democratic Leader Robert Mellow, of Scranton; and another top-ranking agency official, George Hatalowich, of Harrisburg.

Hatalowich faced 15 charges—seven ethics counts for not reporting. He had the most "gift"-type counts piled up. The other major figures faced nine charges. A defense attorney later told me it was consistent with what he considered the Fina case-building strategy: overcharge the defendants and hope one charge sticks. The defense lawyer's concern though was that Brandstetter, who was hired by Fina, would not entertain plea bargains and would if necessary take every case to trial and roll the dice with a Dauphin County jury.

He was probably right.

She had learned extremely well from Fina.

For the record, under Pennsylvania law, statewide grand juries technically don't indict. They issue presentments. The presentments effectively are like indictments in the federal system. State prosecutors then decide whether to file charges based on the presentment.

At the end of 2012, a lot of rumors were swirling that the turnpike case might be spiked altogether. Linda Kelly, Corbett's appointee as his successor, was handing off the case to Kane. No one knew what Kelly or Kane would do. It was secret grand jury material.

Dauphin County jury pools, from in and around the state's capital city, provided the jurors for the major state corruption cases of Bonusgate and Computergate. It was quite a risk to go to trial there on political corruption charges. Of ten political corruption cases that actually went to trial, prosecutors won seven verdicts. Two defendants were acquitted. Those are bad odds if the outcome is prison; the vast majority of the others entered pleas to reduce their exposure to prison time. It's the way it works.

The turnpike officials and vendors were supposedly part of an illegal fundraising machine raising campaign cash for favored elected pols. For some select few vendors, it meant big contracts at public expense.

One big difference between the turnpike case and Bonusgate: more of the top turnpike defendants had top-shelf defense attorneys. And the office of attorney general behind the scenes was in turmoil as a result of a time bomb left by Kane's adversary, former Chief Deputy Attorney General Frank Fina, and the constant internal issue of how to handle her investigation of Corbett's Sandusky investigation that she had promised to the voters. Capitol Hill wags were calling it the "investigation of the investigation."

* * *

(Sources: The state presentment against turnpike employees; Beers' book *Pennsylvania Politics Today and Yesterday* cited in chapter one; Keisling's book *When the Levee Breaks: the Patronage Crisis At The Pennsylvania Turnpike, the General Assembly & the State Supreme Court*; Cupper's book, *The Pennsylvania Turnpike: A History*; a House Republican news release on Oberlander's proposal; Trib stories on the grand jury presentment I wrote with Tom Fontaine; a 2004 article in the Morning Call of Allentown on historic turnpike corruption; the 2005 Trib turnpike series with Chris Osher;

a 1999 piece by Joe Grata and Tom Gibb in the Pittsburgh Post-Gazette on the Jubelirer spouse scandal; Cerelli's 1991 obituary in the Post-Gazette.; federal appellate ruling on Cerelli's case; Michael Wereschagin and Justin Velucci's November 2006 story on former Allegheny County Sheriff Pete DeFazio's guilty plea to a misdemeanor making charge.)

* * *

Next: Anthony Lepore lays out the state's turnpike theory—sort of.

3

"I'M YOUR GUY"

June 24, 2013

Preliminary hearings are typically slam dunks for prosecutors and indeed, no cases were tossed as turnpike case defendants went to court in June 2013. But there was still plenty of drama before District Judge William Wenner.

You would expect nothing less when there are 11 attorneys in the courtroom.

The Commonwealth's first witness, presumably its star witness, didn't deliver any knockout blows. Anthony Lepore, who had been chief of staff to Senate Democratic Leader Mellow, seemed to tread a fine line between trying to help the state's case but also not harming his former boss.

Lepore answered to Senator Bob Mellow, a longtime fixture in the Democratic Caucus. But he also answered to all Democratic senators—especially to former Senate Democratic Appropriations Chairman Vincent Fumo, D-Philadelphia. A former AFL-CIO worker who joined the Senate as a staffer for ex-Majority Leader Bill Lincoln, Lepore was a beefy, amiable guy. He lost a lot of weight since I last saw him. He looked good.

Senators liked him. He was smart and took pride in balancing the senators' interests and getting the job done. He was trusted and well liked—so much so that Senate Minority Leader Jay Costa, D-Allegheny County, who would replace Mellow, decided to keep Lepore in his $170,000 a year job, despite the fact he was implicated in the turnpike case. Lepore was not charged or accused of wrongdoing but he was testifying under a grant of immunity. Based on his testimony, he was in the thick of things—the middle man.

The fact that Lepore could survive the sleaze alleged in the turnpike case spoke volumes about the institutional protection provided by the Senate—the willingness to overlook public perceptions and when possible protect one of their own. And his own savvy.

Costa explained it as Lepore being the under-part of a "master-servant" relationship with Mellow. In other words he did what he was told. You know, it's that defense strategy that didn't work at Nuremberg.

Despite Mellow holding the title of leader, the real power among Democrats rested with Fumo.

"Everything comes from him (Fumo) in a sense," Lepore testified, "and he was a very strong and powerful man." Yet Fumo, despite having the most influence in the caucus, was not charged. Fumo even had a go-to guy at the turnpike in Commission Chairman Mitchell Rubin.

Rubin was Fumo's "super close friend." Rubin "was Fumo's guy," Lepore stated.

That meant Rubin had enormous clout on the commission.

In the past, Lepore said Democratic senators would call the turnpike and say "'we're having an event, we're having a golf outing. I'd like you to sell $10,000 worth of tickets to some of these vendors.'" Those requests were typically relayed to Rubin or Brimmeier, he said. Lepore made a point on several occasions about the "old days" to please his new "master" and let the world know it was no longer going on.

Brimmeier was a known commodity in their caucus and Mellow "was happy" when Brimmeier was appointed, Lepore testified. A few days after his appointment, Brimmeier stopped by Mellow's office and told them, "I'm gonna be your guy."

Fumo was identified in the grand jury presentment only as "Senator No. 6."

Mellow and Fumo were in federal prisons on unrelated corruption charges in 2013. Fumo was convicted of misusing more than $3 million total from a non-profit, the Senate and a seaport museum; Mellow later agreed to plead guilty to conspiracy to commit mail fraud for using state staffers for campaign work and evading taxes when he under-reported the sale of the building he owned that had been used for his district Senate office, the Scranton Times reported. Mellow was in "solitary" confinement following the filing of turnpike charges, his attorneys said.

THE PNC CONNECTION

Mellow was tight with Pete Danchak, a PNC regional bank president in the northeast, and Danchak made it clear to the senator PNC wanted a piece of the bond work at the turnpike. It was the biggest bank in the state yet was missing out on the gravy train.

Mellow and Danchak went to a lot of sporting events together. They were both New York Yankees fans. A limo picked them up and they took in a ballgame and had dinner at an Italian restaurant. Danchak was paying the bills, Lepore stated. At the annual Pennsylvania Society gathering, which Lepore described as a "who's who of Pennsylvania political and business heavyweights," PNC sponsored a dinner at Spark's Steakhouse. The event signaled Mellow's interest in running for governor. The event included "buttered hors d'oeuvres and an open bar and the dinner."

Lepore testified, "PNC paid for it."

It was actually PNC Capital Markets. The tab was $7,082.34.

Under cross-examination by Mellow's lawyer Dan Brier, Lepore seemed to be telling a different story—but just slightly. Asked if he thought the trips to Yankees games were an effort to influence Mellow, Lepore stated, "probably not."

Q. "Well you certainly didn't believe it was?"

A. "No."

PNC garnered almost $2.5 million in underwriter fees from 2007 through 2012, according to the grand jury presentment.

The limo rides to New York were provided in at least nine instances, the grand jury said. Mellow also received tickets from PNC to a Rod Stewart concert, a "Dancing with the Stars" performance and a Bryan Adams concert, according to the grand jury report.

In all years except 2009, Mellow reported receiving no gifts on his financial disclosure statement filed with the Ethics Commission, according to the grand jury report. It was a conflict of interest and a failure to report under mandatory financial disclosure laws, the grand jury stated.

A "BROMANCE"

A gaping loophole in state ethics law allows friends to give gifts above thresholds allowed in the law. State officials must report gifts above $250, except from friends and family members. A $249 gift? No one needs to know. From a good buddy who is a lobbyist? Forget about it.

They are allowed to accept travel, hospitality and lodging up to $650 without disclosing it.

In 2014, Pennsylvania was one of 10 states without a gift ban. Incoming Gov. Tom Wolf, a Democrat, was declaring a gift ban for his employees. Wolf says members of his administration should say "no thank you" even to a cup of coffee. The new governor's push could give gift ban legislation some momentum in the legislature, where it has repeatedly stalled.

Maybe there's good reason.

Legislative leaders and key committee chairmen took $117,000 worth of gifts, lodging, transportation and hospitality from 2007 through 2011, according to a Tribune-Review study in March 2013. Tickets to Penn State games, Steelers games, a Turkish rug and foreign travel were part of the bounty.

Former Senate Appropriations Chairman Jake Corman, R-Centre County, now the majority leader, in 2011 received $3,366 worth of Pittsburgh Steelers tickets. In 2009, the Steelers paid $669 for his lodging and gave him $4,000 tickets to the Super Bowl in Tampa, where the Steelers won their sixth ring by beating the Arizona Cardinals, documents show.

Corman says he's friends with owner Art Rooney Jr. That's how he got the tickets, he told the Trib.

Must be nice.

Corman at least didn't run from his reports. He calls back even on stories that won't be flattering. Most guys dodge.

But Barry Kauffman, lobbyist for Common Cause of Pennsylvania, said Rooney probably has many other friends who didn't get tickets.

Speaking of friends, the loophole became one of the arguments used by Mellow's lawyers in the turnpike case. Attorney Sal Cognetti Jr. told reporters Mellow and Danchak were longtime friends, pre-dating the Yankees trips, and he wasn't required to report under the law. In fact, Lepore testified that Mellow and Danchak had a "bromance"—a slang expression referring to men who are like brothers, extremely close in a non-sexual relationship. Cognetti and Brier had many other arguments—including double jeopardy—that will be explored later. Not only did their friendship pre-date the trips cited by the Commonwealth, Mellow's attorneys in a memorandum cited testimony from a former PNC official stating that the first PNC underwriting contract was dated before the Yankees outings. Mellow also returned the favor and sometimes paid for the trips, the attorneys argued.

I'd covered reporting under the ethics law for years and honestly forgot about the friendship exception. Doesn't it mean you could just say, 'hey, so and so is my friend, so what?' No, Mellow's attorneys said, it's got to be real and verifiable.

Understood. But it still seems like the Wolf proposal—the "no-thank-you rule"—should clarify that it covers friends as well. Friends better than anyone should understand your predicament as a public official and be willing to "go dutch." Wolf told me it would apply to old friends who have business in state government. And how about the legislature, maybe, imposing limits on itself? Wolf deserves credit for at least changing the conversation about the gift culture in Harrisburg. He told me he followed the practice for years, when he worked as state revenue secretary under Rendell. A big Phillies fan, he once after the fact called the Phillies brass to arrange payment for gifts such as autographed baseballs and shirts he and guests received at a game. I think he also said warm-up jackets. He called the Phillies about it and was told in effect you can't pay for the stuff. He insisted he needed to do so and sent the Phillies' office a check for several hundred dollars.

You lead by example he told me. He is careful not to bash others for their gift policies.

TRAVELING MAN

Former Sen. Michael Brubaker, a Lancaster Republican who headed the Senate Finance Committee, apparently logged the most miles—taking trips to Turkey, Taiwan and Nova

Scotia, based on the financial disclosure reports reviewed by the Trib. Those trips weren't underwritten by groups with business in front of the General Assembly, Brubaker argued.

Brubaker reported $10,090 for a trip to Turkey paid for by a cultural exchange group and he brought home the Turkish rug, a gift from his Turkish hosts. The Taipei Economic and Cultural Office paid $5,400 for his trip to Taiwan. He traveled to a Regional Policy Forum in Nova Scotia, which cost $2,364.

These gifts and trips had nothing to do with the turnpike case. But they show the pervasiveness of gifts in Pennsylvania's political culture and why lawmakers may be reluctant to tighten the rules even after the alleged abuses were revealed at the Turnpike Commission.

"My travel doesn't cost taxpayers a penny, and it's not paid by groups with interests before the Legislature," Brubaker told me. "When you are traveling internationally, you are sometimes given a gift. Sometimes it is awkward not to accept."

Former Senate Majority Leader Dominic Pileggi, R-Delaware County, traveled to Dublin in 2010 for a State Legislative Leaders' Foundation conference. The foundation paid his $2,147 travel cost. Corporations comprise the foundation's principal funding source.

Pileggi's then-spokesman, Erik Arneson said the "discussions had direct relevance to issues Pennsylvania was addressing at the time and continues to address."

In the turnpike case, prosecutors noted that Hatalowich received numerous gifts and trips from turnpike vendors and failed to report them.

Hatalowich could not afford to go to prison. His relationship with his son, George, a Harrisburg area high school football star, was at stake. He'd miss his son's best year if locked up in a state prison.

The gifts and trips Hatalowich racked up were eye-popping. According to the grand jury, he received:

- A $4,000 travel voucher from McTish, Kunkle & Associates, an engineering firm.
- Use of the firm's apartment in Pittsburgh and four Pirates tickets. The apartment cost was $480. The tickets cost $320.

- Use of the Orth-Rogers' firm's Las Vegas condo and Vegas shows.
- Travel to Tampa at Orth-Rogers' expense.
- A $600 gift certificate from SP&K Engineering firm for use at the plush Nemacolin Woodlands resort. Former Commissioner Bill Lincoln received a similar gift. Lincoln got immunity from prosecutors and stepped down following issuance of the presentment.

* * *

According to the grand jury report, here's how cozy it got with McTish and Hatalowich, and McTish is only one example:

May 22, 2006

- Hatalowich email to McTish manager: "Hey I wanted to ask you, are we still okay for staying at the apartment from June 30 to July 3rd?" Do you have any baseball tickets for the July 1 game? Let me know. Thanks. G."
- McTish manager replies: "Yes, the apartment is yours. Yes tickets for July 1."
- May 31, Hatalowich to McTish: "Do you know if you have 4 tickets to the game on Saturday? Can you tell me where the seats are located if you do? Thanks. G."
- McTish reply: "4 seats club level section 212 Saturday 7:05 game. Do you have any idea when 0-10 DB will be awarded/ntp (notice to proceed)?"
- Hatalowich response: "Cool. Thanks, the award is on the agenda for June 6. The NTP will be given once all the paperwork is returned. I think it's a 10-day turnaround requirement. G."

McTish received its first contract of $19.7 million in 2003. It was supplemented twice in 2006 and 2007 to a final amount of $21.6 million for part of the Southern Beltway project near Pittsburgh. The firm was selected in 2005 to replace the Allegheny River Bridge for $15.1 million and received a separate roadway contract for $22.3 million. Between 2002 and 2010 McTish and others at the firm donated

$277,515 to candidates including $42,000 to Fumo, other lawmakers and candidates for governor.

Hatalowich, Brimmeier and commissioners took part in fundraising, sometimes extending personal invitations for vendors to attend events, the grand jury alleged.

Principals of Orth-Rodgers, another firm, made $103,700 in campaign donations to candidates with the most influence over the turnpike, according to the grand jury presentment. Engineering firms have been doing so for years. It's legal to do so. The company provided perks such as the Las Vegas and Tampa trips to Hatalowich, the grand jury said. That's also legal as long as the officials report it.

BRIMMEIER "WENT BERSERK"

The warning light went off for me in a big way when a Commonwealth witness testifying for the prosecution at the preliminary hearing in June 2013 effectively handed Brimmeier a central piece for his defense.

Jill Thompson of Uniontown, who works for Orth-Rodgers, a consulting engineering firm employed at the pike, testified that she sometimes went out to dinner with Brimmeier when visiting Harrisburg. She did so shortly after hearing her company had been hit up for a $12,000 campaign contribution just before a contract award was to be announced, according to the grand jury presentment. She told him about it.

"He went berserk," said Thompson, in the hearing before District Judge William Wenner. "Don't ever do anything like that. We're not a pay to play organization," she testified Brimmeier told her in the car. Even over dinner sipping a cranberry vodka, Brimmeier would still not calm down, Thompson said in the hearing's fourth day.

Bill Winning, Brimmeier's defense lawyer, pounced on Thompson's testimony and got Thompson to repeat it on numerous occasions during cross-examination. Winning had repeatedly told me he was representing an innocent man who clearly would be exonerated.

Fina, Patrick Blessington, a former deputy AG out of Philly, and others in the old guard, would never have let this happen. Rightly or wrongly, they'd have had a "come to Jesus" meeting with Thompson.

Brandstetter was tough but not the intimidating type. Still, more cerebral perhaps than the bare-knuckled boys from Bonusgate. And remember, she did not have much help overall in preparing.

Keisling, author of the 1993 book on skullduggery at the Pennsylvania Turnpike Commission, told me early on this did not appear to be a case of "pay to play" but rather was a continuation of "pinstripe patronage," the practice of both parties for decades awarding contracts to big campaign donors.

In reality, it was often not a stated quid pro quo. It was understood that this is how business is conducted.

Such patronage isn't necessarily illegal like bribery. The impact on the institution is, in a way, even more sinister because it is less blatant and may go undetected. A lot of gifts, travel and favors were accepted from vendors, who realized they had to play ball to have a shot at a contract.

An executive with Traffic Planning & Design told the grand jury political contributions in essence were a "marketing expense . . . something we need to do in order to pursue these types of projects."

In other words, so ordinary, so much a part of turnpike business, that vendors didn't think about it as a quid pro quo. Just SOP. Like greasing palms in a Third World country.

POLITICAL ANIMAL

I'd certainly known of Brimmeier back in his days as an official in Allegheny County government, when it was still a Democratic machine under the late former county commissioner Tom Foerster. There's no doubt in that sense he was an old-time pol and extremely experienced at how the game was played. He was Foerster's patronage chief in county government, the Trib's Tom Fontaine wrote in a profile.

Foerster had been one of the last old-style political bosses in Pittsburgh, even though he was one of three county commissioners. He had a hand in or controlled much of the patronage and county contracts on Grant Street. That meant payrollers, who wanted to keep their jobs and who worked on campaigns, and professional service providers and other contractors who donated money to campaigns. Much like what was alleged at the turnpike.

Brimmeier cut his teeth on old school politics.

The connection to Foerster went way back. Brimmeier was a high school football star on Pittsburgh's North Side. He won a football scholarship to Youngstown State University. Foerster had been his grade school coach. It's clear his value was political, according to a Pittsburgh Post-Gazette profile of Brimmeier after he was charged in 2013. With Foerster in a tough primary election in 1983, "Mr. Brimmeier proved himself to his patron that summer when he delivered 58 busloads of seniors to a pivotal Foerster rally in South Park that 7,000 attended, including all the top names in the local Democratic Party," the profile by James O'Toole and Tim McNulty stated.

"He (Brimmeier) knew the chairmen, the precinct captains and the volunteers. He knew the prospective candidates and the failed candidates," wrote Jeff Frantz for Pennlive.com. "He knew the unions. He knew the donors. He knew your name, your kids' names, and your background. He knew who you backed the last time around. He knew who supported you, and who supported the other guy. He knew what you wanted to hear on a key issue, and what you needed to hear."

Brimmeier and Foerster had a falling out in 1991 when Brimmeier decided to run for county prothonotary, the official who oversaw civil legal filings. Foerster was the boss and Brimmeier bucked him. By then Foerster was no longer the powerhouse he had been in the 1970s.

Brimmeier went on to work for Auditor General Don Bailey and later became chief of staff to former U.S. Rep. Ron Klink, a Murrysville Democrat. "He didn't know anything about the legislative process in Washington before he got there, but he did an incredible job," Klink told Fontaine. "He's a great administrator and a smart person."

When Ed Rendell ran for governor in 2002, Brimmeier was his western Pennsylvania coordinator. When I traveled with Rendell on his campaign bus that year, Brimmeier was at one of the stops ahead of us lining things up.

In 2003, Rendell appointed Brimmeier as turnpike CEO.

In that position I clashed with him doing a 2005 series about the agency. First they delayed a request for contracts and other agency records. There were roadblocks inserted along the way to make reporting difficult. I was the "bad cop." I had Chris Osher, a young reporter at the Trib with great investigative skills, play the "good cop." He did most of the interviews with Brimmeier.

THE SUPPORTING CAST

Fast forward to 2013. Thompson testified on the fourth day of the preliminary hearing for six defendants: a powerful state senator and the other top turnpike executives and consultants. Brimmeier, Rubin, Mellow and others were in court defending their very lives. As guys in their 60s a long prison term could mean spending their golden years in the slammer rather than playing shuffleboard at a Florida condo or enjoying their grandkids.

Brimmeier, of Ross Township in Allegheny County, was 65; former Agency Chairman Mitchell Rubin, of Philadelphia, was 61; and former Senate Democratic leader Bob Mellow, of Scranton, was 70. The other defendants were Hatalowich, 47, originally from Uniontown, the turnpike's former chief operating officer; Dennis Miller, 51, of Harrisburg, a vendor vice president; and Jeffrey Suzenski, 63, of Pottstown, a vendor consultant. Unlike the other five facing multiple counts, Suzenski was charged with one ethics violation.

It looked like the turnpike case was falling apart. Brandstetter tried to think hard after the preliminary hearing what went right. Thompson was one of several witnesses to go south. If this happened at trial, Brandstetter could use grand jury testimony—where the Commonwealth witness took firmer stances—to impeach her own witnesses. But that would begin to add credibility problems to the entire case. She was still confident, however, that other company executives from engineering and consulting firms could beef up what these witnesses said.

If she could get it to a jury, Brandstetter believed, she could still win. If Brimmeier could be turned, he provided the road theoretically to Rendell. That presumed there was something to pursue against the former governor and no evidence to that effect surfaced during the proceeding. Rubin likewise was the highway to "Senator No. 6"—to Fumo—assuming he could be implicated.

Asked at the March 2013 press conference why Fumo was not charged, Kane said there was no evidence.

Ruben and Brimmeier provided prosecutors, in theory, with the road map. But they were not breaking.

* * *

After the turnpike case broke in the news, former Republican Gov. Dick Thornburgh told the Trib's Tom Fontaine the corruption case should "serve as a catalyst" to eliminate the agency and place it under PennDOT. That would greatly eliminate duplication of services, material and equipment, Thornburgh said.

The agency was mismanaged and heavily influenced by politics, said Thornburgh, a former U.S. attorney and U.S. attorney general. He acknowledged in the interview with Fontaine that due to politics at the Capitol: "We were unable to get our (turnpike) appointees confirmed in the Senate so we were never able to get into the driver's seat."

Thornburgh fought with Senate Democrats for six years over turnpike appointees. At the time, the battle through the early 1980s was one of the most bitter disputes in Pennsylvania politics. The Senate Democrats held majority control and would not budge.

Thornburgh had booted Camiel after his conviction but that conviction was overturned. Cerelli resigned after his conviction. A compromise in 1985 expanded the number of members from five to six with the governor picking the chairman. The governor was allowed to name two new members without confirmation.

Thornburgh in return agreed to $4.5 billion in turnpike improvements. Critics would later call it the "Noah's Ark deal" because supposedly it required two of everything. If one Democratic consultant was hired for a job, a Republican consultant was as well. That paved the way for Keisling's reporting.

* * *

Footnote: The Turnpike Commission in 2013 spent almost $700,000 in public money on legal fees to defend itself against lawsuits filed by whistle-blowers who claimed that politics and favoritism to campaign contributors or friends dictated business deals, state records show.

In response to a Right to Know law request from the Tribune-Review in 2013, the turnpike acknowledged spending $699,250 on fees for outside lawyers in four civil cases. The lawsuits were filed before the statewide grand jury issued its scathing report alleging cronyism and a "pay to play" culture at the agency. It charged that contracts were rigged to benefit campaign contributors, and turnpike officials received gifts such as travel and costly dinners.

"It's a disgrace," Dave McGuirk, a longtime turnpike watchdog from the Pittsburgh area, said of the legal fees.

* * *

(Sources: A Scranton Times story in June 2013 by Borys Krawczeniuk; a March 13, 2013, Trib story on gifts I reported with Debra Erdley; the 2013 Post-Gazette profile of Brimmeier and the Trib's profile by Tom Fontaine, both cited in the chapter; my own stories in the Trib on the preliminary hearing and the whistleblower legal fees; Jeff Frantz's outstanding piece in Pennlive on Brimmeier; ABC27 TV piece by Dennis Owens on Lepore remaining on the payroll and John Micek on same in Pennlive. Fontaine's Thornburgh interview in the Trib in March 2013. Public documents include the grand jury report and the attorney general's press release and other court documents.)

* * *

Next: Warning signs in pike case.

4

BUSINESS AS USUAL

June 28, 2013

As the preliminary was winding up, turnpike contractor Domenic Piccolomini took the stand and testified that he gave gift certificates every December to top turnpike officials. He gave gift certificates totaling $6,100 from 2005-2010 to agency officials for stays at the posh Nemacolin Woodlands resort. They were Christmas gifts, he explained.

They cost $700 apiece until 2009 when the cost of each certificate went to $1,000.

A grand jury report said Sucevic Piccolomini & Kuckar Engineering received $4.1 million worth of turnpike contracts from 2005-10.

The gifts were not tied to the contracts, Piccolomini, the firm's owner, testified.

This is the way business was done.

Some might call it a thank-you note. Others might suggest it buys goodwill for continued access . . . and continued business.

William Lincoln, former Senate majority leader and a member of the Pennsylvania Turnpike Commission, and Hatalowich received certificates based on evidence submitted by the Commonwealth—one year for $700 and another for $800.

Lincoln needed a free gift certificate—as the cliché goes—like a hole in the head. He retired in 1995 with a pension worth $1.5 million. He took $73,062 a year from the pension.

As a member of the commission, his salary was $26,000 annually. That would help nudge up his pension.

That's $101,562 a year and he was taking "gifts" from contractors?

Excuse me, they are just Christmas presents.

On a local Fayette County blog, an anonymous writer said, "so what? He took some gift certificates? Look at all the good he's done." That's the same argument lawmakers convicted of crimes used in their trials or pleas for leniency at sentencing. Former Democratic Whip Mike Veon, of Beaver Falls, ran a huge constituency service out of his district office. He lined up votes for key Democratic initiatives. Essentially he ran the caucus. He was an extremely effective legislator, maybe the best of his era. But he also authorized the use of state tax money to pay House Democratic staffers "bonuses" to work on political campaigns and in early 2015 he was still behind bars, based upon a Dauphin County jury's verdict. He also was convicted for misappropriating tax money funneled to a non-profit.

Lincoln received immunity to testify but he easily could have been charged. Granted these amounts were minor in the big scheme of things. But it was flat-out wrong. Lincoln did not report the gifts as he was required by law to do. I believe it's why he sought immunity.

Historically, Lincoln was the second-highest profile figure involved in the trial, but few people knew him by then and he received minimal news coverage. On the commission, he was an avid promoter of the Mon-Fayette Expressway, a key turnpike extension project, in his old legislative district.

Lincoln got more than the big bucks.

Commissioners get free vehicles. Retired legislators typically get free health care for life. In 2013, Lincoln was driving a 2011 Ford Explorer that cost more than $33,000. Chairman William Lieberman, less than three months before the indictment announcement and shortly after a toll increase, got a new Jeep Cherokee worth $40,000, according to the Philadelphia Inquirer. His one-year-old Cherokee worth more than $38,000 was turned over to Commissioner Pat Deon, according to the Inquirer story by Paul Nussbaum. Lieberman is an insurance executive based in Pittsburgh. Deon is a prominent figure in Bucks County who owns a beer distributorship. Carlisle lawyer Michael Pratt drove a turnpike-issued 2011 Explorer-like Lincoln, the article said.

The chairman makes $28,500 a year.

The Chief Executive Craig Shuey at that time defended the vehicles as appropriate and necessary. He told the Inquirer, "We ask a lot of our commissioners."

Yet PennDOT Secretary Barry Schoch, then the fifth member of the commission, drove his own car.

Lincoln, of Fayette County in Dunbar, served in the House from 1973-78 and in the Senate from 1979-94. As a pre-1974 legislator he benefitted from a higher pension multiplier that enabled him to draw down more than his salary of $68,097 had been.

I remember him from the '90s as a physically powerful guy. He looked like someone who actually had worked for a living before 1978. He probably never set foot in a gym. To me, he looked "country strong." But maintaining his health and the "stress" of the announced turnpike indictments prompted his resignation on March 22, 2013.

He had been a big cheese in the legislature. In this case he was just an immunized witness.

THE ZINGER

Trial in the turnpike case was less than three months away. Senior Deputy Attorney General Laurel Brandstetter had resigned a few days before and was headed to the private sector.

It was no surprise.

She went out on a high note, not publicly trashing the lack of support from the front office under Attorney General Kathleen Kane. But it bothered her—big time—and it was obvious she wasn't getting much help. Why?

The turnpike was Corbett's case—he had large-scale ownership; Frank Fina supervised the investigation. Brandstetter did the heavy lifting, most of it since Fina was tied up with Bonusgate; Computergate; (a corruption case against House Republicans for using tax money for databases and computer gizmos for campaigns) the case against former House Speaker Bill DeWeese, a Democrat, for using his staff as his campaign team; and of course Jerry Sandusky. Kane had other goals including the consumer-oriented lawsuits her office would launch. Repeating the public corruption success of the Corbett era didn't appear to be her goal. In fact, investigating Corbett's handling of the Sandusky case, despite the successful verdict, seemed to be all-consuming during Kane's first year-and-a-half in office. That put Fina squarely in her crosshairs.

The length of Kane's unprecedented probe of a predecessor attorney general's investigation was due to reconstructing emails from the Sandusky era—millions of them. Her investigators were turning the place upside down to find something. It was that misplaced focus that deprived the turnpike case of oxygen. Add in suspicion of Brandstetter in the front office and you've got the formula that my colleague Steve Esack of the Morning Call of Allentown suggested when he said Kane was "starving" the turnpike investigation. (He said it off camera, I believe, while we were taping Pennsylvania Newsmakers with Terry Madonna, a political science professor at Franklin and Marshall College and an omnipresent TV commentator. That one word summed up the consequences of being on the outs with Kane incredibly well.)

Moreover, this case did include some big Democratic figures, including Mellow from her hometown. By the time trial rolled around, Mellow was out of federal prison and driving around town in a sports car. Much grayer and a bit frailer, he was still somewhat popular in his hometown. Certainly there would be sympathy in some quarters if he went to prison again at his age.

"Frank (Fina) did hire me," said Brandstetter. "He was in Harrisburg and I was in Pittsburgh. He prosecuted Bonusgate, Computergate and Sandusky during my tenure. There were significant portions of our time together where he was un-reachable. He is incredibly intelligent and was an important resource to me as I learned grand jury procedure and how to prosecute public corruption cases in Pennsylvania."

Then came the zinger:

"Frank being my boss and our relationship was held against me throughout my employment with the OAG." She made the comment to me four months after leaving the office, no longer in a state of shock.

Brandstetter had no one helping her at the hearings other than one or two occasions. One was a young attorney, Clarke Madden, a former law clerk for Dauphin County Judge Richard Lewis, along with Susan DiGiacomo, a former federal prosecutor. Madden was removed from the case after Mellow's defense attorneys argued he had a conflict because he had worked for Lewis.

DiGiacomo, a senior deputy out of the Norristown office, was there every day during the turnpike preliminary hearing. "She refused to assist with the presentation of witnesses and my chain of command knew that," Brandstetter told me months after she left the office to join a Pittsburgh law firm.

Refused? The chain of command knew it?

If Brandstetter is right, and I have no reason to doubt her, it suggests the brass in Kane's office, maybe the AG herself, was tanking the case. Or just flat out didn't care.

DEARTH OF EXPERIENCED PROSECUTORS

Laurel Brandstetter was a California girl. She grew up in San Francisco. She graduated with highest honors from the University of California, Santa Cruz. At Hastings College of Law, she won the American Jurisprudence award for best moot court brief. She earned her JD of law in 2000. By 2001 she was trying cases in the rat race of the Allegheny County Courthouse where ADAs flipped case files like accomplished jugglers. So did the public defenders, but the public defenders typically never went up against anyone better than the ADAs. The prosecutors, however, sometimes drew the best criminal defense attorneys in Pittsburgh, or those from other parts of Pennsylvania. Brandstetter cut her teeth on firearms cases, homicides, aggravated assaults, robberies, organized crime activity and of course, drug trafficking. She took 35 cases to verdicts before juries and handled over 60 trials before judges, including nine homicide cases and drive-by shootings.

But these were what Fina would call "gun and knife cases."

It wasn't until she joined the state attorney general's office in 2008 that Brandstetter got her first real taste of major public corruption. She spearheaded the grand jury probe of the Pennsylvania Gaming Control Board. The grand jury issued a comprehensive report and exposed some major problems in the licensing phase. The report blistered the Gaming Control Board. But no one was charged. She then took ownership of the turnpike cases.

Along the way, she prosecuted Veon on the Beaver Initiative for Growth "BIG" case. Fina was co-counsel on that case. She took the lead. The state AG's office again faced Veon's tenacious lawyers Dan Raynak and Joel Sansone.

Sansone gave one of Brandstetter's witnesses a brutal beating on cross-examination. (It's detailed in *Keystone Corruption*, my first book.) I never saw anything quite like it.

She delivered a passionate summation that, in my view, won the case that could have gone either way. Bonusgate, Veon's first case, was far more black and white, with email evidence and former aides lining up to testify against him. The BIG case was more complicated and difficult to understand. Brandstetter nailed it. And Veon got another year tacked onto the 6-14 years he got in 2010 on the bonus case. Veon got the toughest sentence of anyone involved in the corruption scandals. He was paroled in June 2015.

Brandstetter, who was 39 as the turnpike case chugged along toward trial in 2014, had been "one of the guys" back in the day with Fina & Company. The hard-assed prosecutors, especially Fina, spewed out four-letter words like truck drivers. Once, she battled Fina in a challenge where they both dropped down on the seventh floor of the Manor building in Pittsburgh to do 25-30 push-ups. To Fina's chagrin, she won.

Brandstetter cut quite a figure in a red dress and heels. She certainly commanded attention of the men on the jury—at least they weren't dozing. She had plenty of sparkle as a trial lawyer. She didn't get rattled by defense attorneys' shenanigans. If she did, it didn't show. Maybe it was a yoga technique, given she was a certified instructor.

Branstetter wasn't just a Namaste gal, though. She also was a volunteer mentor for the Steel City Boxing Association, working with city kids. Brandstetter did some boxing herself. Boxing tends to keep the mind sharp unless you get your gourd rung a few times. So far, she was clear eyed.

Had circumstances been different after Kane's election, Brandstetter could have become one of the best trial prosecutors in the state in just a short while. In my view, she was still rounding out her style and courtroom presence during the BIG case. By the summer of 2014, she was one of the most experienced prosecutors in the office. Another was Bruce Beemer, who also served his time in the trenches of the Allegheny County Courthouse as an ADA. But he was spending more time as an administrator than a trial lawyer, though he was a good one. Linda Dale Hoffa, a former federal prosecutor, went back to Philadelphia in 2014. Hoffa left in the early wave of departures as Kane's troubles mounted.

Experienced prosecutors were few and far between as the ranks continued to thin after Kane's arrival and unraveling. In 2012, the AG's office had Fina, E. Marc Costanzo and Pat Blessington. Fina was the case architect and a human computer on case details. Blessington and Costanzo were the blue-collar Philly prosecutors with hundreds of trials under their belts. All three wound up working in Philadelphia for DA Seth Williams after Kane's election. Blessington was the lead prosecutor in Bonusgate.

On August 13, 2014, Laurel Brandstetter resigned to set up a practice with Leech Tishman Fuscaldo & Lamplin in downtown Pittsburgh establishing an anti-corruption unit to advise businesses and governments how to stay out of trouble—and help them if the worst happens. The turnpike case crumbled rapidly from there on.

* * *

(Sources: Presentment of the 33rd Investigating Grand Jury, a July 20, 1995 Morning Call story by Megan O'Matz on Lincoln' s pension; the Fay-West.com blog; the Paul Nussbaum Inquirer story on commissioners' vehicles cited above; numerous Trib stories, including my own accounts of the preliminary hearing; an Inquirer story on Hoffa's departure written by Angela Couloumbis in September 2014. I broke the story of Laurel's departure from the office, but the interviews by phone and email took place after she left the AG's office.)

* * *

Next: Why did the turnpike case crumble?

5

"MAKE WORK" AND BIG BUCKS

Nov. 20, 2014

The legislative sting case colored just about everything including a porn scandal that exploded in the fall of 2014 and the relatively quick disposition of the remaining defendants on the turnpike docket.

As the case headed for trial, few believed it would ever take place. It was down to four defendants: Bob Mellow, Mitchell Rubin, Joe Brimmeier and George Hatlowich.

STUNNING CONTRACT

The fire sale began in the summer of 2014 when the attorney general's office accepted guilty pleas from Jeffrey Suzenski and Dennis Miller. Suzenski, a vendor, was a relatively minor figure and he pled guilty to an ethics charge and was placed on two years' probation. That made sense, but Miller? He was the former executive with Ciber Inc., an IT solutions firm hired to consolidate and replace computer systems. He was Ciber's lead guy in Harrisburg.

The Colorado-based firm was the high bidder on a 2005 computer project. Ciber's bid was almost seven times higher than IBM's, and it dwarfed a bid by Deloitte Consulting. Ciber's $3.2 million bid in all topped five other competitors.

You guessed it. Ciber got the contract.

In May 2006, Ciber was awarded an additional payment of $58.3 million, bringing the total contract to $62.3 million. The latter amendment was "dramatic and unprecedented," the grand jury concluded.

Ciber got special treatment because Miller paid for trips and dinners for turnpike officials and donated campaign money to senators with turnpike ties, prosecutors claimed. Miller had a personal relationship with Hatalowich and he donated $19,000 in campaign money to Fumo, the Senate Democratic powerhouse, who clearly had major influence at the agency. Miller approached other consultants to raise campaign money for Fumo, the grand jury said.

Witness after witness told the grand jury the turnpike didn't even need the system Ciber proposed. It was like buying a Cadillac Escalade when a Ford Focus would do, a witness said.

Firmly entrenched at the agency, Miller's crew had a high turnover rate, meaning new consultants needed training and started from the ground up. It was described by the grand jury as "make work."

When Hatalowich was promoted to chief operating officer, Miller took Hatalowich and his family to dinner in a limousine. He gave gift baskets and wine to Brimmeier. Ciber sponsored dinners at international toll association meetings, as did other vendors. Miler paid "more of the expenses" on a trip with Hatalowich and his family to Cozumel, Mexico, according to the grand jury.

Meanwhile, Miller was racking up six figures from his salary, commissions and bonuses from Ciber. From 2003 to 2006, he garnered $309,459 in salary; $253,456 in commissions; and $28,641 in bonuses, court documents show.

There's no way to put a price on the turnpike's chicanery. "The actual cost in dollars and cents is pretty much incalculable," said Jerry Shuster, a professor of political rhetoric at the University of Pittsburgh. Shuster said the "major cost is damage to the public trust and people who administer it."

The attorney general's office agreed to a lenient deal for Miller. He had been charged with unlawful bid-rigging, theft by unlawful taking, theft by deception, an ethics charge and criminal conspiracy.

Miller and Suzenski were both given ARD, Accelerated Rehabilitative Disposition, a program of probation without verdict. There's no plea or admission of guilt under ARD.

It's usually reserved for drunk drivers.

They were both placed on probation for two years and ordered to do 100 hours of community service. They can seek to have their record expunged if they successfully complete the program.

There was no cooperation agreement to testify against other defendants. Of course, why would they flip—given the deal and sentence?

DEAL OF THE CENTURY?

That left only Brimmeier, Rubin, Mellow and Hatalowich.

Their pre-trial motions, seeking dismissal of charges, were pending before Judge Lewis.

First, on Oct. 6, Lewis dismissed six counts against Mellow, leaving only a conspiracy charge. Lewis didn't buy the double jeopardy argument, saying the federal charge concerned his actions as a senator and Senate staff, while the state charge dealt with alleged actions at the Pennsylvania Turnpike Commission. Nonetheless, Lewis kicked most of the case. It appeared to be the prelude to a plea bargain. But it was better than that for Mellow. On Oct. 16, the conspiracy charge was nol prossed in a deal with prosecutors, meaning it was dismissed. "The case was baseless from the beginning," said Dan Brier, one of Mellow's attorneys.

After a thorough review, the attorney general's office stated that it "would be unable to sustain its burden of proof going forward."

Next came Rubin. The former chairman saw all but one of the charges against him dismissed: three counts of bid-rigging, two counts of corrupt organizations, two ethics charges, conspiracy and one count of commercial bribery. The deal? Rubin, Fumo's old pal, pleaded guilty to one count of commercial bribery, a misdemeanor, in November 2014.

Fumo, or "Senator No. 6," was not named or charged in the case.

Rubin could have faced two years in prison. Instead, he received 24 months' probation, 100 hours of community service, and must pay a $5,000 fine.

"Dogman5" wrote on Philly.com's reader comment section: "What a joke. No consequences. Business as usual." That's a facet of Internet news I am still coming to grips with: anonymous writers blasting subjects of news stories. Throughout my career going back to the early 1970s, editorial page editors called people or otherwise attempted to verify the writers were who they said they were. It was entertaining but in many respects unfair.

But it's life today in the Internet and cable TV-driven 24-hour news cycle.

Rubin apologized to the court, saying, "I followed the custom when I should have followed the law." The grand jury said Rubin had a conflict of interest by steering work to City Line Abstract, for which he received payments of $78,927, $76,208 and $65,098 over three years.

Observers were scratching their heads wondering how Rubin avoided going back to prison given he was still on federal probation from the Fumo corruption case. Federal prosecutors alleged Rubin became Fumo's "ghost employee" before former Democratic Gov. Ed Rendell fired him. Rubin in 2010 pleaded guilty to obstruction of justice and was placed on five years' federal probation. The reason it didn't hurt Rubin: there was no overlap in the timing of the offenses. The charge from the Fumo case stemmed from a crime that occurred much earlier than the turnpike case.

That left just two defendants, perhaps the most culpable: Brimmeier and Hatalowich.

Brimmeier pleaded guilty Nov. 20 to a felony and conflict of interest. So did Hatalowich. Both were sentenced to 60 months of probation. They were each fined $2,500 and ordered to do 250 hours of community service. Both "are now convicted felons and will have to carry that badge as a consequence of their actions," said Kane's former spokesman J.J. Abbott. He said the attorney general's office viewed these as "reasonable resolutions of the case."

One way to look at it—of eight defendants charged there were six convictions, albeit several minor ones, comparatively speaking. Another way to view it, is no one went to prison in a corrupt scheme and the loss of millions in public money.

"The final score reads like a boxing match fixed by the promoter: No prison time, no loss of pension, and the defendants walked away with the prize money," said reformer Epstein, offering an analogy.

He compared the prosecution to "a train wreck."

Despite his guilty plea to conflict of interest, Brimmeier received a $43,027 state pension for 12 years of service.

Again, conflict of interest is not an enumerated crime under the pension forfeiture act.

I called Brimmeier on his cell phone in February 2015. He talked to me because he said I'd been fair to him during the legal proceedings.

"I did what I had to do as far as a plea was concerned, for myself and my family," Brimmeier said. "I was not guilty of anything. I didn't do anything wrong in 42 years in government" at the state, local and federal levels. "Now we're enjoying the fruits of my work. I definitely did not do anything wrong. I had to (plead guilty) for my wife, my family, including my grandson."

Well, that statement could have landed him back before the judge. I had no idea at the time but heard it was the buzz the following day in the legal community at the Allegheny County Courthouse in Pittsburgh. You can't plead guilty and then publicly state you were not guilty. Did you lie to the court when you stated you were guilty?

I understand what Brimmeier meant. But he's lucky Judge Lewis in Dauphin County didn't haul him back in court to explain himself.

Was the turnpike case that weak? Were some of the defendants innocent? Maybe so but it looked like Kane's office folded the tent after it was clear Brandstetter would not be around and Kane became immersed in parceling out the porn scandal and defending herself in a grand jury regarding her own conduct. Some believed the legal theory was flawed: you can't blame it on the culture and hope the jury would connect the dots.

Another little known fact about the case: the attorney general's office had to go through 30 million turnpike documents and turn relevant ones over to the defense. That should have been done months ago and trial was fast approaching. Brandstetter didn't have the resources, and had she still been around as trial neared she would have been held responsible for not getting it done.

The lack of cooperative plea agreements by any of the defendants spoke volumes, in my view.

It would take a "legal hazmat team to clean up the damage caused after the Turnpike indictments crashed," said Rock the Capital's Epstein.

"One thing the presentment did point out was there were a lot of weaknesses in controls," said Matthew Haverstick, a lawyer who represented the turnpike commission. Turnpike officials addressed those as quickly as possible as the case was still pending, he said. "At the executive and at the commissioner level we've got to make sure we're doing this the right way. If there are bad procedures, we have to weed them out," Haverstick said.

By January 2015, the turnpike filed a lawsuit against Ciber for more than $45 million, alleging the company orchestrated an overbilling scheme to implement a computer software system that doesn't work properly, the Trib's former reporter Bobby Kerlik reported. It was filed against the Denver-based company and former Ciber Vice President Dennis Miller in Dauphin County Common Pleas Court. The company denied the charges.

The crimes and alleged crimes in the overall turnpike corruption case took place under a Democrat-led turnpike administration. For the next four years, through 2014, no one at the agency was charged with crimes. In January, former Sen. Sean Logan, a suburban Pittsburgh Democrat, was appointed by Wolf, a Democrat. Logan was elected chairman. Logan immediately announced the agency was adopting Wolf's gift ban, which might deter some of the activity alleged in the presentment and admitted by some. Except it should be noted that the state Liquor Control Board also adopted the gift ban. And the state liquor code already made it a crime to accept gifts from vendors. Yet three former top agency officials violated state ethics rules for accepting a combined $23,000 worth of gifts from vendors from 2008-2012, the Ethics Commission found.

It begs the question if a criminal statute didn't deter the behavior why would a gift ban? That applies to the LCB and the turnpike, where gift acceptance simply had not been reported.

In the end, taxpayers also paid almost $300,000 for the legal fees of some turnpike defendants convicted of crimes, records show. The payments covered legal work until they were charged with crimes, said turnpike spokesman Carl DeFebo Jr.

"Pennsylvania is one of the few states where taxpayers get mugged and you charge them for the legal fees," reformer Epstein said.

* * *

(Sources: My Tribune-Review stories on the preliminary hearing, Rubin's plea and my "price of corruption" story; court documents on defendants' pre-trial motions and Commonwealth responses; Judge Lewis' opinions; a November 2014 story by the Inquirer's Angela Couloumbis on Rubin's plea; a Patriot-News photo graphic, summarizing the outcomes of Turnpike cases—used as a guide; a Trib story by Tom Fontaine on the Brimmeier and Hatalowich pleas; the Legal Intelligencer by Max Mitchell on the nolle pros of the last Mellow charge; turnpike documents obtained under the Right to Know law; Kari Andren's Trib LCB stories; and a March 19, 2014, Inquirer piece by Chris Palmer and Tricia Nadolny on the LCB gift scandal; my phone interview with Brimmeier; Tribune-Review Right to Know law request on legal fees; interview with Epstein; Matt Miller's Pennlive story on Rubin's plea.)

Note: The turnpike suit against Ciber was pending.

POSTSCRIPT

In an extraordinary document, former Northumberland County Senior Judge Barry Feudale, who supervised the grand juries for high-profile corruption investigations of the legislature and the turnpike probe, in November 2015 outlined crimes and ethical violations he claims were committed by Kathleen Kane as attorney general. He acknowledged some might consider him biased since Kane helped remove him as grand jury judge and because she lodged a complaint against him with a judicial ethics board. But Feudale said he would swear to his charges in an affidavit. Relevant to the previous chapters on the turnpike was his allegation that a grand jury presentment was sent to him with Senator Vincent Fumo's name (remember Senator No. 6) at the top. "There were 15 officials in that presentment—seven more than the final presentment," according to Feudale. Fumo and others, reportedly vendors, were not named in the final presentment. The suggestion was that Kane for some reason let Fumo walk. That is not necessarily a crime, given the broad latitude of prosecutorial discretion. It implies though that Brandstetter went along, a notion to which she took great exception. Feudale's complaint "raises significant and alarming allegations," Brandstetter said. Her response was limited, she said, due to grand jury secrecy. But Brandstetter stated: "I can say that I have tremendous respect for Judge Feudale, both for his integrity and legal mind. Attorney Generals (Linda) Kelly and Kane made the investigation and prosecution of the Pennsylvania Turnpike cases as difficult as they possibly could.

"That being said, I would never have knowingly participated in an effort to improperly manipulate criminal charges. My oath was to uphold the laws of the Commonwealth and NOT to serve the political whims of either Attorney General Kelly or Attorney General Kane," Brandstetter said.

Feudale's unprecedented statement from a grand jury judge—with a press release and complaint to state and federal authorities—also dealt with the burglary of his office, theft of sensitive documents and unauthorized access of his email. He claimed that Kane and key staffers were behind it. "One of the missing documents was the original grand jury presentment with Fumo's name on it," Feudale said. Kane said through a spokesman Feudale didn't offer "a scintilla of evidence" to support his charges. By late November 2015 Feudale's status as a senior judge was revoked and he could no longer serve as a judge. There's a price to pay for being outspoken. Supreme Court Chief Justice Thomas Saylor removed Feudale on questions of his objectivity, the Daily Item in Sunbury reported. Feudale expected it. Judges don't normally talk out of school much less level serious allegations against a statewide elected officeholder.

Post-Postscript: Brandstetter was again in court with Matthew McTish in April 2016, except in a vastly different role. The engineering firm president pleaded guilty to conspiracy to bribe officials in Allentown and Reading on multimillion dollar contracts, prosecutors said. Brandstetter was McTish's defense attorney. Ironically, it was the type of pay to play case Brandstetter tried to prosecute as a deputy attorney general against the Turnpike Commission.

* * *

Next: A senator's supreme arrogance.

6

"I AM THE FUCKING SENATOR"

Oct. 30, 2014

LeAnna Washington and J.P.Miranda paid a steep price for breaking the law, some might argue. But in reality, nothing could be further from the truth.

Sure, the former senator and ex-House member lost their seats in the 2014 Democratic primary. Philadelphia voters supposedly turn their heads at corruption. But they didn't in these instances and tossed out lawmakers actually charged with crimes.

Here's the rub: neither faced prison time by pleading guilty. Miranda in January 2015, pleaded guilty to conflict of interest and false swearing. Defendants who fess up and save the county and/or state money by avoiding a trial can often but not always get a lighter sentence.

How much more do corruption trials cost? The prosecutors are being paid anyway. It drains resources from dealing with other cases, for one. But the real incentive for prosecutors to take a plea is that it is a sure thing. In the won–loss column, it counts as a win. A guilty plea is a conviction. Going to trial carries some risk though prosecutors win the vast majority of cases.

Miranda's attorney A. Charles Peruto Jr. began by playing hardball claiming Miranda was investigated because Miranda and DA Seth Williams "were both dating the same girl at the same time," according to Chris Brennan's Philadelphia Daily News story in February 2014.

District Attorney spokeswoman Tasha Jamerson denied the allegation and told Brennan the evidence includes "video tape, text messages, bank statements and testimony by Miranda's own staff."

Miranda was 28 at the time. I never saw or heard of him at the Capitol, given he was just off of his freshman year, entering his second term when charged. He'd been elected in 2012. To me the case was noteworthy, at least, because of that last name, as in "you have the right to remain silent . . ." It was also stunning that having a "ghost employee," reminiscent of the 1970s, was still in vogue. Miranda was accused of using a no-show state "staffer" to funnel money to his sister. Ironically, the Miranda case was put together by Frank Fina, now working for Philly DA Seth Williams. Fina? Remember? Kane's nemesis.

Miranda will not be missed. And he's lucky to be on probation and not in state prison.

The reader comments on Philly.com are often quite brutal but when it comes to corrupt politicians they can be downright nasty. Some would argue deservedly so.

"Dumb and dumber," one anonymous writer stated after Miranda's plea. "Justice served," said another.

But the Philly.com hecklers really turned up the heat when Washington also pleaded guilty in October 2014 to that catch-all crime of conflict of interest. It is not one of the enumerated crimes that causes an automatic revocation of pension under the state pension forfeiture act. The idea behind this law was automatic revocation for pols who defiled their office and destroyed public trust by committing a crime hurting the integrity of their office.

So Washington's deal allowed her to keep her $42,879 pension. Miranda wasn't in long enough to get a pension.

The conflict of interest charge often allows corrupt officials during sentencing to avoid the pension forfeiture law. It seems to me that forcing staff to work on campaigns is tantamount to stealing from taxpayers. It's essentially what Bill DeWeese and so many others went to prison for. DeWeese lost a pension he estimated at an annual lifetime value of $3 million. The legislature should remedy the pension forfeiture act to include the conflict of interest charge. Too many pols have used it to keep their pensions. (Of course if the law is adjusted, someone who has earned a good deal with prosecutors will just get a plea to misdemeanors or other crimes that don't trigger the law.) Still a conviction on the ethics charge seems as offensive to the office as perjury.

An elected official convicted of perjury will lose his or her pension. Theft is another crime that requires revocation. So is bribery.

But a state official convicted of murder in a domestic dispute won't automatically lose the pension. Suppose a lawmaker killed a constituent in their office; it might qualify. No, I'm told, that would still not trigger revocation. The law is specific and murder is not one of the crimes.

So Washington pleaded guilty to conflict of interest but not to theft.

The upside supposedly was she would resign immediately. Big deal. November rolled in the day after her plea. The session ends Nov. 30. They do absolutely zilch in November and December.

This is the self-proclaimed "fucking senator" who could do "what I want" and "how I want." She forced taxpayer-paid staff to work on her annual fundraiser, which doubled as her birthday party, from 2005 through 2013. When her former chief of staff Sean McCray balked, he ended up in the dog house and eventually saw his pay cut by $10,000.

She was a hypocrite as well, having co-sponsored a 2010 resolution that forbade campaign activity by Senate staff on state time.

Her state-financed fundraisers were elaborate affairs with ice sculptures and bubble machines, according to grand jury testimony.

The fact she was walking away with her pension—a deal authorized by Attorney General Kane's office—roiled the Philly.com needlers.

One online writer wrote it was "a gross notion that she'll keep her pension after pleading to defrauding the public."

Another complained that using state staff for campaign work is exactly the type of criminal activity that should result in pension loss.

"Townwatch7" said cynically:

> "Did anybody have any reason to think that this would go any other way? Of course she serves no jail time and gets to keep her pension funded by the taxpayers that

> she stole from. What she meant to say was, "I'm sorry I got f--king caught." If someone had stolen $100,000 from a bank they would be sent to prison . . . Absolutely double standards in our courts for politicians."

Kane oversaw Washington's case.

The way Epstein, of Rock the Capital, viewed it: taking away a public official's pension is "one of the few tools we have to combat corruption.

"This is a troubling trend, whereby folks engaged in misconduct are rewarded with a lifetime payout."

Kane's then-spokesman Aaron Sadler said "whether or not an offense should result in automatic pension forfeiture would be an issue for the legislature."

The kicker among Philly.com readers was "Boru" noting that, "By accepting her (Washington's) pension, she's saying F-you again to her constituents. She has absolutely no shame or remorse."

* * *

(Sources: State grand jury presentment against Washington; my Trib story and column about Washington; Chris Brennan's, Philly Daily News stories in January and in February 2014; Inquirer story, January 2015 on Miranda by Julie Shaw; Inquirer story May 22, 2014, by Craig McCoy; piece by Inquirer's Jessica Parks and Tricia Nadolny on Washington; May 21, 2014, Associated Press story on the primary; Angela Couloumbus' and Jessica Parks' March 12, 2014, story on Washington, and Steve Esack's of the Morning Call on the same date; Miranda's official state House bio; Nov. 1, 2014, story by Nadolny and Parks in the Inquirer; attorney general's press release on Washington.)

* * *

Next: The McCord case shocks the political establishment.

7

AN IVY LEAGUE SHAKEDOWN

Jan. 29, 2015

HARRISBURG—Dressed in a dark suit and crisp white shirt, he arrived early and waited in the courtroom. It was a blustery cold day on Feb. 17, 2015, and Rob McCord faced the most embarrassing moment in his 55 years on earth. He carried with him *Changó's Beads and Two-Tone Shoes*, a novel in the Albany series by Pulitzer Prize winner William Kennedy.

For a few blissful moments, he escaped. And he waited for the proceeding to get underway in U.S. District Court.

Pennsylvania's fiscal watchdog was busted by the feds for doing what too many politicians have done for too long. They get caught up in the glory and trappings of office and quest for more. McCord wanted to be governor so badly he became desperate to raise campaign money.

Like other state row officers before him, he crossed the line. Former Auditor General Al Benedict in the 1980s illegally sold state jobs to raise money so he could become governor. He pleaded guilty in 1988 to federal racketeering and tax charges. He once confided to me he wanted to be governor in the worst way. He was devastated when he didn't win the treasurer's race after two terms as auditor general. That would have kept him viable in a potential gubernatorial contest. Former Treasurer R. Budd Dwyer—before his tragic end with a gun in his mouth—in 1987 was tantalized with the prospect of a $300,000 kickback—one third for his campaign, another third for the Republican Party, and $100,000 for himself, according to testimony. A jury convicted him of bribery and he shot himself at a televised news conference the day before sentencing. Hard to say Dwyer was intent on becoming governor, but he was ambitious and had things gone well it wasn't out of the question. Former Attorney General Ernie Preate had his eye on the governor's office and he ran in the 1995 GOP primary. At the outset, Preate was the favorite. But a grand jury found he was too cozy with video poker operators and too casual about the money he collected from them in his race for attorney general. He took their money illegally and pleaded guilty to mail fraud in 1995. He was forced to resign as part of his plea deal. To this day, Preate claims it was an election law violation not a case of selling the office.

Driven by blind ambition and resources he couldn't match, McCord, the two-term state treasurer, saw his dreams crash long before votes were cast in the May 2014 Democratic Primary for governor.

McCord obliterated the law in raising money for the governor's race by threatening two state contractors with potential loss of state revenue if they failed to donate to his campaign. He was charged Feb. 2, 2015, by the U.S. attorney's office in the Middle District of Pennsylvania with two counts of attempted extortion. How many more contractors he may have shaken down we'll never know. McCord, if anything, was aggressive. He was aggressive as a Masters-level squash player. He was aggressive in the gubernatorial debates and at times seemed like he'd enjoy duking it out in the hallway with any candidate foolish enough to get in his face. He was a pugnacious fireplug, compact and muscular.

In fundraising, the Ivy League-educated McCord sounded more like a union thug from the docks, according to federal documents in which McCord's voice was picked up off his cell phone by a wiretap.

McCord told a neighbor, an attorney with a Philadelphia law firm doing business with the Treasury, to carry a message to the firm's managing partner from whom he sought a sizeable contribution: "If (McCord) loses and you stiffed him, every time you are trying to get something done through state government, you are going to have the State Treasurer looking to screw you," federal documents show. McCord wanted $25,000 from the firm, but he knew the firm's managing partner supported the incumbent Republican, Corbett. At one point he went to the partner and suggested using his neighbor as a conduit to disguise the source. The firm was not identified.

Translation: "Nice law firm you have here. Be a shame if anything were to happen to it," York Daily Record columnist Mike Argento wrote later.

McCord also shook down a western Pennsylvania property management company for $100,000 using a campaign "bundler" to send his ominous message.

McCord described the company's executives as being "rich as Gods." So by God, he deserved some money if the firm wanted to continue to get state revenue and/or contracts.

"I stepped over the line," McCord said in his video released by his lawyer Jan. 30, 2015, by "trying to take advantage of the fact that two potential contributors hoped to continue to do business with the Commonwealth—and by reminding them that I could make things difficult for them. I essentially said that the potential contributors should not risk making an enemy out of the State Treasurer."

McCord's downfall was more like a car wreck in a fast lane of the Schuylkill Expressway. He resigned with meager explanation Jan. 29, 2015, via news release. As media pressure mounted, he released the video admitting wrongdoing Jan. 30, and the very next business day, a Monday, he was charged under the Hobbs Act with two counts of attempted extortion by the U.S. attorney's office in Harrisburg, the same office that decades before had investigated and charged Benedict, Dwyer and Preate.

Now it was time to face up to his own words before U.S. District Judge John E. Jones III, who had been quite a political player in his day as the transition co-chair for Republican Gov. Tom Ridge and the chairman of the Liquor Control Board.

DUST UP IN HERSHEY

If you met McCord you would no doubt like him though his ego takes some getting used to. You'd see a man with incredible charisma who is bright, articulate and extremely competitive. He had that natural big smile. Acquaintances say he could not stand to lose. He considered himself an ex-jock. He has Harvard and Wharton School (Penn) degrees in his background. A former venture capitalist, McCord is wealthy and lives in an affluent Philadelphia suburb.

The massive ego was evident in his repeatedly calling the state treasury the "McCord Treasury"—like it was his. I wrote a column about it to hold him accountable. Hell of a lot of good that did. He kept calling it the McCord Treasury. It's the Pennsylvania Treasury that belongs to state taxpayers.

Maybe that should have been a warning sign as the governor's race got underway in 2013. This guy's ego was larger than the Capitol dome.

With two statewide wins under his belt, the Democratic Party endorsement looked like it was his to lose among six candidates. His chief rival for the endorsement was former U.S. Rep. Allyson Schwartz, who represented part of Montgomery County and Philadelphia. The endorsement meeting was held in Hershey, the "sweetest place on earth," at the upscale Hershey Hotel. Again, these state pols often have inflated views of themselves. They believe their own press clippings. Media coverage in the so-called statewide "row office" races is superficial. Look how easily, as an incumbent, McCord had won re-election as treasurer in 2012, he must have thought. Despite disavowals, he had no intention of serving out his second four-year term as treasurer. The governor's race was around the corner and he considered himself the "Corbett slayer" as stated in his press clippings. That McCord moniker first surfaced in Philadelphia Magazine in November 2012 and McCord used it. The truth is any living, breathing Democrat surviving the primary was probably the "Corbett slayer," considering Corbett's unpopularity.

McCord knew he was the favorite of party insiders should they endorse a Democratic candidate. And he was. The hotly debated issue beforehand was whether to hold the state committee vote. It would only be an embarrassment for Schwartz to finish second even if McCord fell short of the needed number to win. Thus, Schwartz and her supporters backed an open primary.

That led to a confrontation at the hotel the night before the vote. McCord had former Philly Controller Jonathan Saidel, Schwartz' campaign chairman "tossed out of a small meeting among leaders," Philadelphia Daily News columnist

John Baer wrote. When Baer asked Saidel about the clash with McCord, Saidel stated McCord is "a f---ing a--hole."

The next day at a Philly caucus meeting, Saidel confronted McCord telling him to "get the f--- out of here," Baer reported. Such is Philly and statewide politics in Pennsylvania. There was no reference to how McCord replied. But I doubt he backed away from the confrontation. Seriously doubt it.

He got the vote.

Still, McCord fell short of the two-thirds votes needed for endorsement even though he won more votes than any of six gubernatorial candidates.

"I thought it was a great win for our campaign . . . and for the party," McCord said.

The endorsement is usually an investment in futility. Or is it merely for bragging rights? Former Democratic Gov. Ed Rendell ran without it and won in 2002. In some statewide row offices, historically, it's been the kiss of death.

Democrat Tom Wolf, a York County businessman, walked around casually greeting committee members the night before the vote. He seemed amiable and relaxed. He was not seriously competing for the endorsement. He was running as an outsider. He had just launched the first sustained TV ad campaign with a compelling biographical ad that won wide acclaim. State committee members and their spouses were buzzing about it. Wolf dumped $10 million of his own money into the primary, took off like a rocket and never looked back. He got only 50 or so votes among the more than 300 Democratic leaders at the meeting and could have cared less. The majority owner of the Wolf Organization, a worldwide distributor of kitchen cabinets, had a plan and he was sticking to it.

The "almost" factor would be a theme for McCord in the governor's race.

For McCord, SEC regulations made regulated financial companies off limits. In the past, politicians serving as treasurer would tap the financial advisers and fund managers as donors. McCord put $2 million of his own into the race but he couldn't keep up. He raised $2.5 million in 2014, a tidy sum but not enough to compete with Wolf.

McCord seemed desperate with an attack ad on Wolf—playing the race card—and reaching back to 1969 race riots in York, Wolf's hometown. Black leaders there were backing Wolf. McCord's TV ad bombed. McCord finished third with Democratic voters in the May 2014 balloting.

THE OTHER SHOE?

He used the power of his office and state-awarded contracts to attempt to bully businesses and lawyers to donate.

The quotes in federal documents were so long and detailed they certainly came from wiretaps. There are only two presumed victims cited, the managing partner of a Philadelphia law firm and a western Pennsylvania property management company. Were there others? Was McCord cooperating? Two charges seemed light. There would be other related offenses they could have thrown at him. He was immediately contrite and remorseful.

Numerous lawyers and criminal justice sources told me there seemed little doubt he cut a deal. When would the other shoe drop?

McCord announced his resignation on Jan. 29, 2015, and later acknowledged he hoped to keep the federal investigation secret. I came to work that morning with no clue about McCord. Sometimes, you catch wind. This was not one of those times. Donald Gilliland, a Trib editor with experience in Harrisburg, spotted a tweet early that morning about the resignation. As soon as I read it, I thought "indictment." How so? He said he was leaving for the private sector but he mentioned no job.

"It is time for me to return to the private sector, where most of my life's work has been," his resignation letter read. He went on to cite his accomplishments in office like it was an obituary. McCord was giving up a $156,264 job that he had campaigned for and won twice. He finished third in the governor's race. Disappointing but no reason to drop out of state politics. Former Democratic Gov. Robert P. Casey had been known as the "three time loss from Holy Cross," winning for governor on the fourth try in 1986. Casey was a study in perseverance.

Former Lt. Gov. Catherine Baker Knoll had no talent to speak of but she too was persistent and kept throwing her name on the ballot, losing and trying again. She was elected treasurer on the third try in 1988. She ran for governor then won for lieutenant governor.

Why would McCord give up? Was he offered the CEO job at Google? Why throw in the towel?

Democrats were stunned by the announcement. In no time, strong persistent rumors were in the wind. Media reports surfaced that McCord was under federal investigation.

Asked whether the treasurer's office received federal subpoenas for documents or McCord received notice that he was the target of an investigation, his spokesman Gary Tuma offered what had been called a "non-denial denial" in the Watergate era. He would not lie to a reporter. Tuma had been a fine reporter for the Pittsburgh Post-Gazette.

Tuma said McCord deferred to "the law enforcement authorities on whether to comment on, or even confirm, any such inquiry."

It's clear McCord was trying to use the treasurer's post as a stepping stone to become governor. His 2012 opponent, Republican Diana Irey Vaughgan, told me McCord had no real commitment to the office and had set his sights on becoming governor.

So even if he was bored with being treasurer, as some suspected, he had plenty of time to make a comeback if his story were true. But it wasn't and the feds weren't talking that day, at least for the record.

That evening, a Philadelphia TV reporter showed up at McCord's house. He gave a brief statement—a polite no comment. But it was a sign of what was to come if McCord didn't come clean. The drumbeat got louder the next day, with "investigation" stories swirling.

On Jan. 30, 2014, McCord's attorney Robert Welsh released a video of McCord making a statement saying that he would resign immediately and he planned to plead guilty to two charges in federal court.

THE VIDEO

Pennsylvania Treasurer Rob McCord on Friday acknowledged that he "stepped over the line" when raising campaign money for his failed gubernatorial bid, and his lawyers said he intends to plead guilty to federal charges for strong-arming two unnamed state contractors.

"I owe an apology to the people of Pennsylvania," McCord said. Addressing the public, his staff and family, McCord said: "I am sorry I let all of you down."

He was contrite, apologetic. It was sad. His resignation took effect immediately.

In the Democratic primary, McCord, 55, of Bryn Mawr, warned the potential donors of a possible loss of state business, he said in the video.

"Clearly that was wrong," McCord said. "It was wrong. It was a serious mistake, and I stand ready to pay the price for that mistake. I have always believed in accountability. Now I have to live it."

McCord received almost $2.5 million from hundreds of donors who made more than 560 contributions in 2014, according to campaign finance records compiled and analyzed by Trib reporters Brian Bowling and Mike Wereschagin. Since he took office in 2009, the Treasury Department signed nearly 900 contracts with about 190 contractors, according to the department's data.

McCord began 2014 with $6 million in his campaign account. He raised nearly $2.2 million before the primary and ended up with just over $31,000 in the bank after the primary. Still on the books is $2.2 million in debt, all but $25,000 of which he owes himself, campaign finance records show.

"Immediately upon being contacted by federal agents about these matters, Mr. McCord acknowledged that he had overstepped the line of legitimate political fundraising," Welsh said.

Wolf said he would move quickly to nominate McCord's replacement. The Senate approved Wolf's pick, Timothy Reese, an investor and entrepreneur.

McCord said he hopes people will eventually judge him by the work he did as treasurer, but he acknowledged, "I know my improper efforts to raise campaign money will forever be a stain on my reputation."

Welsh noted that McCord made $2.1 million in personal loans to his campaign.

REALLY, THE OTHER SHOE

Christopher Craig, the office's chief counsel, became acting treasurer until Wolf named a replacement. Craig is the consummate professional and widely respected staff lawyer who had the misfortune to have earlier worked for former Sen. Vincent Fumo, D-Philadelphia, who was also convicted of corruption charges.

Voters will elect a treasurer in 2016. Reese is a caretaker and as usually happens with interim nominees, he had to agree not to run.

Meanwhile, McCord waited throughout 2015 to be sentenced and likely was singing like a song bird to garner a better deal.

"The mistake and fault here is mine and mine alone," McCord said.

The McCord wiretaps would haunt other state officials who spoke with him in 2014. His pre-sentence conference was delayed in June and by February 2016 he still had not been sentenced. McCord also wore a body wire briefly at the state Capitol in 2014 on behalf of the FBI, the Philadelphia Inquirer disclosed in April 2016.

What was going on? The FBI was investigating others on the tapes and several other shoes were expected to drop. A campaign consultant, Michael Fleck, who worked for Allentown Mayor Ed Pawlowski, also did some work for McCord in the 2014 governor's race after Pawlowski bowed out. Fleck was wired by the feds in what analysts said appeared to be a pay to play investigation. Reading Mayor Vaughn D. Spencer was another Fleck client.

In the summer of 2015, the FBI served subpoenas for records in Allentown and Reading City Halls.

In another case linked to the McCord investigation, federal prosecutors announced in April 2016 that John Estey, former chief of staff to Gov. Ed Rendell from 2003 to 2007, would plead guilty as part of a plea deal to federal wire fraud charges. Estey, then 53, of Ardmore, had earned $783,000 as a top executive at the Hershey Trust and he lobbied as a lawyer for Ballard Spahr in Philadelphia. He was Adrian King's brother-in-law. Estey began working as a lobbyist in

2008. Estey co-owned the Enterprise Fund, a political action committee that donated $125,000 to McCord one day after the 2014 gubernatorial election, in which McCord finished third. The Estey case was part of a probe of lobbying in the Pennsylvania General Assembly, federal prosecutors said.

* * *

(Sources: Michael Wereschagin and Natasha Lindstrom, Pittsburgh Tribune-Review, on McCord's plea in federal court in February 2015; A report by Robert B. Swift, Scranton Times-Tribune, on McCord's plea; My Trib stories on his resignation and intention to plead; McCord's video announcing his intention to plead posted by the Welsh & Recker law firm; Wereschagin and Brian Bowling's research on McCord's campaign finance data for the governor's race in 2014; John Baer's Daily News Column on "Democrats in Hershey, Not Too Sweet" from the Democrats' endorsement meeting in governor's race; Philadelphia Magazine article on McCord from 2014; Michael Argento's York Sunday News column from February 2015; My Trib column in August 2013 about McCord calling the state Treasury the "McCord Treasury"; Trib stories on Fleck and the McCord fallout in July 2015; Morning Call story on Fleck being wired, by Emily Opilo, Scott Krauss and Matt Assad on July, 13, 2015; April 2016 story by Tom Fontaine, Pittsburgh Tribune-Review, on Estey being charged; Philadelphia Inquirer story on that same announcement by Angela Couloumbis, Mark Fazlollah and Craig McCoy, of the Philadelphia Inquirer; Bumsted and Mike Wereschagin stories in 2005 about the mysterious Enterprise Fund controlled by Estey.)

* * *

Next: Why Kane didn't prosecute.

8

"NOT PROSECUTABLE"

March 17, 2014

The days after the sting story were chaotic in the attorney general's office and in the Capitol newsroom as we tried to catch up to the breadth of the story's implications. The attorney general, after the governor, is the second most powerful position in the executive branch of state government. Arguably with arrest power, the ability with court approval to tap phones, search homes and run investigative grand juries, the attorney general is the most powerful figure in the executive branch.

Kathleen Kane, the 2013 darling of the media, had taken a direct hit.

She blamed Frank Fina.

Fina would later say he did not leak the story and had even posed objections to its publication.

But he was not unhappy. He did drop a time bomb in her lap as he left the attorney general's office for Philly in early 2013. It's not as if this began as some grand conspiracy against Kane. The case began long before she even became a candidate for attorney general.

However, Fina knew he'd wind up in Kane's sights when she promised in 2012 to investigate why the attorney general's investigation of Sandusky took so long. Candidate Kane said the delay was "probably" political.

"How long should it have taken?" Tom Corbett once asked me.

Frank Fina was dead meat if he stayed to work under Kane. They seized his hard drive—an act of outright aggression to a prosecutor—shortly after taking office.

Aides were stunned during Fina's exit interview with Kane when Fina laid out the sting case. No one claimed to have known about it. Indeed, it had been kept tightly under wraps. Kane's office would suggest it was a rogue investigation by Fina under Corbett, interim AG Bill Ryan and Corbett's successor Linda Kelly.

Fina had a lot of latitude in previous administrations because he delivered. One need only look at his success with Bonusgate, Computergate and Sandusky. He sent that serial child predator, with his sick smirk, to state prison for the rest of his life. Running a probe targeting lawmakers needed to be akin to a covert op.

* * *

So on the day after the Inquirer story broke, Kane called a news conference. Fina and the Inquirer would be directly in her sights.

Kane looked chipper, considering. It was, after all, St. Patty's Day, and Kathleen Granahan Kane, the descendant of Irish ancestors, began her news conference with "Top of the mornin' to you." Kane is tall, thin, with long brown hair and high cheekbones. She is telegenic and her presence on TV ads undoubtedly helped her.

President Obama got into a bit of trouble when he ventured into "looks" of female attorneys general. At a California fundraiser in April 2013, he said California Attorney General Kamala Harris "happens to be by far the best-looking attorney general in the country."

Kane's then-spokesman Dennis Fisher told Pennlive that Kane had no comment but "her (former) husband Chris respectfully disagrees with the president."

Gary Rothstein, of the Post-Gazette, wrote: "Pennsylvania has an attorney general who's also rather hot, and there's a big risk that you just insulted her, if she cares about that sort of thing. I know that I, as a Pennsylvanian proud of my top lawyer, am offended the president doesn't put Kathleen Kane anywhere in Ms. Harris' league."

A female attorney once told several reporters in a casual chat that she believed Kane feels the need to be the "prettiest woman in the room." Whether true or not, it may tap into the massive ego that seemed to be steering her off-course in 2014.

* * *

Angela Couloumbis sat near the front of the room. I joined her on one of the few chairs along a wall with a side view of the lectern. Most of the reporters were seated in rows of chairs facing Kane, with TV cameras in the rear. I'm sure Angela didn't know what to expect. I certainly didn't. Would Kane directly attack her in going after the Inquirer? Former Gov. Ed Rendell was never shy about calling reporters out at a news conference, asking them questions to try to turn the tables.

But Kane's presentation this day was well prepared and delivered in a professional manner.

The arguments were much the same as she had laid out in broader detail in my interview the night before.

The 2,000-plus fraud charges against Ali were dropped, by agreement, "just 24 days after I was elected and weeks before I was sworn in."

"I will not sit back and allow lies from those who seek to destroy the public's trust in me or my office," Kane said.

Her office found "disturbing information" that there may have been "a racial focus to the targets of the investigation" as well as "improper reporting, inadequate resources and inadmissible evidence." She claimed the agent on the case was told to "focus only on members of the General Assembly's Black Caucus." The agent was told to ignore wrongdoing by white lawmakers, Kane alleged.

Kane stated that Bruce Beemer, chief of staff to Kelly, only learned of it Jan. 17, 2014, the same day she did. Little wonder.

Fina held Beemer in low regard.

But Kane said she did not have "any animosity towards the lead prosecutor of this case." She barely knew him, she said. She didn't mention Fina by name. And she hinted at the dares to come.

"If the former prosecutor (Fina) believes the case is strong enough to move forward, he currently has concurrent jurisdiction in public corruption matters (in Philadelphia)," Kane said.

Beemer reviewed OAG Case File No. 36-622 and found prosecution was "not advisable or warranted," Kane reported. Beemer had a great reputation from his days in Pittsburgh as a trial prosecutor in the district attorney's office. Kelly brought him on board. I thought his endorsement of Kane's position carried some weight.

The sweetheart deal for Ali was so lenient that it undermined his credibility, Beemer reported.

Kane called it the "deal of the century."

At the news conference I asked Kane whether she would allow Beemer, standing behind her, to come to the microphone and explain why it was not prosecutable. She brushed off the question. I didn't doubt her, but I wanted to hear from him.

Kane stated that 80 percent of the recordings were made 18 months before she took office. The case was dormant when she took over, she said.

Three attorneys general, Corbett, Ryan and Kelly, didn't file charges, Kane said. There was no "quid pro quo" between the would-be lobbyist and lawmakers, she said. The sting ran for three months under Corbett, a total of 22 recording sessions. Under Ryan, 67 recordings were made from January through April of 2011. In 2011-12, Ali made 34 recordings while Kelly was AG. The last seven sessions were made in April of 2012.

Kane was elected in November 2012.

Up to $20,000 paid in bribe attempts by Ali was gone and could not be recovered, Kane said.

In short, it was a "half-assed investigation," Kane contended.

At first blush, I thought Kane seemed to present a credible defense on why she didn't prosecute. In an op-ed piece sent to the state's newspapers, Kane began saying the "thought of elected officials taking money and violating the public's trust makes me sick." She added she will "never shy away from prosecuting public corruption."

Later, as her argument began to unravel, former prosecutors told me her mistake was saying too much. Prosecutors have wide discretion to prosecute or not. She should have said she made a decision not to bring charges, period.

Kane was either being naïve or too honest about her actions. One might also conclude she doth protest too much.

* * *

(Sources: My interview with Kane and story that ran in Trib March 17, 2014; Associated Press—Mark Scolforo's March 16, 2014, AP story based on his interview with Kane; public documents released by the attorney general's office Sunday, March 16, 2014—including a written statement by Kane; Background news release from Kane's office; "fact sheet" released by Kane's office; Chris Mautner's Pennlive article on AG Harris and Kane; Gary Rotstein's April 2013 Pittsburgh Post-Gazette piece; Op-ed piece entitled "Taxpayers are the true victims of dead case by Kathleen G. Kane"; Kane's statements at a news conference on March 17, 2014; numerous Inquirer stories, including Dec. 18, 2014, by McCoy and Couloumbus; May 2015 Philadelphia magazine story; a December 2014 story in the Legal Intelligencier on Seth Williams' news conference; Time line of Case File No. 36-622 of 113 tape recording sessions provided by attorney general's office.)

* * *

Next: Kane's legal threat backfires.

9

THE SPRAGUE THREAT

March 20, 2014

There were several momentous moments in Kane's downfall. I witnessed most of them. But one I didn't see ranks as her worst public relations decision, permanently straining, if not ruining, her media relations at numerous outlets across the state. It was in short, a PR disaster that could not be reversed.

Kane arranged a meeting with the Philadelphia Inquirer's editorial board. The meeting was held four days after the sting story was published.

OK so far, right? But unbeknownst to her top advisers, Kane showed up with famed Philadelphia libel lawyer Richard Sprague, whom she had retained privately. Every newspaper editor in the state knows and perhaps fears the legendary litigator. It wasn't just that Kane made a unilateral decision to hire Sprague. The woman elected statewide just 17 months before by the voters of Pennsylvania, announced through Sprague that she would not talk at the meeting she requested. Sprague would do the talking. Attorney Thomas A. Sprague, his son, accompanied them to the meeting.

"The meeting began on an unusual note when the elder Sprague announced that Kane was his client—and that she would not speak," the Inquirer's ace political reporter Thomas Fitzgerald and Craig McCoy, the paper's investigative reporter, wrote. "Her office had asked for the meeting following the newspaper's story Sunday that disclosed the corruption investigation and her decision to halt it. 'She would like to speak to you,'" Sprague said Thursday. "'Unfortunately, a mean ogre representing her is preventing it. So put the fault on me.'"

Asked if she agreed with her attorney's advice not to talk, Kane answered, "I do."

Sprague suggested that the Inquirer may have been used by the sources of its stories—"wittingly or unwittingly" as a "weapon" to attack Kane to defend themselves from potential charges of wrongdoing in the management of the probe, according to the Fitzgerald and McCoy story.

"I intend to look at the investigation from the very beginning to the conclusion of it, and in terms of what has been published, by this paper and others, to take appropriate action on behalf of the attorney general against those responsible for the defamatory and the false publications that have been made," Sprague was quoted by the Inquirer as saying.

Inquirer Editor William K. Marimow said the paper stood by its story.

But the damaging "evidence" suggesting Kane abandoned all conventional rules of dealing with the press—a press that by and large had fawned over her through the last election cycle—was the photo. The Inquirer's picture of Sprague at a table wearing a windbreaker included Kane by his side, looking at him adoringly, as if she found her champion.

What a fearsome move she must have thought. Sprague's best-known media case is a suit against the Inquirer that brought a record-setting libel judgment. At last count, the paper owed $24 million after a tortuous 23-year history in the courts. The case was settled for an undisclosed sum in 1996.

But reporters, editors and politicos I know were blown away by her decision. Several senior staffers of Kane's considered it a mistake. A former top aide would call it the "worst political decision in this state since (Treasurer) Budd Dwyer decided to kill himself" at a widely covered news conference. Dwyer on Jan. 22, 1987, shot himself in the mouth with a .357 magnum handgun the day before his sentencing on federal corruption charges. Hyperbole, perhaps, on the former advisor's part. But the point is well made.

King, Kane's first deputy, was later quoted by investigators saying it was "a very, very unwise move" and "cast the whole office and everybody who worked for her in a bad light."

It was, quite simply, "madness," King stated. It was "embarrassing" and "possibly fatal."

The best editorial reflecting the outrage against Kane was written by the Trib's Colin McNickle. He saw it clearly as an effort "to intimidate the free press."

Colin didn't say this, but I wondered at the time. What small to medium newspaper in the state would allow Kane to visit the newsroom or editorial board since Sprague might come along?

Colin McNickle wrote that Kane who "at least now, appears to have the facts in the disputed prosecution on her side, no less—retains private counsel in a hardly tacit attempt to intimidate a newspaper. Not only does it smack of attempted official oppression in hoping to win a urination match with her political foes, it's incomprehensibly stupid."

Kane—even though she wasn't charging the taxpayers for Sprague's advice—had blundered in such an amateurish way. Later, she would let it be known that she no longer employed Sprague. But the damage was done with the state's newspapers—a former top aide became convinced he had to get out and one of the best press secretaries she had would resign shortly thereafter. The week after the editorial board meeting, Joe Peters, from Kane's hometown of Scranton, resigned. Peters was overqualified to be a press secretary but he was knowledgeable and articulate. He was an attorney and former drug and Mob prosecutor.

He would not say why but everyone knew.

* * *

(Sources: The Inquirer story and photo referenced above in March 2014; the Trib editorial by McNickle also in March 2014; an April 1996 story by Emilie Lounsberry with a McCoy contribution on settlement of Sprague's libel suit with the newspaper; The Affadavit of Probable Cause filed in Montgomery County on Aug. 6 by Detective Paul Michael Bradbury. My background interviews with former Kane staffers; *Keystone Corruption* by Brad Bumsted, Camino Books.)

* * *

Next: The dispute between Kane and Fina goes public.

10

"I AM AN ATTORNEY"

March 21, 2015

If you ever met Frank Fina, you would know cynicism and sarcasm permeate his verbal landscape. So it was absolutely no surprise to me, at least, that an op-ed piece he sent to the Inquirer in the sting's aftermath used a mocking tone about Kane's decision to have Sprague speak for her at the editorial board.

"I have been a lawyer for 22 years, and a public servant for almost all of that time," Fina wrote. "I have not retained a lawyer to advise me to speak, or to remain silent. I am an attorney."

He challenged Kane to sit down with him and answer questions in a televised event with questions from reporters on why the sting case was dropped. "I invite her to bring her personal lawyer, or to bring with her any of the dozens of lawyers she directs at the Office of Attorney General," Fina wrote.

Of course that was not happening.

Fina would have crushed her.

Fina was writing in response to Kane's repeated public suggestions that racism was an underpinning of the case. Her charge of racial targeting incensed Fina's new boss, Philadelphia District Attorney Seth Williams. Fina and agent Claude Thomas, along with another state prosecutor, E. Marc Costanzo, left the attorney general's office and went to work for DA Williams. They wanted no part of Kane.

"As a black man, I have seen racism. I know what it looks like. This isn't it," DA Williams said of the dropped investigation.

The lead agent on the sting case, Thomas, is black. He had a reputation as someone who advocated for raising issues of fairer treatment and pay for black law enforcement agents. The idea that he'd target blacks seemed absurd on its face. Thomas allegedly confessed to two people in Kane's office to taking orders to target only black officials.

Or so Kane asserted.

Thomas filed a civil lawsuit against Kane.

I've met Thomas. I would feel sorry for anyone who would accuse him of that in person. He is a big, strong man, prone to dressing in dapper outfits. He shows a steely resolve beneath the surface.

Seth Williams asked Thomas about it in a face-to-face meeting. "I have looked into his eyes," DA Williams said. "I believe he is telling the truth." If Kane believed members of his staff were guilty of "serious ethical and legal issues," DA Williams said, why didn't she raise it sooner?

"BLIND AMBITION"

Seth Williams was insulted by the accusations because he had hired Costanzo, Fina and Thomas. If they were racists, then he was harboring racists. Kane "publicly attacked respected career prosecutors and investigators in a desperate effort to absolve herself," DA Williams said.

Here was one of the state's top prosecutors from Pennsylvania's largest city taking on the Commonwealth's chief law enforcement officer. Both are Democrats. It was highly unusual. Was it because, as Kane supporters carped, DA Williams planned to run against Kane in the 2016 primary? Not so, his staffers said. No, Seth Williams told me when I asked at a press conference. Politicians change their minds and stories all the time. He would be a formidable candidate coming out of Philadelphia if he did decide to run. A former staffer, however, said DA Williams has his "dream job." As the 2016 race approached, there was far less talk about Seth Williams as a candidate.

"Kane accused her predecessors of racism, blind ambition and simply made things up—things that were disproven the moment they sprang from her lips," wrote Dennis Roddy, a former Corbett staffer who wrote for Pennlive.com as a columnist after the governor's defeat. He transitioned back into reporting and writing because of his record as an investigative reporter for the Pittsburgh Post-Gazette.

His column on Kane appeared in the Times Leader of Wilkes-Barre.

An example of Kane gone astray was the unequivocal blame she laid at Fina's feet for dismissing 2,088 criminal charges against Ali, the informant, in late 2012. He had been charged for defrauding the Department of Education through his day care center. Ali got the "deal of the century" and his credibility as a witness was shot, she argued. Never mind, DA Williams would later say, that prosecutors every day give deals to "very bad men" including murderers in exchange for testimony. A prosecutor from another jurisdiction told me privately he would have loved to have had Ali as a witness, compared to the bad-ass criminals who testified in his cases now.

SOCIAL GENIUS

Also, it seems obvious filing voluminous charges was an effort to turn Ali into a state informant and witness. He is a smooth-talking young man, often dressed to the nines in pinstripe suits. The Trinidad native is as articulate as a college professor even though he never graduated from college. According to a Philadelphia Inquirer story, Ali worked as an unpaid informant and was involved with an investigation of threats against public safety. Ali had extensive dealings with the FBI. I talked to him a few times.

He called me and my caller ID showed a "blocked" cell number. We talked off the record so I won't reveal what he said. Suffice it to say, he was impressive, perhaps brilliant, though he also struck me as eccentric.

I saw an opportunity several weeks after the sting. More than a year later, as the case against Kane progressed he called me out of the blue while I was eating dinner at a Wegmans near Norristown. "You haven't heard from me in a while," he said.

"Who is this?" I asked.

"Ty," he said.

"You were pretty convincing on the tapes," I told him. He then offered a treasure trove of interwoven links of politicians and investigations.

Back after news about Ali came out in March 2014, I asked Kane's office for expenses from the undercover investigation. I knew I would get it quickly without a Right to Know law request because it was in Kane's interest to provide it. Turns out there was $12,600 for a "safe house," a food and booze tab exceeding $8,000, more than $1,400 for cigars, $6,700 worth of hotel expenses, and $22,000 in payments to suspects. The OAG stated the $32,600 spent overall violated longstanding operating procedures of the office. It looked bad for a moment from a 60,000-foot view, but it was truly peanuts for an undercover operation.

Compare that, for instance, to the cost of rented jets or even the fuel to run a luxury yacht needed in Abscam to impress New Jersey and Pennsylvania pols that their guy making the payoffs represented an "Arab sheik." The yacht had been seized from drug dealers by U.S. customs. The thrust of Abscam (Arabscam later changed to Abdulscam) involved payoffs to New Jersey officials and members of Congress in an investigation of a sophisticated influence-peddling scheme. They were selling supposed influence to obtain Atlantic City casino licenses.

"The elaborate sting ensnared seven members of Congress, including six in the House of Representatives and a veteran U.S. senator, along with a powerful New Jersey state legislator, three Philadelphia councilmen and a number of high-level political operatives," said an NJ.com story comparing the real Abscam to the Hollywood version in the movie *American Hustle.*

Abscam involved "phony, oil-rich Arab sheiks with suitcases full of cash, stolen artwork, payoffs for Atlantic City casino licenses and backroom influence-peddling that generated worldwide headlines and set off political shockwaves for years thereafter."

This Pennsylvania sting was teensy-weensy by comparison, and a far better bargain.

VIDEOCAM IN GLASSES

The state attorney general's office filed more than 2,000 fraud charges against Ali for supposed violations by his day care center in Philadelphia for allegedly overcharging taxpayers more than $400,000. Recall earlier that Kane cited in effect Ali being such a bad guy that no one could prosecute a case and use him as a witness.

Financial documents provided by Ali substantially exonerated him, according to a memo from his attorney Robert Levant.

Eventually the U.S. attorney's office in Harrisburg reached agreement with Ali and the day care center. The 2015 agreement saw Ali pay $67,167 to resolve allegations of failing to provide accurate charges for meals through the federally-funded Child & Adult Care Food program. There was *no admission of guilt* by the day care center.

The overcharging of Ali by the state, the dismissal of the state charges, and the agreement absolving him of guilt by the feds suggests a tug of war over who would use him as an informant. Documents strongly suggest he worked for the federal government as an informant. I remember thinking, "he was that good?" It would take release of actual tapes to find out how good.

Documents obtained by a legal motion filed by the Tribune-Review's law firm revealed at least 12 legislators, lobbyists and a former traffic court judge took cash or meals and drinks from Ali when he worked as an undercover OAG informant, who typically wore a wire.

The secret documents were unsealed by Dauphin County Judge Todd Hoover as result of a motion filed by Ron Barber, an attorney with Strassburger McKenna Gutnick & Gefsky. Kane immediately jumped on board. Other newspapers across the state also filed.

Four lawmakers and an ex-judge had been identified at that point.

My guess is other cases weren't substantial enough to pursue, or time and resources were cut short after the Sandusky case and corruption trials, with a change in administrations looming.

Ali paid case bribes to "no fewer than eight elected representatives in exchange for favorable votes on a variety of public laws," the unsealed documents asserted. To this day, not all the legislators have been named.

For the state sting investigation, Ali wore the video camera installed in his glasses. The sound was recorded in a pen with a carefully hidden microphone.

Fina dismissed the case against Ali before Kane took office, Kane flatly asserted. In actuality, it was a cooperation agreement that Fina signed on Nov. 30, 2012. It required Ali to testify truthfully at any subsequent trial while dismissing the charges that had been reduced by then. It wasn't a final dismissal.

It was, in fact, Kane who dismissed the charges in October 2013, documents showed. Conveniently, she never mentioned that little fact.

She had no choice because Ali's attorney requested it and case law made it clear she had to do so, Kane and top deputy Adrian King later contended. She was grumpy when she called me to acknowledge that. She seemed resentful and irritable on the phone. Again, she didn't think she was wrong. It was a sign of her outright arrogance I should have spotted then. She wasn't wrong that she had to sign the document. She was wrong in not admitting upfront she had a role in dismissing it.

There's little doubt that case law requiring dismissal was a valid point. But Walter Cohen, a former acting attorney general, who early on was a Kane supporter, told me she could have challenged the deal if she felt so strongly about it. She could have argued that this was a decision that should have been saved for the new attorney general.

The bottom line is, the problem stemmed from the way she mishandled it. That may be more PR than legal but it dented her credibility. Had she stated on March 16th that Fina signed a cooperation agreement—and that she later signed it because she had no choice—she would have acknowledged her role in it from the beginning. To have it come out later looked suspicious, given the high-voltage nature of the sting case.

Kane maintained: "It's not that we killed it. This case was dead."

ABSCAM FACTOR

The 2012 memo from Fina sought to expand the probe to Harrisburg by establishing a fictitious business, complete with office and staff. The long-term goal was exposing under-the-table dealing by certain non-profits and relationships between lawmakers and lobbyists. Fina wrote that "manpower security and financial concerns" prevented the probe from moving forward. In fact, he referred to it as uncovering "Abscam-type actions."

The July 26, 2012, memo was copied to former Attorney General Linda Kelly, William Conley, then first deputy, and Richard Sheetz, former director of the criminal law division. Sheetz confirmed to me he saw it. Sheetz said the investigation was "by the book."

King, Kane's first deputy, said the document appeared to have been "improperly taken from the office."

"The investigation remains highly sensitive and secret," Fina wrote. "It's why few people even internally knew about it," Fina said.

The first goal was to establish Ali in the "political lobbying community" of Pennsylvania. He laid out the options including the investment of more resources, moving ahead and charging legislators implicated to that point, confronting the lawmakers and trying to obtain their cooperation.

Sources familiar with the investigation also said Ali had conversations with a racially diverse group of Democrat and Republican legislators. Some lawmakers he approached were white. Ali bought drinks and lavish dinners in an effort to boost his influence in Harrisburg.

* * *

(Sources: Letters from Fina, Seth Williams and Thomas released to the media; the plea agreement with Ali; Kane's 2013 dismissal, first reported in an Inquirer story by McCoy and Couloumbis on March 26, 2014; my March 26, 2014, Trib story—leading with Kane's dismissal of the sting case; Dennis Roddy's June 2015 column on Kane; court documents unsealed in response to a request filed by the Trib and other newspapers; Trib story in April 2014 by Adam Smeltz and myself on the unsealing of legal documents; my interviews and conversations with parties involved; an April 13, 2014 profile of Ali written by Jeff Gamage in the Inquirer and the 2012 Fina memo; a March 2014 Trib story about it; and an April Trib story on the broader nature of the investigation; NJ.com article on Nov. 25, 2013, by Ted Sherman on Abscam.)

* * *

Next: The Sandusky report and how Kane's claims backfired.

11

THE SANDUSKY REPORT—"INEXCUSABLE DELAYS"

June 23, 2014

Attorney General Kathleen Kane campaigned in 2012 on a couple key promises:

She was "a prosecutor not a politician," despite having been a deputy district attorney in Lackawanna County from only 1995 to 2007—never as an elected DA. (Tom Corbett by contrast had served as a U.S. attorney and completed a previous stint as appointed AG, before he was elected as the top state prosecutor in 2004. Corbett began as an assistant district attorney in Allegheny County and served as an assistant U.S. attorney.)

She also pledged that she would take on the "old boys' network" in Harrisburg. While under investigation by a statewide grand jury, it became one of her explanations of why she claimed Republicans were trying to do her in.

Her theme would be "transparency" and she would be an advocate for children; she stated repeatedly she would get to the bottom of why it took then-Governor Corbett, when he was attorney general, 33 months to investigate and charge Jerry Sandusky.

The former Penn State assistant football coach had been convicted of molesting 10 young boys in 2012, before Kane took office. But public suspicions about the "Freeh report" implicating other top Penn State officials for allegedly ignoring complaints about Sandusky to protect the university's reputation and above all the football program, reached a feverish pitch during the fall campaign, especially within driving distance of Happy Valley. The report by former FBI Director Louis Freeh was commissioned by the university.

Running for re-election as governor, Corbett was already extremely unpopular for having carried through on his pledges to cut spending and bring the state budget under control. It is part of why he was elected in 2010.

Kane stoked the Sandusky coals during the attorney general's race against Corbett's handpicked candidate, Cumberland County District Attorney David Freed.

She told the Scranton Times that Corbett had "probably" played politics with the Sandusky investigation but her investigation would find out for sure. Remarkably, as a Democrat, Kane racked up healthy vote totals in Central Pennsylvania, which is Nittany Lion country and largely Republican outside the PSU campus. The Penn State football team is often worshiped, not only in University Park but throughout the state except for pockets of Pitt and Temple supporters. The difference between Penn State's support and the others is devotion.

The fate of legendary football coach, Joe Paterno, rudely fired in a phone call by the university's board of trustees, had Corbett's fingerprints on it. "I reminded the (Penn State) board we must remember that 10-year-old child (an unnamed Sandusky victim) and the other children," said Corbett, a member of the university's board of trustees by virtue of his position as governor.

Anger about Paterno, a backlash against Corbett, and Kane's fresh face in politics, fueled her campaign. The "non-politician" had helped Hillary Clinton's 2008 presidential primary campaign in Pennsylvania. Bill Clinton appeared on her behalf and she ran it as an ad. Being a woman definitely helped her, given neither a female attorney nor a Democrat had held the office since it became elective in 1980.

The suspicion behind political foot-dragging went like this. The arrest of Jerry Sandusky did cause shock waves on campus, resulting in the firing of Paterno and University President Graham Spanier.

Sandusky's arrest took place in November 2011, after Corbett had been in office as governor for 11 months. Suppose it had happened in March 2010, when a deputy state prosecutor pushed for an indictment? Would the backlash have hurt Corbett's gubernatorial bid built on his successful prosecutions as attorney general? Corbett was on the ballot in November 2010 against Democrat Dan Onorato.

Kane's inexperience—having only been an assistant district attorney in Lackawanna County—was almost universally overlooked by the media. I plead guilty for not pushing to report more at that time on her lack of serious credentials.

THE MOULTON APPOINTMENT

Kane shortly after taking office named academic H. Geoffrey Moulton Jr. as special deputy to handle the Sandusky investigation. The Widener University law school associate professor, appointed in February 2013, had a reputation for thoroughness and fairness. He had done big-league investigations including how the Bureau of Alcohol Tobacco and Firearms handled the raid of the Branch Davidian compound near Waco, Texas. He is a former federal prosecutor in the Eastern District of Pennsylvania.

The issues included whether Sandusky should have been arrested after the attorney general's office became aware of the first victim and whether it was appropriate to conduct the investigation through a statewide grand jury.

As a county prosecutor, Kane said she had never handled a child sex abuse case through grand juries. Corbett said it was necessary to compel witness testimony and because the trail led to top university officials. It wasn't a simple molestation case, he suggested.

By its very nature, the statewide grand jury was slower. The grand jury only met one week per month.

Moreover, Sandusky had been a revered figure in State College known for his charitable work on behalf of disadvantaged kids. It turns out the Second Mile Charity he founded was the place where he "groomed" his future victims with visits to the field during Penn State games and sleepovers at his house. Going after him on one kid's word—or even two—wasn't good enough, Corbett said. Predators like Sandusky are usually serial offenders. Corbett said he wanted a strong irrefutable case.

CONFLICT OF INTEREST

Centre County District Attorney Michael Madeira referred the case to Corbett in March 2009, citing a conflict. Madeira, a former deputy attorney general, cited a brother-in-law who was an adopted son of Sandusky. A draft grand jury presentment was prepared by the state prosecutor on the case, Jonelle Eshbach, in March 2010 based on one victim's testimony. The victim, Adam Fisher, claimed Sandusky had performed oral sex on him, according to the report. He had "great difficulty" testifying and his answers were mostly one-word answers, the Moulton report stated. Fisher was identified because he outed himself in a book on which he collaborated with his mother and psychologist: *Silent No More: Victim 1's Fight for Justice Against Jerry Sandusky.*

From April through August 2010 Eshbach pressed on seeking answers through email from her superiors but was told it would not move forward with one victim. More victims were needed.

It wasn't till November 2010 that investigators got a tip that Penn State Assistant Football Coach Michael McQueary had information about the case. McQueary's statements served as confirmation to investigators that Sandusky had molested other kids even though he would later testify that while what he saw was "extremely sexual"—he heard rhythmic "slapping sounds"—he did not see "insertion." But Sandusky was showering with a boy and McQueary said he believed the boy was molested.

This book won't recount the entire background of the Sandusky investigation and how it came together from there. Suffice to say it gained considerable steam after McQueary was located and moved forward rapidly (as much as grand jury probes do) until Sandusky's arrest on Nov. 4, 2011.

INVESTIGATION OF THE INVESTIGATION

I had mixed feelings from day one about Kane's investigation. It is probably bad precedent for a prosecutor to investigate a predecessor's investigation unless there's some suggestion of wrongdoing. This was, after all, a successful prosecution that sent Sandusky to prison for 30-60 years. But the public drumbeat driven by the media on "why did it take so long?" deserved an answer. Corbett once asked me, "How long should it have taken?" He firmly believed the case could not proceed based on one victim given Sandusky's stature in the community prior to charges.

But people see school teachers arrested the next day if there are substantiated allegations of sexually assaulting a child. Kane did those types of simple investigations as a prosecutor in Scranton. She was right: she didn't need a grand jury for those.

This was no garden variety molestation case and it allegedly involved a cover up by three top administrators, who were eventually charged: Spanier, the university president; Tim Curley, the athletic director; and Gary Schultz, vice president of finance, as part of an alleged cover up to protect the university's image.

There was considerable speculation within the political community on what the Moulton report would say—whether it would rip Corbett, find something new or even vindicate Corbett.

The general mood around the office was dark. Kane was not happy at all with the report's findings, an aide said. It portrayed her campaign statements as incorrect. And worse, there was no "smoking gun." True there was some criticism of Corbett but by and large employees knew she was not a happy camper. So Kane wanted to go beyond it if at all possible and there were multiple top-level meetings on whether there were additional 2009 victims. In other words, kids were molested while Corbett was supposedly asleep at the switch? That was the idea. Kane wanted to do it and felt there was just enough to say so. The decision was if she got that question she'd let it rip and there was some suspicion she had someone plant the question with a reporter.

"CRUCIAL MISSTEPS"

When it was finally released by Kane in late June 2014, the report found:

- Using the grand jury "proved valuable" and was a "reasonable exercise of prosecutorial discretion."
- "No direct evidence that electoral politics influenced any important decision made in the Sandusky investigation."
- It's impossible to know in hindsight whether additional resources earlier in the investigation would have helped uncover additional victims.

- The decisions not to charge Sandusky earlier appear "to have fit within the bounds of prosecutorial discretion."

A press release from Kane highlighted "crucial missteps and inexplicable delays in bringing a serial child molester to justice."

The release read a lot differently than the neutral tone of the Moulton report, which even the Corbett people thought was even-handed. But it did point to problems in the investigation.

For instance, OAG did not search Sandusky's home for more than two years after the office received the case, 21 months after it was suggested by the lead investigator and more than a year after Eshbach wrote the draft presentment, according to Kane's office.

Still, it resulted in convictions for abuse of 10 victims. Remember, Fina helped direct the case and prosecute it in court. He *won.*

It's ironic that Kane talked about inexplicable delays given that her investigation began in February 2013 and wasn't released to the public until late June 2014. A 16-month report on a 33-month investigation? The first response from Tom Corbett, Frank Noonan and Frank Fina should have been, "Why did it take so long?"

Reconstructing millions of deleted emails delayed the probe, Kane's office had said. The email retention policy was dramatically shortened under Bill Ryan, Corbett's top assistant who served as acting attorney general after Corbett. The retention policy was shortened from five years to six months in February 2011, three months after Sandusky was arrested and more than a year before he would go to trial.

Kane's former aides and supporters hinted maybe the loyal Ryan had cleaned things up for the Corbett team. There is no evidence of that. The official explanation was an overload in computer storage. I saw Ryan in the Capitol cafeteria the morning my story ran on the email deletion policy change. He was not happy with what Kane's staff had released to me. He was a well-respected former Delaware County DA then chairing the Gaming Control Board, a plum appointment by Corbett that paid $150,000 a year.

* * *

Kane's Sandusky report was marred by her own announcement, an ad lib rant, during a question and answer session with reporters after her June 23, 2014, news conference releasing the report.

What was significant about Kane's delivery of the report on stage in the Capitol media center—with a mortified Moulton by her side—was her postscript. She added an explosive element that wasn't in the report and was not true. She claimed Sandusky molested two additional boys in the fall of 2009 while Corbett's investigation plodded along.

It didn't have the ring of truth. If it were true, it would have been the lead paragraph in the news release. It roused the Capitol press corps into an aggressive round of questioning.

* * *

Kane: "We do have two individuals who indicated that they were abused by Sandusky, both in the fall of 2009."

I asked: "Can you elaborate? What happened? (Was it investigated?)"

Kane: "Those cases were already known before we took office."

Another reporter: "Are these new victims?"

Kane: "OAG received the case in March 2009, and two individuals indicated they were abused by Sandusky in the fall of 2009."

Reporter: "Were they among the victims in the criminal case?"

Kane: "They are not."

Reporter: "Will there be more charges?"

Kane: "You have respect for abuse victims. We don't want to give any identifying information for these individuals. Because Sandusky is in jail, there were also victims we found who were not found previously. Those victims have indicated that because he is in jail and the appeal went well for the office of AG, they do not wish to prosecute at this time."

Reporter: "Are there more victims?"

Kane: As to whether anyone said he was abused after the OAG got the case: "Two individuals have indicated they were abused by Sandusky in fall 2009 . . . I can't give you any more identifying about the victims."

It was a dash of hardball Scranton politics. It was a sign she would use whatever she had to go against her perceived enemies. You throw it up against the wall and hope something will stick.

But this press gambit was slipping and sliding off the wall at a remarkable rate of speed.

Moulton, the professor who wrote a largely neutral report, sat onstage stone-faced. He didn't say a word after this little exchange.

My take: Kane couldn't get Moulton to say things any more harshly about Corbett.

So she'd do it herself.

DOUBLING DOWN

One of the victims was in fact part of the Sandusky trial.

Later, Kane was adamant about not wanting to correct it. She feared reporters would say she lied, a staffer said.

That afternoon she decided to double down on it with an additional statement from four top staffers. "It is absolutely true and factual that evidence exists of two individuals who allege they were victimized into the fall of 2009. It is shameful for others to re-victimize these individuals by denying their existence," said the statement by First Deputy Bruce Beemer, Regional Director Anthony Sassano, Chief Deputy Attorney General Linda Ditka and Special Agent in Charge David Peifer.

Meanwhile reporters were going with the prosecutors and agent on the case saying it was flat out wrong. It was at that point a she 'said–he said' story.

But Couloumbis took it a step further. She confirmed with an attorney general's source that it was not correct. Couloumbis included an acknowledgment in the Inquirer's a.m. story by Kane's office that her statement was inaccurate.

We were still stuck with the she said-he said portion of the story. It was still a powerful story given the ferocity of the ex-Sandusky prosecutors' statements challenging Kane.

Kane was said to be furious at the acknowledgment of error and still did not want to send out a statement.

J.J. Abbott, a young press aide who had worked for Controller Chelsa Wagner in Allegheny County and Joe Sestak for U.S. Senate, ironically had argued for releasing a clarification. Abbott and I clashed his first day on the Kane beat months earlier but I came to realize for a guy in his twenties he was damn good. He'll probably be a gubernatorial-level press secretary someday. He was a University of Pittsburgh grad and only a few years ahead of my daughter at Pitt. He knew what he was doing.

But Abbott's worst day—a PR guy's worst nightmare—was yet to come.

I was persistent, and got an on the record statement from Abbott the next morning acknowledging one of the victims had been part of the case. Maybe another reporter or two got the same, but it didn't go out to everybody. There had been an email crash and Abbott would later see about 30 emails from others.

Sometimes it pays to pick up the phone and call and keep pounding it.

But Abbott had been told to send it to everyone.

I remember Steve Esack of the Morning Call absolutely furious that they wouldn't send out a general statement. He was frustrated as hell they weren't producing it. He left a brutal voicemail with Renee Martin, then ostensibly in charge of Kane's press.

Abbott was sent to the Capitol Newsroom to hand-deliver the statement and apologize to reporters. He was sweating profusely. I remember telling him to forget about it. He'd have better days. It should have gone to everybody at once the day before. But he was swimming upstream with Kane not wanting to correct anything.

Kane should have arranged a conference call and admitted she'd been wrong.

It's that simple.

It was a sign of how Kane's mind worked. If challenged she would double down. She could not admit a mistake.

* * *

I tried to put the report in perspective in a Feb. 22, 2014, Tribune-Review column looking at the set of facts.

It depended on your point of view and your like or dislike of Tom Corbett. He's the Republican governor who, as former AG, put corrupt lawmakers behind bars and began the investigation that led to the conviction of serial child molester Jerry Sandusky nine months after he became governor.

If you support Corbett, you saw the development, perhaps, as another annoying stage in a political move by Democrat Attorney General Kathleen Kane. She's conducting an unprecedented investigation of a highly successful criminal probe that resulted in Sandusky's conviction on 45 of 48 charges of molesting boys.

If you're against Corbett, who is seeking re-election as governor, the deletion of up to 1 million emails by Corbett's longtime top assistant Bill Ryan, as acting attorney general, was proof that a guy who convicted public officials with emails that were, in many cases, five to seven years old, caught a break with the dumping of his own emails. You would feel Kane is warranted in looking into the almost three years it took to convict Sandusky. Many of those critics see the email policy change as a cover-up to protect Corbett and other old-hand prosecutors.

In the least, it is a head-scratching and surprising development in Kane's investigation to unravel the events surrounding the Sandusky case. About the only thing you can safely conclude is that it helps explain why her investigation—a campaign promise—has taken over a year. She is reconstructing up to 1 million emails—a figure believed to be extremely conservative.

The set of facts was bad for Ryan and Corbett, though their longtime former Information Technology Director James Ignalzo told the Trib the email deletion was a 'cost' and 'management issue,' not a cover-up. And there's no proof of any wrongdoing, misconduct or bad intent.

Perhaps the biggest discovery of Kane's techs combing through the emails was not about Sandusky at all. It was the finding of trails of emails and images involving pornographic, religious and racially insensitive posts among prosecutors and other AG employees. She would later blame that as the root cause of her downfall—the old boys' network trying to thwart the one person who could expose it. But Kane at that point was not playing the porn card and she had her techs digging up more.

POSTSCRIPT

In April 2016, Spanier, Curley, and Schultz received welcome news. The attorney general's office declined to appeal a Superior Court ruling that had dismissed the most serious charges against them, according to accounts on Pennlive and Philly.com. Lesser charges were still pending as of that time.

* * *

(Sources: Report to the Attorney General on the Investigation of Gerald A. Sandusky, May 30, 2014, by H. Geoffrey Moulton Jr., special deputy attorney general; Adam Fisher's book *Silent No More: Victim 1's Fight for Justice Against Jerry Sandusky.*

Referenced above: Kane's June 23 news release on the report's release; Scranton Times 2012 story on Kane's campaign comment about Corbett "probably" delaying for political reasons; WFMZ.com, Nov. 7, 2011, video on ex-Attorney General Linda Kell's news conference on charges filed against Sandusky; Feb. 4, 2013, story by Pennlive's Charlie Thompson on Moulton's background; Centre Daily Times story, Dec. 11, 2013, on Centre County DA's referral of Sandusky case to Corbett, citing a conflict; numerous Trib stories on why the investigation took 33 months, the Moulton report and deleted emails; Sandusky trial analysis by Sara Ganim of Pennlive.com on June 12, 2012; McQueary's testimony; Dec. 16, 2011, on McQueary's testimony by the Trib, nbcnews.com, espn.com and abcnews.com; the transcript of Kane's postscript to her news conference recorded and transcribed by the Trib's former reporter Adam Smeltz; story by Smeltz and Bumsted on Kane walking back her claims; Kane's press release—after her press conference—from four top aides attempting to back up her claims; Pennlive June 23, 2014, timeline on Sandusky; the most "overlooked" part of the Moulton report by Charlie Thompson on Pennlive.com. On June 25, 2014; Pennlive editorial on Kane getting "sloppy" in pressing Sandusky report.)

* * *

Next: Seth Williams launches grand jury probe.

12

SETH

June 18, 2014

Seth Williams was on fire.

He went directly after Kathleen Kane, responding to her taunt suggesting that three of his employees with vast public corruption experience conducted a racist undercover investigation while in the attorney general's office.

But his statement that he had taken the unusual step of publicly announcing a grand jury for the sting case was even-handed. The grand jury could recommend charges or issue a report without criminal charges, Williams said.

The investigation focused on allegations that "several Philadelphia legislators accepted gifts and money in exchange for political favors and votes." Williams said.

In my mind there was no doubt where this was heading. The legislators had been videotaped taking money from an undercover informant for the attorney general's office. It was not a cakewalk; there might be legal hurdles but these folks were caught dead to rights.

RACISM IN STING CASE?

Williams was an imposing man, built like a Division III linebacker. He was quick on his feet. He was forceful and deliberate. He backed up his guys.

Normally, Williams said at a news conference, he would not even acknowledge there was a grand jury investigation. But the public deserved to know about it given the "unusually high profile of this case."

Right—and Kathleen Kane had ticked him off. Calling the sting probe racist seemed to be what did it. If his guys who used to work for Corbett were racist, what'd that say about him? He's an African American. Why would he tolerate racists working for him? He wouldn't. And he played Philly hardball politics.

The sting probe began under Republican Attorney General Tom Corbett, continued under Acting Attorney General Bill Ryan and Corbett's handpicked successor Linda Kelly, a career federal prosecutor. Kane, as the Inquirer put it, "secretly" declined to prosecute.

Most decisions to prosecute—or not—are secret.

'You dare me?' Williams seemed to be saying. Maybe Kane figured in Philly politics, Williams, an African American, wouldn't really want to touch a case Kane had branded as racist?

Did race play a role as Kane suggested?

Veteran homicide prosecutor Mark Gilson, appointed by Williams to head the probe, said Kane produced no evidence to support that claim.

Kane had cited an internal document stating a former investigator in the case claimed African Americans were targeted. The investigator, Claude Thomas, vehemently denied it and later filed a lawsuit against Kane.

But Gilson said no such affidavit had been turned over to prosecutors.

ETHICS COMMISSION CASE?

While Williams launched a grand jury, former Acting Attorney General Walter Cohen would tell me much later he would not have initiated a grand jury investigation. Cohen said he would have filed a complaint with the Ethics Commission for conflict of interest for failure to report cash gifts. But he would be the first to tell you prosecutors have broad discretion on charging decisions. Kane would have had much more of a legitimate defense if she had stated that the matter was being resolved by the Ethics Commission. Again, she made her own fate by seemingly picking a fight with Williams, whom she likely viewed as an extension of Fina. Defense attorney William Costopoulos, a widely respected criminal law expert, earlier had argued for criminal cases such as Corbett's against Bill DeWeese and former Sen.

Jane Orie, to be ethics rather than crimes code violations because of relatively small amounts of money involved.

* * *

By October 2014, the first sting defendant was charged: former Philadelphia Traffic Court Judge Thomasine Tynes. The traffic court was enveloped in a federal scandal over politically-connected people getting their tickets trashed. In July 2014, six former judges including Tynes were acquitted of conspiracy and ticket fixing by a federal jury. But Tynes was one of those convicted of lying to federal authorities.

Tynes was arrested by the DA's office for taking a $2,000 Tiffany charm bracelet from Ty Ali, the informant. In return, Tynes promised special access to Ali's "client," a businessman seeking an exclusive, lucrative contract.

The ex-judge "promised to deliver," Williams said.

Tynes and the "businessman" later toasted over a drink "to making some money together."

The investigation was "not dead on arrival," as Kane had stated and it definitely wasn't over, Williams said.

I remember asking Gilson afterward about obstacles in the case. That's when he told me about Lex Street.

* * *

(Sources: Public letters from Seth Williams to Kane and Kane to Williams; Williams' press release and news conference on launching a grand jury and my Tribune-Review story on the same; Trib story and Inquirer story on charges being filed against Tynes; an interview I did with Walter Cohen in 2015 and several with Costopoulos from 2012-2015; CBS Radio (KYW) report July 23, 2014 by Tony Hanson on the traffic court verdicts.)

* * *

Next: The Lex Street Massacre.

13

THE LEX STREET MASSACRE

May 2014

Three days after Christmas in 2000, masked men brandishing semiautomatic handguns and wearing rubber gloves charged into a crack house at 816 North Lex Street in West Philadelphia. They rounded up the 10 people in the house and ordered them into the dining room. They were told to lie face down on the floor. The people were shot execution-style. Seven people were killed; three survived.

It was Philadelphia's worst mass murder in recent history, the Philadelphia Inquirer wrote.

You might wonder what this horrific event has to do with Kathleen Kane or Pennsylvania corruption.

It took place 13 ½ years before Seth Williams took office. Kane would publicly argue over her decision not to pursue charges in the legislative sting case and her claim that the case amounted to racial profiling of suspects without predicate.

The tie is a feisty city prosecutor, Assistant District Attorney Mark Gilson, who was tapped to handle the second prosecution of defendants in the "Lex Street Massacre." He was brought in after the first case blew up on then-District Attorney Lynne Abraham.

Four suspects initially were charged in the killings. But the DA's office admitted it had the wrong guys in what at first was believed to be a drug dispute. As the case was about to go to trial in 2002, charges were dismissed against the four because prosecutors developed new evidence. The suspects spent 18 months in jail. The falsely accused defendants later successfully sued the city and won a $1.9 million judgment.

Eventually, ballistics and testimony of new suspects led to charges against four different defendants in 2003. The dispute was actually over a car trade gone south, not a drug deal. It was a robbery to recoup money from the trade that soured over a clutch that didn't work. The gunmen took $200, drugs worth $400, and a silver pendant and chain.

Two brothers were among those charged with murdering the victims, aged 15 to 54, the Associated Press reported. The defendants were Dawud Faruqi, Khalid Faruqi, Shihean Black and Bruce "Snoop" Veney. Gilson and Assistant DA Vernon Chestnut had the task of proving the case in the backdrop of a high-profile failure. The second prosecution arguably was tainted by the first, at least in the public eye. If prosecutors got it wrong the first time, who could be certain they didn't blow it again? Whether potential jurors admitted it or not, the massive publicity on the botched case might color their perception of the second.

But prosecutors pulled it off, winning the case despite its twisted history.

The Faruqi brothers were each convicted of seven murders in March 2004. They also went down on three charges of attempted murder, robbery and weapons possession. Veney and Black were also convicted. The Faruqis and Black are serving life sentences and Veney is doing 15-30 years.

Perhaps because he pulled this off, Gilson was not bothered by the idea of taking the sting case, tainted by Kane's repeated statements of its flaws.

Gilson, though, was a prosecutor who handled "blood and guts" cases. He had tried 215 homicide cases and boasted a 96 percent conviction rate. But he conceded in an interview he "knew nothing about public corruption." He said he was "a little surprised" he was selected to head the sting prosecution. At 56, he was at the top of his game in the courtroom. He was savvy from 28 years in the trenches—23 as a line prosecutor. For reporters, he was a quote machine in and out of the courtroom.

"They shot them like fish in a barrel," he told me regarding the Lex Street victims.

Never tell Gilson a case is "unwinnable." He also got all of the defendants to confess their guilt in open court and waive any and all future appeals.

Gilson knew the DA's office had some of the state's best public corruption prosecutors in Frank Fina, Marc Costanzo and Patrick Blessington and he could rely on them, if needed, as resources. Claude Thomas, the agent who supervised Ali in the sting case, was also in the same office.

Gilson's first questions were:

- "How good are the tapes?"
- "Is there any evidence of racial targeting?"

After he spoke with Thomas and Fina, he said he knew Kane's allegations were bogus.

After listening to the tapes, it was clear the legislative defendants hungry for cash "passed Ali from one person to the next.

"He was like their own private ATM machine," Gilson said.

Gilson knew tough cases, such as the Lex Street Massacre. As far as he was concerned the sting case, despite Kane's ranting about its deficiencies, wasn't one of them. He would say so in his direct style as DA Williams' investigation of the sting got underway and started producing results.

* * *

(Sources: My interview with Gilson in June 2015; story on Philadelphiaweekly.com Feb. 14, 2001 by Solomon Jones on the shooting; an Associated Press story in November 2002 about four new suspects charged; a September 2003 story by the Inquirer's Jacqueline Soteropoulos on the city's settlement with the wrongly accused suspects who each spent 18 months in jail; Soteropoulos' story from January 2003 on the preliminary hearing where two brothers were held for trial; her story in March 2004 on the conviction of two brothers in the Lex Street killings.)

* * *

Next: The Dunmore accident.

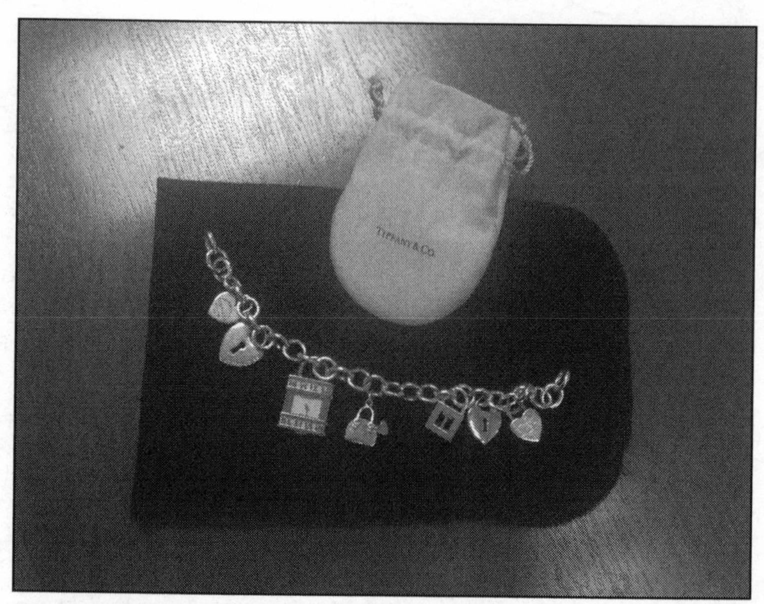

$2,000 Tiffany bracelet—this silver charm bracelet was a gift to former Philadelphia Traffic Court Judge Thomasine Tynes from an undercover informant posing as a "lobbyist" with business clients seeking contracts. Photo provided by Philadelphia District Attorney's Office.

Assistant Philadelphia District Attorney Mark Gilson, an experienced homicide prosecutor, heads task force prosecuting the bribery sting case. Photo by Brad Bumsted for the Tribune-Review.

Kari Andren, the Tribune-Review's LCB news hawk at the rear of the state Capitol in Harrisburg. Photo by Evan Sanders, Tribune-Review.

Chuck Ardo, spokesman for Attorney General Kathleen Kane, in gaggle with reporters after Kane testified Nov. 5, 2015, in a closed door session ordered by Judge John Cleland, who presided over Gerald Sandusky's trial. The issue was Kane's suggestion in a press release there had been leaks from the Sandusky investigation under her predecessors in the attorney general's office. She had no evidence of that sort. Photo by Brad Bumsted, Tribune-Review.

Former Traffic Court Judge Thomasine Tynes, who was the first official charged by the Philly DA's office in the case Attorney General Kathleen Kane said was "not prosecutable." Provided by Philadelphia District Attorney's Office.

Former Chief Supreme Court Justice Ronald D. Castille talks to reporters at the Pennsylvania Society in New York City in December 2014. Castille had authorized the statewide grand jury investigation of Kane. Brad Bumsted, of the Pittsburgh Tribune-Review far left; Amy Worden, former Philadelphia Inquirer reporter; and Lynn Marks, executive director of Pennsylvanians for Modern Courts. Photo provided by Pennsylvania Manufacturer's Association.

Former Republican Gov. Tom Corbett, a career prosecutor, whose successful investigation of serial pedophile Jerry Sandusky was challenged by Attorney General Kathleen Kane. Photo by Brad Bumsted for the Tribune-Review.

Former Rep. Ronald Waters, D-Philadelphia, as videotaped by undercover informant Tyron Ali. Waters pleaded guilty in the bribery sting case. Photo provided by Philadelphia District Attorney's Office.

Laurel Brandstetter, the former senior deputy attorney general, who prosecuted the corruption case against the Pennsylvania Turnpike Commission, until she resigned and later cited lack of support from the front office. Submitted by Laurel Brandstetter.

Ex-Turnpike CEO Joe Brimmeier, who pleaded guilty to conflict of interest in November 2014 in a plea bargain and salvaged his pension. Photo by Eric Felack of the Valley News Dispatch when Brimmeier was still with the Turnpike Commission.

Gov. Tom Wolf the day before his inauguration in January 2015. His gift ban covered all employees who worked for him. Photo by Brad Bumsted for the Tribune-Review.

Attorney General Kathleen Kane arrives with phalanx of security for her arraignment on criminal charges in Norristown where she was fingerprinted and a mug shot was taken on Aug. 10, 2015. Photo by Brad Bumsted for the Tribune-Review.

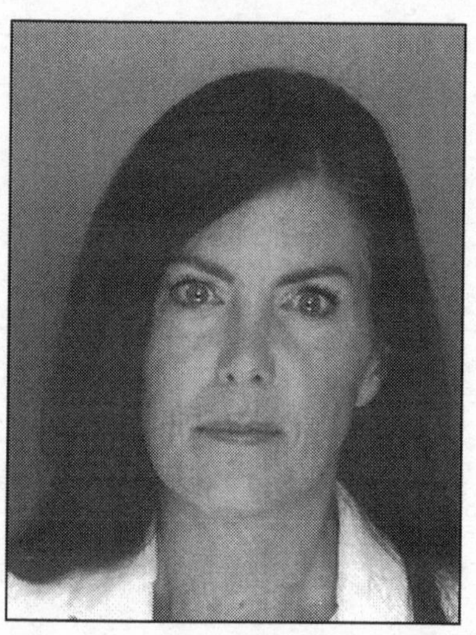

Kathleen Kane's mug shot when she was arraigned on perjury and obstruction of justice charges Aug. 8, 2015, in the Montgomery County Detective Bureau. Photo posted on Montgomery County's web page.

Gerald Shargel, the Manhatttan defense attorney representing Attorney General Kathleen Kane, holds an impromptu news conference after Kane was bound over for trial on criminal charges in Montgomery County on Aug. 24, 2014. Photo by Brad Bumsted for Tribune-Review.

Attorney General Kathleen Kane's photo provided by Pennlive.com

The Montgomery County Courthouse, scene of enormous statewide interest during the investigation of Attorney General Kathleen Kane in 2015. By Brad Bumsted for the Tribune-Review.

Former Montgomery County District Attorney Risa Vetri Ferman, who conducted an independent investigation of a statewide grand jury presentment against Attorney General Kathleen Kane. Photo provided by Risa Vetri Ferman.

The Pennsylvania State Capitol, itself a monument to corruption, given the early 20th Century criminal charges levied against the architect and others for over charges. Photo provided by Tribune-Review.

Philadelphia District Attorney Seth Williams conducts an interview after a news conference on his investigation of the so-called "sting" bribery case that Attorney General Kathleen Kane declined to prosecute. Photo by Brad Bumsted for the Tribune-Review.

Press corps from Harrisburg and Philly awaiting Kathleen Kane's press conference in the Capitol Media Center, August 2015. By Paula Knudsen Burke.

Eric Epstein, co-founder of Rock the Capital, a government reform group founded in 2005, after speaking at a news conference in the Capitol Rotunda in 2015. Photo by Brad Bumsted for the Tribune-Review.

Former state Treasurer Rob McCord pleaded guilty to extortion in February 2015 under the Hobbs Act. This photo was taken on an earlier date by Stephanie Strasburg for the Tribune-Review.

State Sen. Jay Costa, a Forest Hills Democrat, introduces Attorney General Kathleen Kane to acting Pittsburgh Police Chief Regina McDonald at a community drug forum at the Penn Hills Library on Aug. 5, 2014. Photo by Jasmine Goldband, Tribune-Review.

Rep. Mike Vereb, a Montgomery County Republican and former police officer, pushes for a new special prosecutor law for procedures establishing a special prosecutor when the attorney general or an official in that office is suspected of crimes. Photo provided by Vereb's office.

HARRISBURG, PA

Subpoena Duces Tecum

In the Senate of Pennsylvania

From: Special Committee on Senate Address

To: Kathleen Kane, Attorney General
Commonwealth of Pennsylvania
16th Floor, Strawberry Square
Harrisburg, Pennsylvania 17120

You are hereby ordered by the Special Committee on Senate Address to supply the following documents listed below. This material shall be delivered to the Chair of the Special Committee on Senate Address, The Honorable John R. Gordner, at Room 177, Main Capitol Building, Harrisburg, Pennsylvania, no later than Friday, November 13, 2015 at 4:00 p.m.

- Any and all documents, including electronic communications, detailing or describing the operation of the Office of Attorney General following the suspension of the Attorney General's law license which became effective on October 22, 2015.
- Any and all communications from the Attorney General to the employees of the Office of Attorney General related to the suspension of the Attorney General's law license.
- Any and all communications sent to the Attorney General from or produced by employees of the Office of Attorney General related to the suspension of the Attorney General's law license.
- A description of any duties or functions the Attorney General has delegated to other employees of the Office of Attorney General which cannot be performed or effectuated due to the suspension of the Attorney General's law license.
- Any opinion or explanation of the legal authority of the Attorney General to delegate any duties or functions to her First Deputy since there has not been a "vacancy in the position of Attorney General" as required under Section 202 of the Commonwealth Attorneys Act.
- All filings and documentation required under Section 217 of the Pennsylvania Rules of Disciplinary Enforcement related to formerly admitted attorneys.

This subpoena is issued pursuant to permission granted to the Chair of the Special Committee on Senate Address and in accord with the Constitution and Rules of the Senate of Pennsylvania.

John R. Gordner

Senator John R. Gordner, Chair
Special Committee on Senate Address

Attest:

Meg Mart

Megan Martin, Secretary
Senate of Pennsylvania

11-6-15
Date

14

THE VERY QUESTIONABLE ACCIDENT

Oct. 31, 2014

Renee Martin, Kane's eminently likeable but inexperienced spokeswoman, called me about 8:15 a.m. Renee, daughter of former Pennsylvania AFL-CIO president Bill George, a union powerhouse in the state, knew I was not hostile toward Kane. The embattled AG clearly believed some reporters were out to cast her in the worst light.

The truth is, Kane made much of that happen herself.

"Pennsylvania Attorney General Kathleen Kane's slide from political stardom to possible criminal defendant appears traceable to one place. The mirror," Steve Esack of the Morning Call would write later as Kane's grand jury woes heated up.

Chris Kelly, a Scranton Times-Tribune columnist, may have put it better, shortly after the accident: "Enemies have been gunning for Kathleen Kane since she took office. None has had better aim than the state attorney general herself."

The accident was a case in point.

* * *

I talked to Martin fairly often. Still, I was surprised to hear from her this early. She was driving to work. Renee Martin was filling in as an acting press secretary (without the title). She had been the agency's education and outreach director.

"What's up, Renee?" I asked.

"The general's been in a car accident."

I asked if Kane was OK and Martin said she was recovering at home from a concussion. I said I'd have to have the police report in hand.

"When did it happen?" I asked her.

Oct. 21, she said.

Say what?

That was 10 days before. I pressed her on why they didn't release it right after it happened. She said she was not going to release it at all except a reporter inquired.

That reporter was not me. But Martin said in an email "someone mentioned that you were asking about it as a story. I wanted you to have the correct information. I wasn't really releasing anything."

I told her it was absurd. The attorney general is the second most powerful executive branch official after the governor. If the governor (then Tom Corbett) were hurt in an accident and his office failed to inform the public for 10 days, reporters would collectively blow a gasket.

But I did not have this key fact at the time. Oct. 21 was also the date Kane missed her second appearance before a statewide grand jury sitting in Trooper, near Norristown, Montgomery County, the Philadelphia Inquirer reported Nov. 1. This was the grand jury investigation of Kane for leaking documents from a 2009 grand jury probe—before she took office in 2014.

Martin would tell the Scranton Times-Tribune later it was "bull crap, absolutely" that Kane used the accident to avoid anything. In an email to the paper, Martin stated, "We did not notify the press because the accident did not (affect) the operation of business at the (office)."

HOW IT HAPPENED

Kane was involved in the accident at 6:55 a.m. in Dunmore, a small borough outside of Scranton. Kane's two security agents were with her in her black 2011 Chevrolet Tahoe, a sport utility vehicle.

It is curious that her two agents were both former Dunmore cops. What was she doing there that early on the morning of her much-awaited grand jury appearance?

Agent Robert Ruddy, then 49, was driving. Patrick Reese, the former Dunmore police chief and another Kane driver and bodyguard, was in the rear seat with Kane. Ruddy dropped his iPad, according to the police report, and hit a parked vehicle.

Reese, then 47, was a Kane confidant. He later would be identified at key meetings with staffers, some of whom called him her "chief of staff."

Kane's car hit a parked 1999 Jeep Cherokee at an estimated speed of 10-15 mph, the investigating officer said. Her SUV turned right on Chestnut Street. The Inquirer reported in mid-November 2014 that a neighbor said the Cherokee hadn't been moved in at least two years. It was said to be "brimming" from floor to ceiling with clothes and assorted possessions. The car's then 69-year-old owner didn't respond to calls.

The repairs on Kane's vehicle cost the state $964.10, records show. The estimate report was dated Oct. 22, 2014. The work was done at an "auto paint" shop in the Scranton area, according to the Department of General Services. It's not clear there were any claims by the owner of the parked SUV. I checked months later and there were still none.

Kane was treated and released from the Scranton Regional Hospital, the police report said. Kane and Ruddy were listed on the police report as having injuries of unknown severity.

Noting the many media calls, Dunmore Police Chief Sal Marchese told the Inquirer's Couloumbis, "There is nothing to this. Nothing. There is nothing out of the ordinary."

Kane's condition as a result of the accident would worsen, according to Martin, though we never heard from Kane personally.

An "Automobile Accident or Loss Notice" report on file in the attorney general's office stated that Kane had injuries of the head and back. Ruddy reported his knee was injured and Reese was listed as injuring his "left abdominal (area) and back."

SCRANTON AREA CONTEMPORARIES

A star football player when he attended Dunmore High School, Ruddy and his twin, William, led the 13-0 Dunmore Bucks to the 1985 Eastern Conference Class A championship, according to Scranton Times-Tribune stories.

William Ruddy died in a car accident in January 1986 while the brothers were on a football recruitment trip to Mansfield State University.

Reese and Ruddy are not listed on Pennwatch.org, the state's salary database. In response to inquiries, Kane's office said Reese is paid $99,658 and Ruddy, $96,763.

Reese's salary as police chief was $65,744, according to borough records. He's a former patrolman and captain who praised Dunmore businessman Louis DeNaples for spending $400,000 for a police and fire station. DeNaples, owner of the Keystone Landfill, also donated equipment, including four police vehicles, worth about $130,000, according to the Times-Tribune.

DeNaples was charged with perjury in 2008 in Dauphin County, accused of lying about alleged mob ties to get his license for Mount Airy Casino Resort. The charges were dropped in 2009.

"I don't believe the man gets enough credit for what he does in the community," the Times-Tribune quoted Reese in 2010. "Everybody knows it. He deserves the credit."

Kane, 49, a former Lackawanna County assistant district attorney, has known Reese at least 20 years. She is a 1984 graduate of West Scranton High School.

The initial police report said the three were wearing seatbelts but Martin said that report was wrong; Kane was not buckled in and she hit her head on the back of the front seat. That raised the question: if she had been wearing a seat belt, as the first report indicated, how could she suffer a concussion in the back seat hitting her head on the back of the front seat?

Kane asked that the report be changed, Martin said. Dunmore police later said the report contained a "clerical mistake." Patrolman Joseph Hallinan told me it was a "typo."

The report, of course, was changed at Kane's request.

Kane's SUV turned right on Chestnut Street. The speed limit is 15 mph.

RUNNING THE OFFICE IN PJs

Questions began to mount when it became apparent Kane wasn't reporting to work in Harrisburg, or Scranton for that matter. She didn't come to the AG headquarters every day anyway. But reports bubbled out of the office that she was AWOL.

Kelly, the columnist, reported that the Times-Tribune sent a reporter to Kane's door because her absence from the office sparked news reports. A boy answered. It was likely one of her two sons, Kelly wrote. The boy came back and said she was in the bathroom and couldn't come to the door. "Ms. Kane's refusal to come to the door is inexcusable, considering the newspaper tried to reach her through less personal means," Kelly wrote.

She was working from home, Martin acknowledged.

Martin strongly denied that Kane was attempting to avoid the grand jury investigating a leak from her office.

"Absolutely not," she said, though she said she could not acknowledge the grand jury's existence. It was by then 3 ½ weeks since the accident. In stronger terms, Martin told the Scranton Times-Tribune it was "Bull crap."

Steve Corbett, a commentator for WILK FM, wrote that "You can be attorney general in your PJs."

Martin told me she did not know what medication had been prescribed for Kane. She said she could not talk about her condition or release her doctor's name. At the time, Kane's salary was $156,264.

The attorney general's health is a "legitimate concern" for the public, said Cohen, the former acting attorney general.

All the while, the grand jury's investigation of Kane, led by a special prosecutor appointed by grand jury Judge William Carpenter, continued. Carpenter chose Thomas Carluccio, a Plymouth Meeting defense attorney with prosecutorial experience, to lead the grand jury. There are typically three statewide grand juries, all under the auspices of the attorney general.

Then-Supreme Court Chief Justice Ronald D. Castille had given Carpenter permission to appoint a special prosecutor. It was highly unusual. It would be vigorously challenged by Kane's legal team. Here was a statewide grand jury, nominally under the OAG, investigating the AG herself. But as Castille would later say: the attorney general can't investigate herself.

Carluccio, with as thick a Philly accent as one will hear anywhere in the City of Brotherly Love, is a solo practitioner specializing in real estate, commercial litigation and defending people accused of crimes. He worked as a deputy attorney general in Pennsylvania and special assistant to the U.S. attorney in Delaware. You can't miss him in a crowd. He's got to top 6'4" and he was a former basketball player at the University of Delaware. He is married to Montgomery County Judge Carolyn Carluccio.

His initial involvement on the case, whether he actually was a special prosecutor for the statewide grand jury, was not a matter of public record. There had been an initial story in the Inquirer but calls to his office went unreturned. Carpenter wasn't talking. This was, after all, a grand jury investigation conducted in secret.

And it appeared Kane was doing her best to avoid it. Her absence became a big story.

"If I were the grand jury judge, I'd move the grand jury on a bus to see her," said former Montgomery County District Attorney Bruce Castor, a Republican county commissioner who ran unsuccessfully for attorney general in 2004. Castor said he had no firsthand knowledge of the grand jury and based his remarks on published reports.

Nonetheless, there was growing awareness something was amiss and talk that perhaps she needed to turn over power temporarily to her first deputy.

"Since the accident, the pain in her neck and back has intensified," Martin stated. Her office issued a statement from Kane's neurologist saying she suffered from "cervical back trauma" and that she had a return-to-work target date of Nov. 24, 2014.

But Kane would be in the public eye sooner.

By Nov. 17, she would testify before the grand jury investigating her conduct at the attorney general's office in Trooper near Norristown.

Was it the accident? Grand jury-related stress? Was it both? Was there really an accident?

THE KANE STAKEOUT

We arrived at the attorney general's office near Norristown at about 8 a.m. on Monday.

I thought this was the right place. But grand juries, despite all the talk about leaks, are not exactly publicly scheduled. Among three potential locations, the attorney general's office in Trooper was an educated guess.

Would Attorney General Kathleen Kane show up here? I was with Angela Couloumbis, the Inquirer reporter, who was in on breaking most of the major Kane stories.

We waited—and waited—in a lobby that was partially under construction. There were no benches or chairs, but there were power receptacles, which was what we needed. A Philadelphia Inquirer photographer also waited. An Associated Press reporter showed up mid-morning.

Then I was pretty sure we were on the right track. Carluccio blew by us without comment. A Philadelphia Daily News reporter trickled in. A reporter from the Times-Herald in Norristown followed.

By noon or so, Judge Carpenter arrived and headed upstairs, Couloumbis told me. I missed him and I'd only seen his picture so it would have been hard to be sure.

At least we were inside. Rain was coming down hard most of the day. There were no food trucks on the street. If there was a lunch room with vending machines, we could not access it. We had stale bagels and apples to eat from the buffet breakfast that comes with rooms at the Springhill Marriott in King of Prussia. A real feast.

Was Kane actually coming? I had advanced the story very generally, according to sources, that she was expected to testify on Nov. 17. Where was she?

On stakeouts, reporters check the entrances. Where else could she come in or leave? Not that she would necessarily try to duck us. But plenty of officials over the years have sneaked past the press. We figured Kane was coming through the front door.

At 1:20 p.m., in a light rain Kane showed up with a security officer, New York City lawyer Gerald Shargel, and Lanny Davis, her crisis communications specialist. It was a new legal team, both high-priced options from New York City and Washington, D.C., respectively. Davis was nationally known as the former White House scandal spokesman during special prosecutor investigations of former President Bill Clinton. He was close to the Clintons and had attended law school with Hillary.

Kane looked like she lost 15 pounds. She didn't have it to spare. She looked emaciated and sick. Was that from the accident or the stress?

Kane read a statement and headed for the elevators to go to the grand jury room on the third floor. "I will tell the Special Prosecutor the truth and the facts surrounding the disclosure of information to the public that was done in a way that did not violate statutory or case law regarding Grand Jury secrecy," Kane told reporters.

She was expected to testify on whether she had leaked grand jury information. It is potentially a violation of the law. She would eventually say she approved giving out a memo but it wasn't covered by grand jury secrecy.

We waited until she was done testifying. She had little else to say. She appeared to be famished and scarfed down a Twix bar. Davis, her PR specialist, talked plenty.

Nearing the end, with the star attraction gone, a middle-aged woman leaving the building looked at Couloumbis, sitting cross-legged in a corner with her laptop, writing her story. "What did you get?" the woman asked her. "A time out?" (like some toddlers get from parents.)

Neither Carluccio, the special prosecutor, nor Carpenter, the judge, spoke to reporters.

Asked afterward whether it was over, Kane said, "It's up to Mr. Carluccio."

Kane testified for about 2 ½ hours.

"She did not commit a crime. She did nothing wrong," Shargel, of the prestigious Winston & Strawn law firm, said afterward. He accompanied her into the grand jury meeting room.

Kane knew that her office leaked information to the Daily News but believed it was not grand jury material, Davis said.

DENYING LEAK OF CONFIDENTIAL INFORMATION

"I'm stunned by her testimony. I'm flabbergasted," said Castor, a Republican. The judge, in starting the investigation, had determined it was grand jury material, Castor said. "What she is saying is she'll decide what's a grand jury leak, not the judge." Castor made the remarks by phone after her appearance.

The grand jury was nearing an end. It appeared to expire Dec. 31. In reality it would go through mid-January 2015. Taxpayers weren't paying her legal bills, Kane's office said.

Kane was going through a divorce and her husband Chris' family was wealthy. That's a huge stressor along with your job and career in jeopardy.

But Kane's testimony was complicated and previewed a case with many twists and turns and seemingly inexplicable events, we would later learn. Here is Kane's written statement that she read on her way into the grand jury. It resurrected the porn and the conspiracy she would lay out in coming months by an "old boys' network" of Republicans out to get the first Democrat to hold the elective office of attorney general.

Kane's statement:

> "As many of you know, I initiated an independent inquiry into the way the Sandusky investigation was conducted—a central concern raised during my campaign for attorney general. During that investigation, thousands of emails were discovered sent and received by Pennsylvania public officials that contained pornographic materials. As a result of multiple requests to the Office of Attorney General under Pennsylvania's broad Right to Know law, I released most of these emails to the media and the public.
>
> "The Chief Justice of the Pennsylvania Supreme Court, in a recently published opinion, described the attachments to these emails as 'clearly pornographic' and possibly criminal. As a result, many senior public officials involved in these emails resigned. But others remain on the public payrolls, as the Chief Justice pointed out.
>
> "Today I am due to testify before a Pennsylvania Grand Jury, as has been publicly reported. However, due to continuous, even overlapping court orders since last March, I am not allowed to explain why I am testifying or what my testimony has to do with the release of the pornographic emails under the Right to Know law. These court orders also expose me to legal risk if I do my job as Attorney General that I was elected and trusted by the people of Pennsylvania to do. I am not allowed at this time to explain why.

"The Office of Attorney General has cooperated from the beginning of this process and I will do the same. I will tell the Special Prosecutor the truth and the facts surrounding the disclosure of information to the public that was done in a way that did not violate statutory or case law regarding Grand Jury secrecy.

"Despite my present situation that restricts my ability to answer your questions, I remain committed to the central theme of my campaign—transparency in government. The public has a right to know what public officials are doing or not doing with taxpayer dollars and whether they are doing their jobs properly or attempting to investigate or prosecute possible criminal conduct.

"I promised I would expose corruption and abuse of the legal system. The winds of change can only blow through open windows. My administration is being prevented from prying open the windows that corruption has nailed shut. But that change is coming.

"The right of the public and media to know what public officials are doing is vital and should be protected by public officials, the media, and the people of Pennsylvania. I am fighting for the right of the attorney general to do my job without interference.

"But more importantly, I am fighting for an end to abuse of the criminal justice system, for transparency, and for better government. That doesn't come without cost to us. But if this can be done to me as attorney general, the chief law enforcement officer of the 5th largest state in the country, I am sickened to think what can and may be done to regular, good people who don't have the resources that I have to challenge it.

"In conclusion, I wish I could say more and answer all your questions but I cannot. But I can promise you this: The truth and the law will prevail."

Indeed, it would.

* * *

(Sources: Steve Esack's Morning Call story on Jan. 27, 2015; Chris Kelly's Nov. 14, 2014, column; Dunmore police report; my Trib stories on the accident and Kane's absence;

Couloumbis' Inquirer blog piece on the accident; state records on the vehicle damage and the accident; WNEP's web page with Steve Corbett's comments on Kane's accident; the Scranton Times-Tribune story on the accident; Inquirer story on Carluccio's appointment in September 2014; my Trib "back story" blog piece on the stakeout in Norristown; letter from Carpenter to Castille on his appointment of special prosecutor; my subsequent interviews with Lanny Davis; Wikipedia for background on Carluccio; Kane's statement released by Davis before Kane's grand jury appearance.)

* * *

Next: Happy Birthday, Ron Waters.

15

"HAPPY BIRTHDAY, RON WATERS"

Dec. 16, 2014

A Philadelphia grand jury delivered a stinging rebuke to Attorney General Kathleen Kane shortly before Christmas, 2014, in what had been a very bad year for her. But it was not anything like what awaited her in 2015.

The minority-dominated grand jury sharply rebutted Kane's charge that racism under her predecessors' probe was one of the reasons she did not charge black officials with crimes after they were videotaped taking cash payments. You'll recall Kane declined to prosecute the case in 2013, citing legal flaws, poor supervision and racial targeting.

This was hardball politics: payback for Kane, and some would argue, the right thing to do by law. We found that out later when the tapes were released.

It was Seth Williams' first major volley in the sting case involving lawmakers. He announced at a Philadelphia news conference that based on the grand jury's findings he charged two legislators with bribery, conspiracy and conflict of interest for failing to report cash payments they received from Tyron Ali, the undercover operator who filmed the encounters for the attorney general's office under ex-Attorneys General Tom Corbett, Bill Ryan (an acting AG) and Linda Kelly, Corbett's appointee after he became governor.

Charged were Rep. Ronald Waters and Vanessa Brown, both Democrats and both black.

Williams was the first black elected DA in Pennsylvania.

You'll recall Kane declined to prosecute the case in 2013, citing legal flaws, poor supervision and a taint of racism.

"(Kane) said it was dead on arrival," DA Williams said. "Like Lazarus at Bethany, it was resurrected."

Kane's supporters and legal experts in general would tell you that a prosecutor can get a grand jury to do just about anything he or she wants. One might say whatever the prosecutor wants is a highly likely outcome though occasionally grand juries won't indict.

In the sting grand jury, two-thirds of the 23 grand jurors identified themselves as black. They said in a report they found Kane's claim of racism "simply false," and determined "the only thing flawed was the internal review by the current attorney general."

DA Williams called it a "press and play" case—hitting the video button and playing for a grand jury, if necessary a jury.

Even though DA Williams' assistants controlled the grand jury it's hard to believe a grand jury with a super majority of black people would endorse a case with even a taint of racism.

"The evidence in this case has always been there; it's just finally seeing the light of day," the grand jury report said.

HOW IT WENT DOWN

Waters was a star, of sorts, on the videos.

The OAG investigation logged 113 recordings and meetings with legislators, public officials and others. Twenty-six of those recordings featured Waters.

Waters, 64, took cash on nine occasions for "promising to peddle his influence," DA Williams said. In all, he took $8,750 in cash.

Brown, 48, on five occasions, took a total of $4,000. "Ooh whee—thank you twice," she told Ali when he handed her an envelope of cash with $2,000 in her Capitol office, according to the grand jury report.

Both Waters and Brown admitted to the grand jury they "knowingly took illegal cash payments," DA Williams said.

The cash payments shocked many of both parties in the state Capitol. Under Pennsylvania's liberal law it is not illegal to take cash as a gift as long as it's reported. Of course, reporting it would raise a whole lot of questions and maybe interest from the IRS. Two exceptions made this case different. For one, the lawmakers didn't report the gifts to the Ethics Commission. Second, an element of bribery was alleged which made it not only illegal but a crime.

BIRTHDAY BONUS

Waters was a Philadelphia Parking Authority supervisor before he won the House seat in a special election in 1999. He served on the powerful appropriations committee.

Ali told Waters he was paying him "to exercise that God given right of leverage." Ali had rich "clients" who wanted special access. Ali had several requests, one of which was an exclusive collection contract at the parking authority, where Waters still had contacts. His clients were pushing liquor store privatization

At Waters' birthday party in 2011, Ali paid $400 for a Michael Jackson impersonator. He also gave Waters expensive cigars and $1,000 because Ali's "client" was pleased with the progress. Waters, according to the recording, said "My man, happy birthday to Ron Waters."

Waters understood how the game was played. "I'm going to tell you the fucking truth. You have money, then you can get something done."

LANGUAGE OF BRIBERY

I wrote a column about it in December 2014, intrigued by the patter between Ali and Waters. It is rare that you get to hear bribes being offered to public officials.

In their first meeting, Ali and Waters described the "setaside," which meant the kickback.

Ali told Waters he had control of the project by fictitious bank clients.

"That helps," Waters said. Ali asked if Waters needed money for his next election. No, Waters said. But he added, "I got stuff I always need."

"Here this is for you. That's a grand," Ali said.

"OK, my man," Waters replied.

And on another occasion he gave Waters $500 cash. "It's the usual amount," Ali said.

"OK, my man," said Waters.

Ali: "All right."

Waters: "My man."

When Ali asked Waters whether he wanted a scholarship fund or kickback from the authority contract, Waters replied, "why not both?"

OUT OF THE ORDINARY

Bruce Antkowiak, a law professor at Saint Vincent College in Latrobe said, "It is unusual to see a prosecutor decline a case completely and then have another one come in and have such a completely different assessment of it."

Much was made of the fact Ali had more than 2,000-plus criminal counts dismissed. To even be charged with 2,000 counts smacked of overcharging far beyond the attorney general's office usual MO. It was clearly, in my view, an effort to snare Ali as the state's sting informant.

* * *

Tynes, the former traffic court judge, had been the first to cut a deal. Tynes agreed to take a plea deal after she was charged in late October 2014 for accepting a $2,000 Tiffany bracelet. Tynes pleaded guilty on one count of conflict of interest. The other state charges against her were dropped. The plea deal came as a federal case against her was being resolved. Tynes faces no additional prison time beyond the two years she'll be serving for committing perjury in the feds' ticket-fixing case.

Her plea and filing charges against legislators in the sting case did not bode well for Kane's already eroded public image.

"From the perspective of selling Kane's decision to the public on why she didn't proceed, this absolutely undermines her claims and further adds to the questions that have built up during the last year among Pennsylvanians about her performance in office," said Christopher Borick, a political science professor at Muhlenberg College in Allentown.

* * *

By 2015, Kane had a glimmer of hope that pornographic emails released by the Supreme Court, those from the Corbett era, especially would give a breath of life to her racial targeting claims. They were emails from the OAG that Kane had attached to a legal filing with the court.

Williams would later say there were "offensive" emails in those that Fina and Costanzo were linked to during their days as state prosecutors.

"They contain numerous graphic images with captions that are derogatory towards women, a few that have racist connotations, and a smaller number with negative comments about gays. As the father of three daughters, as an African-American, as a law enforcement official, I was disappointed, and angry, that these messages were considered acceptable," Williams said. But he declined to fire Fina, Costanzo and Pat Blessington, another ex-state prosecutor on the DA's payroll. The National Organization for Women (NOW) was clamoring for their heads through the Philly papers. Instead, DA Williams sent them to sensitivity training.

It was essentially the same standard Kane had used.

* * *

(Sources: Story by Bumsted and Natasha Lindstrom on Seth Williams' new conference in December 2014; Philadelphia grand jury report released Dec. 16, 2014; Seth Williams' press release and Q&A at his news conference; Philadelphia Inquirer story by McCoy and Couloumbis on arrest of Waters and Brown; my column Dec. 20, 2014; McCoy and Couloumbis original sting story on March 16, 2014; Inquirer piece on Tynes' sentencing in federal court; Seth Williams' press release in September 2015, on porn emails.)

Footnote: Brown launched a defense fund and hired the Scranton firm of Dan Brier, who got charges thrown out against Mellow in the turnpike case. As of September 2015, she was planning to go to trial. The porn emails, a few with racist overtones, may have given defense attorneys something to work with.

* * *

Next: A bizarre 24 hours for Kane.

16

BIZARRE 24 HOURS

March 11, 2015

What an amazing, topsy turvey 24 hours for Kathleen Kane on March 10 and 11 of 2015.

The day before Supreme Court arguments on her motion to throw out a grand jury investigation of her, Seth Williams held a news conference to announce three more legislators would be charged in the sting case that Kane declined to prosecute.

The timing seemed more than coincidental. It was an announcement that blistered Kane. It brought to six the number of officials, four sitting lawmakers, a former legislator, and Tynes, the ex-traffic court judge, charged with crimes in the sting case. Kane is "her own worst enemy," DA Williams said.

That afternoon, Kane received fawning praise from members of the Republican-controlled House Appropriations Committee for her efforts battling drug abuse. No one really grilled her. Kane was seeking a near 6 percent budget increase. Lawmakers liked Kane's "mobile street crime" unit that moved from one city to the next focusing on street crimes and drug abuse. The unit made typically small-scale busts but provided fodder for legislators who wanted to appear to be doing something about the state's "heroin epidemic."

It was parochial politics at its best or worst, depending on your viewpoint.

The following morning Kane's motion that could determine the rest of her life would be argued before the Supreme Court. It was a huge legal and media event. Afterward, it would become a spectacle.

"THE QUEEN"

Seth Williams held his news conference a short walk away from Philadelphia City Hall where the Supreme Court would hear arguments the very next day.

Three additional legislators were charged: Rep. Michelle Brownlee, Rep. Louise Bishop, and former Rep. Harold James. Brownlee and James admitted to the grand jury they took money from Ali, DA Williams said. Bishop appeared before the grand jury under subpoena. She declined to answer questions. Bishop would challenge the charges.

The tapes allegedly showed Bishop accepted three cash payments from the informant totaling $1,500; Brownlee took one payment for $2,000 and James took one payment for $750.

The charges included bribery, conspiracy, conflict of interest and failing to file statements of financial interest for the cash gifts.

Bishop at the time of the presentment was 81 years old. She was well known beyond her West Philadelphia District. Bishop hosted a gospel radio show for decades. She believed her celebrity and friendship with DA Seth Williams would keep her from being charged, the grand jury said.

"You don't get a pass just because you are a friend, or a member of my political party, or race," DA Williams was quoted as saying by the Philadelphia Tribune, a black newspaper. "I've known and looked up to Rev. Bishop almost my entire life. I've been to her home often. My mother listened to her gospel radio show. Mrs. Bishop thought all of that would save her in the end, that I wouldn't prosecute her. That is what she told many people. But it can't. That's the nature of my oath—to do my job. We had to follow the evidence."

Bishop was first elected to the House in 1988 and she was re-elected to 13 two-year terms.

Like the others, Bishop took money and promised to perform official acts, the presentment said.

Bishop was confident in her staying power as an incumbent believing she could ward off any potential challenger.

"I'm not bragging, but I'm revered in this area," Bishop told Ali on tape. "In my area I'm the queen."

Queen or not, Bishop warmed up to the idea of getting money for her campaign, the grand jury suggested.

QUO WARRANTO

The filings and answers that led to a March 11, 2015, hearing before the Supreme Court might bore you to tears unless you're teaching a law school class or consider a "quo warranto" motion fascinating for some other reason. It's an archaic term that means "by what warrant." In essence it is to challenge whether someone has the authority to take a certain action. That's what Kane was doing in challenging Carpenter's appointment of Carluccio as a special prosecutor. If she won, the action would nullify a statewide grand jury presentment that had been issued but was not yet public record. The case already had been referred to Montgomery County District Attorney Risa Vetri Ferman but any action on her part was on ice pending the outcome of Kane's appeal.

If she lost, she likely would be eventually charged with crimes.

The Supreme Court argument on Kane's challenge in Philadelphia City Hall became a spectacle. She attended and sat near the rear of the courtroom. Kane looked elegant in a black jacket, black sweater, and bright print flowered skirt with a black background. She wore a single strand of pearls.

As she clearly enjoys, Kane was the center of attention. After the hearing it became a media circus.

THE HEARING

As pre-arranged with sheriff's deputies by James Koval, a Supreme Court spokesman, TV camera crews would be prohibited from filming in the hallway outside the courthouse following the arguments. But this was, after all, Philadelphia. I suspected it would be a mess. So before hitting the media crush that I anticipated, I maneuvered across the rear of the courtroom and caught Kane on the way out. It was insurance to have something in case she didn't stop at all.

Kane said very little. She told me she was "grateful" the court took time to hear her arguments because it was an important matter for the Commonwealth. I went outside the courtroom door and was shocked at the lineup of dozens of TV cameras and print reporters. She was probably more stunned. I grabbed a spot beside the door with my back up against a wall. There had to be an exit for her and it was likely to be past me. Kane had two agents with her as bodyguards and they cut a path past me through the crowd for her to get through.

So much for the sheriff deputies' orders.

I did not expect her to say much. Why should she? She just ran up billable hours for former President Judge of Superior Court Joseph Del Sole, who was retired, to represent her before the Supreme Court. An attorney attending the hearing told me privately hiring former judge Del Sole—just for these arguments—was the only good decision she made in 2015. His argument was smooth and articulate.

Outside the courtroom, Kane said roughly the same thing she told me inside the court. What did reporters expect? TV needed film and they would get it.

Kane seemed calm and relaxed considering her life's work and career were on the line. She told someone later it did rattle her, but she had a knack for not showing it. OK, she was a lawyer and argued cases but this was media-shock therapy.

The amazing thing about this particular ambush was how long it continued. Most of the TV crews followed her down a very long hallway in City Hall firing questions each step of the way. Some ran ahead of her to turn and get shots. Her bodyguards could only keep reporters and cameras from jostling her. It is a public hallway.

THE RULING

In a very short period, for the Supreme Court or any court in Pennsylvania, a decision was handed down on March 31. By a 4-1 majority, the court turned Kane down on her argument that Judge Carpenter illegally appointed Thomas Carluccio, the special prosecutor, to investigate a grand jury leak to the Philadelphia Daily News.

"Although we recognize that there are legitimate concerns arising out of a judicial appointment of a special prosecutor, we follow the approach of the United States Supreme Court and the many other jurisdictions which have found such appointments proper as an essential means to vindicate the courts' own authority," Chief Justice Thomas Saylor wrote.

Justice Debra Todd voiced the lone dissent. Carpenter "acted within his authority and sound prerogative" in appointing Carluccio, the court said.

The prevailing view among political and legal observers was that Kane seemed likely to be charged in Montgomery County.

On April 1, Ferman announced that she would conduct an independent investigation of the charges recommended by the statewide grand jury. She was running as a Republican candidate for judge that November but said she would not be pushed by any artificial timetable.

"ANGRY REPUBLICAN MEN"

Del Sole's appearance for Kane stood in stark contrast to another one of her lawyers, Lanny Davis, a former scandal spokesman for the Clinton White House, who earlier tossed Molatov cocktails at Carpenter and Carluccio.

Davis was a "crisis communications specialist," but the Washington D.C.-style smokescreens only aggravated judicial officials here in Pennsylvania.

Davis wasn't there for the hearing. In January, he had charged at a press conference in Philadelphia that "angry Republican men" were after Kane. The implication without saying his name was that Fina and other Corbett-era prosecutors were trying to cover their involvement in sharing pornography on office computers. Davis continued with Kane but quietly dropped out of sight shortly after the Supreme Court arguments in March 2015. There was never any announcement about his departure.

Back to Philly.

The Philadelphia Inquirer in January had reported that the statewide grand jury had recommended criminal charges against Kane. Davis wasn't confirming it. But he held the press conference in a Philly hotel in January to say if it were true, then that material was a grand jury leak that also needed to be investigated.

He referred to a mysterious court order that limited what he could say and who he could name at the news conference.

He had made it sound like a star chamber proceeding against Kane. "You have to wonder what is motivating this pseudo-legal effort to take down Kathleen Kane," Davis said.

What had unfolded was "a stacked deck, a railroad train process, shameful, contrary to all principles of justice and fairness," Davis stated.

He referred to porn emails discovered by accident in Geoffrey Moulton's review of the Sandusky investigation at Kane's behest. "They weren't looking for the pornography emails, they stumbled over them. And you know the rest of the story, those of you in the room. Those emails which I started to look at and couldn't continue—and I'm no shrinking violet—some of the most disgusting, misogynistic, repulsive, incredibly racist, awful stuff that I've ever seen in my lifetime were being circulated by a group of men, many of them the same prosecutors who were investigating the child molester, Sandusky," Davis said.

"This is an investigation of the attorney general—the first elected female Democrat in Pennsylvania history—triggered by individuals, I believe they happen to be men—with a personal and political agenda that smacks of politics through and through. A railroad, politicized process is not what Pennsylvania stands for.

"To me, it smacks of the politics of personal destruction," Davis said borrowing a phrase from the Bill Clinton era. He noted the judges involved from Castille to Carpenter, plus the special prosecutor Carluccio, were all Republicans.

Translation of his entire remarks: Kane was a woman, a Democrat, who promised transparency. The old guard in the attorney general's office, Corbett's people, were trading porn around on government computers. They supposedly concocted a scheme to block Kane and turn the tables on her. They were aided all the while by Republican judges in their efforts to put Kane in a legal bind, according to Davis' theory.

It's not clear whether going political and playing the gender card was Kane or Davis' idea but in my view it poisoned the well not only with Carpenter but other judges.

By April 2015, Davis was gone from the public scene on Kane's behalf. With Seth Williams, a Democrat, in high gear and Ferman, a Republican woman, now handling the investigation of Kane, the GOP-male conspiracy became much harder to sell. But Kane would still use a variation of it charging an even more sinister conspiracy by a "good old boys' network" of prosecutors.

Davis served a purpose. He lit the torch and helped fuel Kane's offense through the Supreme Court hearing. He foreshadowed what would eventually become a central element of her defense. But there is no doubt in my mind he aggravated Carpenter, former Chief Justice Ronald D. Castille and perhaps current justices who know Carpenter or knew of his solid reputation. Castille had approved the statewide grand jury investigation of Kane.

But Kane's disastrous press operations began to improve in April 2015 when she hired Chuck Ardo, former press secretary for Gov. Ed Rendell.

* * *

(Sources: My Tribune-Review column on a "Surreal 24 Hours" with Kane on March 14, 2015; Seth Williams' press release from March 10, 2015; Philadelphia grand jury presentment; March 31 Tribune-Review story on Supreme Court decision; the court ruling on Administrative Office of Pennsylvania Courts web site; March 11 Tribune-Review story on House Appropriations Committee hearing; story on hearing by Terrie Morgan-Besecker in Scranton Times-Tribune; Craig McCoy and Maria Panaritis, Philadelphia Inquirer on Supreme Court hearing; Ferman press release; my January 2015 Trib story on Lanny Davis' press conference with Davis.)

POSTSCRIPT

In December 2015, Bishop took a plea bargain and entered a plea of no contest to a misdemeanor charge and agreed to resign immediately. Most significantly, her attorney Charles Peruto withdrew the racial targeting motion he had made on Bishop's behalf and told the court that after reviewing unsealed grand jury files and other documents provided by the Philly DA's office there was no evidence black lawmakers were targeted. The prominent defense attorney known for bare-knuckled lawyering apologized. Vanessa Brown's case was still pending by the end of 2015, but it brought the sting case tally to four quilty pleas, one no contest plea, and Brown's case outstanding.

* * *

Next: Was he out of his mind?

17

DIFFICULT TO MANAGE

April 21, 2015

Kane's press operation finally stabilized when she brought in grizzled veteran press operative Chuck Ardo in April 2015. But by then, it was too late. The damage had compounded from the repeated legal shots she had taken and from her self-inflicted wounds. But Ardo helped her in several ways. The Capitol press corps found Lanny Davis difficult to deal with—too Clintonian in his hair-splitting and mind-numbing challenges. For instance, he kept texting me New Year's Eve demanding to know what else Chief Justice Castille had said when I earlier had asked for a response for a potential story. If I wasn't printing it I was under no obligation to tell him. Some of the email exchanges with him on nailing down her position on the grand jury leak were mind-blowing, shifting ever so slightly here and there, expanding and contracting. In person, Davis was likeable. But he was more Yale lawyer than press operative. Chuck by contrast was easygoing and he'd survived nearly eight years of Ed Rendell, who thought he was his own best press spokesman. He also had real life experiences that gave him a broad perspective.

Ardo served as Rendell's press secretary for most of his second term in office. According to newsroom lore, Ardo had to go when he told the Inquirer's Couloumbis, who was doing a profile of Policy Director Donna Cooper, that Cooper was the "T.O." of the Rendell administration. It was a reference to ex-wide receiver Terrell Owens whose trouble making with the Philadelphia Eagles resulted in only a brief stay in the City of Brotherly Love. Everyone in Philly who could breathe knew what calling her "T.O." meant: prima donna.

Given Cooper was arguably the most powerful staffer under Rendell, Ardo this time was really out. He says Rendell on numerous other occasions had fired him but in an hour or so would cool off and ask where a certain document or a revised statement was. "But you fired me," Ardo would say. Rendell would tell him to forget about it. Ardo once said working for Rendell was like walking behind an elephant and cleaning up the dung.

Ardo actually resigned in 2010, he says, because of "personal differences with Rendell."

Ardo was well-liked and effective as a gubernatorial press secretary for several reasons: he was quick on his feet and could spin a quote out of nowhere, he was responsive and returned all calls, he didn't take much of anything personally and he made his regular "rounds" spending about an hour every day schmoozing with reporters. Most of all, he was candid. He'd give you his best shot at getting a positive on-the-record quote for his boss, then tell you the truth.

In retirement, he served briefly as a press spokesman for troubled Harrisburg Mayor Linda Thompson. But Ardo quit and talked publicly about his boss because he thought she had crossed the line with anti-gay comments, calling Controller Dan Miller, for instance, that "evil little homosexual" and for talking about how a Jewish developer would bring "Israel money" into Harrisburg for new construction. As the son of Holocaust survivors, Ardo did not find that acceptable or funny.

Ardo lost his grandparents, aunts and uncles in the Holocaust. He was born in Slovokia. His family fled to Israel after the Communist takeover. They lived in Swedish-built prefab housing near Tel Aviv, one room and a kitchen for a family of four and a shared outhouse. He had polio at age 4. He woke up one morning and "couldn't move." It took months to recover. His parents brought the family to the U.S., landing in New York Feb. 8, 1954. They went to live with an aunt in Stamford, Conn. He went to school and couldn't speak English. "Much to my amazement the teacher didn't speak Hebrew," he said. He remembers the name of the young African American girl in his class who took him by the hand and led him to the boys' room when he couldn't explain it to the teacher. (Hint: she saw him squirming in his seat.) He went to Ohio State University where he majored in English and History. He left without a degree but picked up the necessary credits years later—in all, seven years for a bachelor's degree. Much of his life was spent in various business enterprises, some successful some not, from a second-hand jeans store to making and selling wall plaques to running or owning restaurants, beginning as a street vendor in Athens selling tostadas to college drunks at businesses such as "Chico's Chicken" and "Mexigo," a Mexican home delivery restaurant in Columbus. He gave up restaurants and started for a political consulting firm and worked on both of Bill Clinton's campaigns. Then he was picked up by Rendell's 2002 campaign in Pittsburgh.

So after the Linda Thomson gig he was really retired. Or so he thought. He could only tell one day from the next by his standing schedule of breakfast with one friend on one day and lunch with another friend two days later. He worked at a food bank till his shoulder gave out from moving boxes. In the meantime, he was an abysmal failure at growing much of a lawn and usually pulled the wrong perennials rather than weeds much to his wife Nancy's chagrin. He was writing a novel on the Kennedy assassination. He wasn't suited to being a "full-time house husband," Nancy Ardo said.

When he got a voice message from Kathleen Kane to call her back, he was on a long walk with his Boston Terrier. He told Nancy he knew what it was about but he wouldn't go back to work. He called back and at least agreed to meet Kane in Scranton for breakfast. He was impressed with Kane, thought she was easy to talk to and that she fully understood the situation she faced. He was offered a job.

It had Rendell's fingerprints all over it. Rendell liked Kane and he knew Ardo was good. But Ardo, then 68, called Rendell. "He denied being behind it but he encouraged me to take it. He told me I was too old to worry about my reputation." So Ardo agreed to a six-month contract as the attorney general's spokesmen—her seventh since January 2013.

I called Ardo and left a voice mail for him "Are you out of your f---ing mind?"

"They'll have to get used to me," he told me in an interview. "I'm not that easy to manage."

He told Kane he had only one requirement for the job. He wouldn't lie for her.

Seldom has the appointment of a press secretary prompted so much interest at the Capitol. It's because of who he is—Chuck Ardo—and whom he's going to work for—the embattled attorney general.

The others have been fired, quit or they've been pushed out the door. If you count Lanny Davis, an outside the office spokesman, Ardo was the eighth. Since Davis technically was a lawyer, Ardo more accurately was the seventh.

Ardo was being paid $10,000 per month.

Kane knew she might face possible criminal charges based on a presentment by that statewide grand jury alleging she authorized release of confidential grand jury material to a newspaper. She was at that time under investigation by the Montgomery County district attorney.

Kane has said on numerous occasions she'll fight as long as it takes.

"Chuck is well known throughout the commonwealth as a 'tell-it-like-it-is' professional who will help us get our message out," Kane said in a written statement.

It's the "tell-it-like-it-is" part that might get tricky with Kane. She is the only one who seems to like to tell-it-like-it-is . . . in her mind, at least.

As I mentioned in a column shortly after Ardo was hired he now had "front-row seat at the circus."

He began to help Kane immediately by getting reasonable comments defending her into news stories. Most importantly, he helped her deliver on her promise of transparency by getting documents for reporters rather than having them go through the arduous Right to Know law process. It was an unofficial policy under Rendell. Kane's office had been anything but transparent. With Ardo there, it stated to feel a bit more transparent though the career bureaucrats sometimes won.

Still, it was unclear who would last six months: Kane or Ardo?

By January 2016, they were both still there and Ardo was on a contract extension.

* * *

(Sources: Interviews with Ardo in 2015 and some from prior years from Rendell era; Tribune-Review story on his hiring and my column on him joining the Kane team; August 2009 Inquirer story on Donna Cooper by Angela Couloumbis.)

* * *

Next: Porn scandal explodes.

18

"POLITICAL PEEP SHOW"

Sept. 25, 2014

Beneath my desk in the Capitol Newsroom is a stack of pornography about three inches thick. The smutty images show men and women having sex, women with other women, sex toys, and genital close ups. Some are clearly over the top. There are plenty of relatively tamer photos of bare breasts and derrieres. Many are intended to be funny and probably wouldn't qualify as "porn." Raunchy, yes. Distasteful, undoubtedly. Some are racially offensive like a white guy carrying a bucket of Kentucky Fried Chicken fighting off two black guys trying to grab it. The caption reads "BRAVERY" at its finest.

They're not from Hustler Magazine, Penthouse, Playboy or raw web sites. I got them in August 2015, courtesy of the state Supreme Court for a hefty copying fee paid by the Tribune-Review.

It was the second batch of porn publicly released—the first by Kathleen Kane in late September 2014. Court officials used good sense in making them available only for copying or review. If the court had posted them, the porn would be assuredly linked by some web site making it appear Pennsylvania's highest court had gone rogue.

Editorial and Opinion Editor John Micek, of Pennlive, wrote that "mostly they're just crass and sophomoric. They're the posters that hung on the wall at your frat house, stuff that maybe you found hilarious at 18 when you were presumably too dumb to know any better."

In fact, they were forwarded and received by high-ranking prosecutors, supervisors and agents, on email chains within the state's highest law enforcement agency, the Office of Attorney General.

Most were sent by government employees on government time on government computers. What was odd: just a week before the Supreme Court's release, the justices ruled that Kane could release them in an "appropriate manner." They were not grand jury material, the court said. But she didn't do it despite claiming at a press conference in August 2015 they were vital to her defense. Even the grand jury judge she blamed for holding them up had written that the emails could and should be released.

The problem was Kane "has cherry-picked" which emails to "selectively release," Judge William Carpenter wrote in a Dec. 12, 2014 court filing. Carpenter added he believed all of the images "should be released."

HARRISBURG'S "DELTA HOUSE"

So with that green light from the high court "naturally you'd expect the scheduling of a very glitzy press conference, starring a triumphant Kane, smiling beatifically before the cameras as she enjoys her 'I told you so' moment against her rivals, including former OAG prosecutor Frank Fina," Micek wrote.

Micek wrote they were the emails that were "supposed to blow Harrisburg's old boy network wide open, exposing senior members of the Office of Attorney General as superannuated frat boys who turned Strawberry Square into their own personal Delta House, as they allegedly exchanged sexist and possibly racist missives on their taxpayer-funded computers during work hours."

Those involved in the email chains saw it a lot differently. For numerous high-profile trials, they often worked 15-hour days, six or seven days a week. They were blowing off steam—a minute here or there. Some officials said they didn't open any. They didn't surf the web for them. Most came in from outside the office. It was wrong, one of them told me later, but it wasn't for the thrill. It was dark humor intended to get a laugh and to then get back to work. One of them told me it was wrong to say on "government time" if it happened at 10 p.m. on a day that—for them—started at 8 a.m.

Women in the office and outside the office received them and sent some, sources and records say. But the complete "porn" link diagram showing where all came in and everyone who forwarded them and where they landed wasn't made public. We didn't have full evidence on the email chains.

SPEAKING WITH "FORKED-TONGUE"

But Kane wouldn't release them claiming that protective orders in Montgomery County prevented her from doing so. The Supreme Court suggested that's not what the protective orders did.

It would get so bizarre that Kane, while calling for the emails to be released, had her attorneys argue before Commonwealth Court that remaining emails in Kane's possession were not public records and should not be released.

Contrast that with Renee Martin's comment on Kane's behalf when the first batch was released in the fall of 2014 aimed at Republicans.

"Attorney General Kane believes it is in the public's best interest to have a good understanding of how its public servants conduct their business," Martin said in a statement. "She also believes transparency on this issue is a very good way to help ensure that the exchanging of sexually explicit materials through internal emails on state-owned equipment, during official work hours doesn't happen elsewhere."

It was transparency for political enemies and rivals. It was opaque for those Kane protected.

Terry Mutchler, lawyer for the Inquirer in the Right to Know law case, called it "forked-tongue advocacy."

* * *

I was still finishing a salad at my desk when the call came in from Renee Martin. It was about 12:30 p.m. on Sept. 25, 2014. Martin told me to come over at 1 p.m. to look at material available as a result of our RTK requests. She scheduled reporters in groups of three. I went with Couloumbis and Steve Esack. Agent Braden Cook sat at a laptop in a large conference room calling up images. But there were no emails identifying who sent the images, or even who received them. Eight former attorney general employees under Corbett and his successor Linda Kelly were identified.

The emails were discovered during law professor Geoffrey Moulton's review of the Sandusky case for the attorney general in 2013. It didn't unravel all at once. It took months to recover them. When Capitol Newsroom reporters wrote the first porn release story, we only had the agent's descriptions of which former OAG employee sent or received them. Martin, Kane's then-spokeswoman, told us those provided were in response to Right to Know law requests from the Inquirer, Trib and Morning Call. I never asked for these specific people. I requested all current and former employees who sent sexually explicit emails. It appeared to be some type of compilation of our requests, which is not provided for in the Right to Know Law. That's flat out wrong. They were looking for an excuse to release them.

NEMESIS FINALLY NAMED

When Kane first learned the object of her obsession, Frank Fina, was on the email chains she must have thought she hit the winning number in the state lottery. But when she later learned there was a protective order preventing her from essentially naming him in any way or in any action that might be deemed threatening, she must have been crushed.

The names of Kane-nemesis Fina and another extremely talented prosecutor, E. Marc Costanzo, were redacted in the material Kane released in 2014. I believe then she was concerned she'd get hauled in for contempt of court.

But they were not redacted on the Supreme Court's release of 398 pages in August 2015. Fina and Costanzo were named. A lot had changed by then. So she got her wish, right? They'd both be fired in the Philly DA's office, Kane figured.

These were now public documents.

Kane's modus operandi has always been, in my opinion: "if I'm going down I'm taking people with me." But given that Fina and Costanzo didn't send any such emails in their new job and because they weren't serial senders based on the material released and were among hundreds involved, DA Seth Williams didn't fire them.

Defendants that Fina, Costanzo and Blessington had prosecuted in part for doing campaign work on state time were outraged. Most were still on parole and couldn't speak out. But they saw it as blatant hypocrisy. Their hours of using state employees for campaign work were compiled by prosecutors to provide part of the equation for calculating the severity of theft and restitution. In reality, the cases were far more complicated than that with the theft of expensive data equipment in Computergate and the theft of taxpayer money for campaign bonuses in Bonusgate. But the defendants were right, essentially, about the parallel. In reality though glancing at an email no matter how nasty, or hitting a button to forward 20 images as Fina apparently did once, takes seconds. And several people from the Corbett prosecutorial team like Blessington were merely recipients. There's no way to tell if those messages were opened.

I understand the outrage of Bill DeWeese, John Perzel and probably others who thought this was fundamentally wrong. But it is not the same. A lawyer from the Computergate case told me, however, that Fina set the standard that misuse of government computers is a crime, therefore it is comparable.

But is the cost negligible in dollars and cents?

As Commonwealth Court Judge Dan Pellegrini would later say in the Right to Know law case over the emails Kane still wouldn't release, if receiving a questionable email were the standard for judging someone "we're all in trouble." He's right. Anybody can get a dirty email.

* * *

Martin in 2014 would later provide totals of how many each official forwarded or received. It seemed unfair these officials were being outed without knowing the universe of all current and former employees sending and receiving racy emails. I didn't like it but I could not ignore it. This was an official release from the attorney general.

Chris Brennan, formerly of the Daily News, who was in a different viewing group, gave the best accounting:

"Explicit emails put on display for reporters yesterday by Attorney General Kathleen Kane—in perhaps the strangest political peep show in history—included videos of women masturbating by inserting a bowling pin and a lit cigar," Brennan wrote.

"In another video, a man who looks like a race-car driver shakes a bottle of champagne, uncorks it and then inserts the spouting mouth of the bottle into a woman's vagina while others watch. He then takes a big gulp of the bubbly. And not from the bottle."

Some made fun of fat women.

I recall one called "Alabama Death Penalty Execution" in which a woman I first thought was a male Sumo wrestler and must have topped 350 pounds squats over a man's face and drops down with all her weight.

That's the "execution."

Many of these images already released were not in the attachment Kane made to the Supreme Court.

The 2014 release covered email attachments from 2008-2012.

Kane would release transcripts of the eight Corbett staffers about a week after the "peep show." So what that gave us was: the viewing and our notes from it, and separate email transcripts. But they were not together in one document proving that person X sent email X that we'd already seen.

I didn't disbelieve it. All I'm saying is it was not done in a way that would be considered reliable evidence in court, not that anyone would ever be prosecuted. Transmitting porn even on a government computer isn't a crime unless there's child pornography involved. And there wasn't any kiddie porn though Kane would later wrongly imply in a CNN interview that there was. And then back off of it through spokeswoman Martin.

A prominent figure among those named was ex-prosecutor E. Christopher Abruzzo, a member of Corbett's Cabinet as secretary of the Department of Environmental Protection. He resigned Oct. 2, 2014. He received 46 racy emails and forwarded eight while working in the AG's office under Corbett. Abruzzo, to his credit, stepped up. He said he took responsibility for any lack of judgment in 2009 and said he didn't condone it. But he had "no recollection" of the "specific accounts described by the media." The emails were not reflective "of the person and professional that I am."

By contrast, the second prominent official implicated was State Police Commissioner Col. Frank Noonan, who received 338 pornographic emails. There's no evidence he opened any and Corbett said that Noonan did not. Noonan headed investigations under Corbett in the AG's office. To me, it was believable he didn't open any. He was old-school FBI. He didn't seem the least bit tech savvy or the kind of guy to use a lot of email. Moreover, instinct probably told him to leave them untouched. Was that the right thing to do? As a supervisor in the AG's office did he have a responsibility to say: Knock it off? And based on the "subject lines" I saw it was clear these were not about obtaining search warrants or finding probable cause. A glance at them over time would have suggested there was a problem. Noonan was probably spared because he was leading an extensive manhunt in northeastern Pennsylvania for a cop killer in late 2014. Moreover, Corbett, as expected, lost the November election. Noonan had a few weeks left on the job anyway. Others resigned and even some former deputy state prosecutors in the private sector lost their jobs.

The porn disclosure by Kane a little more than a month before the election didn't sink Corbett. He was consistently down in the polls for a variety of reasons too lengthy to discuss here, principally a widespread perception he made massive cuts in state education funding. That was based on truth but also was not 100 percent accurate. He did get the legislature to cut spending just as he promised to do in the 2010 campaign and people ultimately didn't like it. Moreover, there was a "failure to communicate," as a prison warden once told Paul Newman in the movie "Cool Hand Luke." Bottom line: Corbett was a career prosecutor, not a politician, and it showed.

The irony is Kane had too little prosecutorial experience and it caught up with her. Corbett had been a prosecutor most of his life, including U.S. attorney in Pittsburgh, and he acted like one in the governor's office. It didn't help he'd just put a lot of legislators and staff in prison.

It's fair to say though that Kane's two-stage porn disclosure before the gubernatorial election didn't help Corbett increase his margins in the polls.

No evidence ever surfaced that Corbett personally received any dirty emails while AG. Whether he heard about them is another matter. He was informed by Moulton the emails existed prior to release of the Sandusky report in June 2014.

In a debate with Wolf at KYW Radio, Wolf said Corbett was responsible for the culture in which the emails flourished. Corbett called it a "cheap shot."

"That's not my culture and everyone knows that's not my culture," Corbett said. "I can't believe they were dumb enough to send them on public emails."

THE ROAD TO PORN

It was a long tortuous legal path to get to the point of Kane's selective porn release in 2014.

To make a long story short, Kane's office turned down my Right to Know law request. I appealed. Kane appointed a hearing officer, Debra K. Wallet, a Camp Hill attorney, to decide the issue. It pointed out one of the major flaws in the RTK law. The email provisions applied only to the governor's office and executive branch agencies, but NOT to the legislature or the independent row officers. Normally an appeal would have gone to the independent Office of Open Records. But I am not complaining. After a phone conference with Wallet and the AG's office, Wallet agreed with my position essentially that because these emails were sent on government computers and on government email systems they constituted misuse of the AG's email system based on official policy. Therefore, they represented an agency transaction or activity. It was very similar to the Inquirer's case which landed in Commonwealth Court while mine was stayed there.

That's when we hit what Mutchler called "Wizard of Oz" land—where Kane was arguing both for release and for withholding the remaining porn emails, of which there may be thousands.

Why? As of this writing it's unknown. One theory of mine: the totality of the record might show the "core" portion of the email ring (Fina and Costanzo), as Kane called it, wasn't the "core" at all.

Another is she held them back for leverage—on whom wasn't clear.

Within a week though she would be threatening a scorched earth policy that she hinted would reveal porn sent by officials previously undisclosed. "Our preliminary review has generated emails of government officials, including law enforcement officials and judges, heretofore unknown to us," Kane said. "These emails will be fully released either as public documents defined by the Commonwealth Court, or at my discretion."

Yet another change of direction. Mutchler said one needed a "legal GPS" to keep track of Kane's positions on porn.

TWO JUSTICES IMPLICATED

Steve Esack did plenty of "door knocks" as a reporter. He'd knocked on doors at homes of soldiers killed in battle, cops killed in the line of duty and for five kids killed in a house fire. Door knocks are one of the hardest things reporters do. Asking for comments from a grieving widow or mother. It's an awful side of the business. Knocking on the door of a Supreme Court justice, a former police officer, after attending a gubernatorial debate in Philadelphia, was not really a much bigger deal. "Door knocks" are one of the hardest things reporters do. Asking for comments from a grieving widow or mother. It's an awful side of the business. Esack was a Philly guy and knew his way around the area near Pennypacker Park.

He showed up on Seamus McCaffery's front porch at 9:10 p.m. on Oct. 1, 2014, having viewed some pornographic emails McCaffery sent from his private email address to an old friend from the police force working as an agent in the attorney general's office. What McCaffery wouldn't necessarily have known was that the former agent was sending them to a lot of other people in the office. They in turn sent them to others. It multiplied from there.

When Esack showed up, McCafffery was wearing shorts and a black golf shirt that said "Pennsylvania Supreme Court."

What Esack did was ballsy. He showed up at the justice's door for comment before publishing his story. It was one of the bigger scoops of what some called "porngate."

His story said McCaffery forwarded at least eight sexually explicit emails to the agent in the state attorney general's office who later shared them with more than a dozen others.

McCaffery was the first judge implicated in the blossoming scandal. Esack set off a firestorm.

"Not only do I not have any comment, since when does the news media pry into personal emails?"

McCaffery then asked Esack to leave his property.

The Morning Call story identified McCaffery as a recipient or sender of 54 emails.

The justice forwarded some with subject lines "tan lines XXX" and "centerfold," but most of the emails reviewed by the newspaper and bearing McCaffery's name were not sexually explicit, Esack wrote.

Castille earlier that week during a conference call with reporters said a judge should not be fraternizing too closely with either prosecutors or defense attorneys by sending personal emails of any kind.

He had demanded Kane provide him with emails of any judges. Earlier Inquirer stories hinted at top jurists being involved in the porn email scandal. As I look at it in retrospect, Castille had a whiff of this.

Kane, for a few days, resisted Castille's stepped up demands. That was a clear path to suicide. She's an independently elected official but still an officer of the court.

One way or another, Castille was going to get them. Kane relented and sent Agent Cook to Castille's office. Castille and McCaffery had a long history. There's no question, in my view, that Castille's distaste for McCaffery was enormous. The animus from both was clear.

And now Castille had the goods.

Nineteen days after Esack's door knock the Supreme Court suspended McCaffery, who the court's opinion stated "publicly accepted responsibility for exchanging hundreds of sexually explicit emails with a member or members of the Office of Attorney General . . . which surfaced in the Gerald Sandusky investigation."

The court also cited Justice J. Michael Eakin's assertions to the Judicial Conduct Board that McCaffery threatened to embarrass him with porn. "In my opinion, that sort of threat borders on criminal conduct," Castille said in a concurring statement. Eakin used a "John Smith" address on Yahoo and he stated there was only one email. He self-reported to the judicial conduct board. But as of October 2015, more Eakin emails surfaced and the board was doing another review. Kane sent 1,000 personal emails of Eakin's to the board. Meanwhlile, the Philadelphia Daily News came up with copies of some very raunchy material allegedly received or sent by Eakin.

Documents were released by the Judicial Conduct Board from December 2014 saying Eakin had been cleared of two complaints. A letter to Eakin said he'd been a "passive recipient."

However, Kane's assertions in 2015 prompted the Supreme Court to hire a Pittsburgh law firm to take another look at Eakin's emails.

In 2010, Eakin claimed McCaffery threatened him with release of the emails unless he could persuade Castille to retract comments that McCaffery was the only justice who received sexually explicit emails.

The material McCaffery forwarded to the attorney general's office included a video of a "woman in sexual congress with a snake," Castille asserted.

Castille implied McCaffery was a "sociopath." Through a spokesman, McCaffery blamed "malicious intent" by the chief justice for his suspension.

The court's order called the material "extremely disturbing" based on Castille's review of the emails.

This was a backyard brawl and Castille had McCaffery in a choke hold.

Both were ex-Marines. Castille lost his leg in the Vietnam War.

Bruce Ledewitz, a Duquesne University law school professor, told me at the time the action against McCaffery set "a terrible precedent" and is "absolutely a power grab."

"They can suspend any person they don't like," Ledewitz said.

A week later, while Gov. Tom Corbett was speaking to the Pennsylvania Press Club luncheon, I got a text at the Hilton from one of Corbett's guys: McCaffery resigned. He submitted a letter to Corbett. The Judicial Conduct Board dismissed its investigation of McCaffery. It was over.

Or was it?

McCaffery's conduct brought the court into "enormous disrepute," Castile previously wrote in his concurring statement on the suspension.

"It would be impossible for this Court to function effectively while Justice McCaffery sits on this Court," Castille said. His so-called "lapse in judgment" lasted, at least, for many years as an adult, Castille said. "It is more than a lapse in judgment—it has caused unmitigated turmoil in the justice system and has indirectly cost several state prosecutors and high ranking state officials their public careers."

Castille said McCaffery was correct in "one of his assertions about me. I have been attempting to remove Justice McCaffery from this court. In two decades of my experience on this court, no other justice, including (convicted) ex-Justice Joan Orie Melvin, has done as much to bring the court into disrepute." He referred to other controversies including McCaffery meeting with the "main traffic court ticket fixer" to "discuss" his wife's ticket, and his wife's legal referral fees while working in McCaffery's Supreme Court office.

McCaffery, contacted for this book, provided the following statement. I had several off-the-record talks with him about a wide range of matters, but he was limited in what he could say about leaving the court. Here is his statement in its entirety. It is the first time he has responded in a detailed way on his resignation.

* * *

> "I appreciate the opportunity to make a statement concerning what led up to my retirement from the Supreme Court of Pennsylvania. To those who are not familiar with my career, I spent forty years in our Nation's military—I joined the Marine Corps as a private and retired as a Colonel in the Air Force Reserve. I spent twenty years in the Philadelphia police department, and by the time of my election to the Pennsylvania Supreme Court, I had spent fourteen years as a trial and then an appellate court judge.
>
> "During those years of public service, I don't recall ever having had a complaint filed against me. However, after my election to the Supreme Court, all of that changed. It began with an anonymous complaint to the Judicial Conduct Board ("JCB"), based upon my having been honored by the Marine Corps Law Enforcement Foundation for my service to our Nation, the Commonwealth of Pennsylvania, and my city. I was cleared, in writing, by the JCB, of having improperly "lent the prestige of my office" to the MCLEF.
>
> "Then I was accused of trying to influence the outcome of a traffic ticket that my wife had received.

After a full and complete investigation by the Judicial Conduct Board, it was determined that I had done nothing wrong. Then I became the target of a federal investigation into "referral fees" received by my attorney wife. This investigation, along with the traffic ticket investigation, received a great deal of media attention. The stories cited "sources," and although I have my suspicions, as of this writing, I have still not been able to learn what the specific allegations were and/or who made them. After two and a half years of being under the relentless spotlight of the media and the microscope of the F.B.I. and the U.S. Attorney's Office, my wife and I were notified through our attorneys that the federal investigation was being closed. . . . This investigation was the most intense and stressful experience that either I or my wife have ever endured.

"After being publicly cleared by the U.S. Attorney's Office, I then began to hear rumors about 'pornographic' emails that were found in the email servers of the Office of the Attorney General that I allegedly had sent. Let me be clear: I never sent ANY emails to ANY attorney in the OAG, from ANY email account whatsoever.

"Like most people today, I have a private email account. This email account was not connected in any way to the Supreme Court of Pennsylvania, it did not reflect any connection to the Court, and did not bear my name. I have a group of friends from my military and law enforcement careers who have stayed in touch via email. One individual in this group, who is NOT an attorney, happened to have been employed in the OAG, although he retired from that office many years ago. Unbeknownst to me, this individual had been passing our private, personal emails to other individuals inside the OAG. I have since learned that one or two attorneys in that office made and kept copies of these private emails. Then, after they left the OAG, one or both them 'leaked' these private, personal emails—that I had NOT sent to them—to the media. Obviously, this was done for the sole purpose of embarrassing me. (Although I have asked Attorney General Kane to show me copies of any emails in the emails strings of the OAG that were allegedly "mine," she has, to date, failed to respond to my requests.) My private email address was one of the many emails found in the email strings of the OAG. The rest is not only history, but is history still in the making.

"I want to be perfectly clear: I DID NOT LEAVE MY POSITION AS A JUSTICE OF THE SUPREME COURT BECAUSE OF ANY EMAILS (caps emphasis by McCaffery.)

"I decided to retire after the October 2014 'suspension' order by the Court, even though the order was an interim one. Included as part of the justification for my "suspension" were the traffic ticket allegation (I had been cleared of any wrongdoing by the (Judicial Conduct Board in March 2013), and my wife's referral fees. (As noted above, we were cleared by the U.S. Attorney's Office when they closed their investigation in June 2014.) While the order also sets forth allegations that I had been involved in the sending of "sexually explicit" emails to the OAG, emails had absolutely NOTHING to do with my reasons for retiring. The interim suspension order was the culmination of what I perceive to have been a well-orchestrated effort to force me off the Court. The amount of vitriol contained in certain portions of the interim suspension order was literally shocking not only to me, but to many, many others, including judges and lawyers, to whom I have spoken in the aftermath of the issuance of that order. It was perfectly evident to me that it was time to retire and leave this all behind me.

"After a lengthy career of blemish-free public service, I had become the target of the media and law enforcement. Cowards, using the cover and shield of anonymity, had finally succeeded in persuading me, after years-long, coordinated efforts to humiliate and bankrupt me and my family that it was time to stop the train and get off. I was no longer willing to endure one baseless attack after another, attacks which I could not stop at their source. Despite having been cleared in regard to the attacks by the relevant and involved investigative bodies, I was unwilling to continue to incur additional legal expenses and to have my family suffer further embarrassment. Retirement, not resignation, was not only my best path, but was an opportunity to which I looked forward after what I had endured, especially during the latter part of my tenure on the Court.

"Sadly, my many years of stellar public service have been obscured by the storm involving sexually explicit emails that has swept so many into its vortex. While I cannot speak for others, I know that any emails I sent to an old friend from a personal email account that were leaked to the media by those who sought my downfall, were just that—personal emails to an old friend that had nothing to do with my job or performance as a Justice of the Pennsylvania Supreme Court. Instead of being remembered for all of my many wonderful achievements, such as the creation of the largest number of Veterans' courts in the country, the long overdue reform of the Philadelphia court system that saved and continues to save taxpayers millions of dollars, giving medical coverage to all same-sex employees of Pennsylvania's courts, and creating mental health and domestic violence specialty courts, to name but a few of the programs that I was instrumental in creating, my good name is now forever and unjustly linked to scandalous emails. It pains me greatly that the media has reduced the totality of my long and productive career and personal life to a single embarrassing episode that I and my family are forced to relive, over and over again."

* * *

Note one phrase McCaffery used: "history still in the making."

* * *

(Sources: Steve Esack's Oct. 2, 2014, story on his review of McCaffery's emails; Supreme Court opinion on McCaffery's suspension, and Castille's concurring statement; AP story in October 2015 by Mark Scolforo and Marc Levy on judicial board's letter to Eakin; my Trib story on the suspension in in October 2014; Philadelphia Inquirer editorial in August 2015; Daily News' Chris Brennan's story in September 2014. My Trib story from September 2014, on the first email release; Inquirer's McCoy and Couloumbis from September 2015 on whether Kane really wanted emails released; Commonwealth Court hearing I attended and wrote about in September 2015; Brennan's Oct. 27, 2014, story on McCaffery's resignation; my October 2014 Trib story on McCaffery's response to the order; William Bender's October 2015 Daily News stories on new Eakin emails; McCaffery's statement to me for this book.)

POSTSCRIPT

By mid-November 2015, Kane's porn charges were gaining traction in Philadelphia.

Sen. Anthony Williams, a powerful voice on virtually any topic, was hammering away at Justice Eakin, Judicial Conduct Board officials and others he contended took part in an attempted 2014 cover up of Eakins's emails.

DA Seth Williams, and the former prosecutors who worked for Corbett in the OAG, were also under fire.

Williams, a Philadelphia Democrat, said the emails that Justice Eakin sent and received from his state-issued account were more than X-rated.

"This isn't 'porngate,'" Sen. Williams said at his press conference. "This is 'hategate.'" It is noteworthy that Eakin's wife Heidi, an experienced criminal defense attorney with William Costopoulos' Lemoyne law firm, initially was representing him.

"These emails are riddled with hate speech," Sen. Williams contended. "All of them undermine the integrity of our judiciary and they raise serious questions about Justice Eakin's impartiality and his common sense, especially as it affects women and minorities."

A report was expected from the conduct board, which would then, if warranted, go to the Court of Judicial Discipline.

Professor Ledewitz told me when he appeared as a guest on a popular news talk show on WHYY in Philly, the buzz was about porn.

It resonated with many in the City of Brotherly Love. Fina, fairly or unfairly, was the focal point of that anger among some women.

Philadelphia city councilwomen in conjunction with the National Organization for Women, were banging the drum for Fina and Costanzo's dismissal.

Meanwhile, DA Williams said the assistant DAs, including Fina, underwent a day of sensitivity training by a leading expert. That made their critics even angrier.

The flipside is it is not a crime and they didn't swap around any porn while working for DA Williams. It was a miniscule portion of their email.

Fina and Costanzo, among other former state prosecutors and an ex-agent, were suing Kane in federal court claiming their constitutional rights were violated.

"Kane has misused the power of her office, and its publicly funded resources, for the purpose of silencing her critics through a pattern of intimidation, attempted blackmail and vindictive resolution," the lawsuit claimed. It was filed by attorney Mark Tanner on behalf of Fina, Costanzo, Blessington, former Executive Deputy Rick Sheetz and Randy Feathers, an agent who supervised agents the Sandusky investigation. The suit seeks costs and punitive damages. Kane will defend herself vigorously against the allegations, Ardo said.

The case, for instance, cites the "horrific allegation" by Kane on national TV, which was false, that the former OAG staffers sent child pornography. It was "devastating" to their reputations, the suit claims.

It's fair to say Porngate was quite a mess.

Here is a comprehensive analysis of Porngate in an interview with G. Terry Madonna, a political science professor at Franklin & Marshall College. "It transcends every other major controversy including Bonusgate. That had, at least, a level of simplicity. This has multiple moving parts. It involves judges, prosecutors and defense attorneys. It involved at least two grand jury leaks. You have multiple lawsuits against Kane by people who worked for her. This has tentacles everywhere in the state. It caught Cabinet members, two Supreme Court justices, prosecutors and others in the attorney general's office, even people in the private sector who had worked in the

AG's office. The other thing is the duration. It's two years in length and still ongoing and now there's an attempt to remove an official (Kane) from office by means of a constitutional provision not used since 1891 and there is a special prosecutor appointed by Kane looking at the emails."

* * *

(Additional sources for postscript: Anthony Williams and Seth Williams' news releases; November 2015 Philadelphia Inquirer story on the porn ruckus on city council; brief interview with Heidi Eakin; my coverage in the Tribune-Review on Fina's lawsuit; copy of the Fina-Costanzo federal lawsuit.)

* * *

Next: Mania: paranoia, vindictiveness rule the day.

19

"UNHOLY MESS"

Any work day, March 16, 2014–Sept. 24, 2015

This is my best effort to give you a snapshot of what it was like working in the Pennsylvania Attorney General's Office for most of 2014 and 2015.

It's based on many sources from her office who bravely came forward to tell me about the poisoned atmosphere as Kathleen Kane unraveled under the stress of three investigations: a statewide grand jury investigation of confidential 2009 documents in 2014, a Philadelphia grand jury investigation into the sting case she dropped, and Montgomery County District Attorney Risa Vetri Ferman's probe into the leak and related potential charges. Kane was not under investigation for any crimes in the sting case but numerous staffers were called as witnesses and the grand jury's conclusion pointedly challenged her assertions about racial profiling.

The Kathleen Kane we saw in 2015 was not the same woman who entered office in 2013 as the fresh face who would reshape Pennsylvania politics. She went from potential U.S. Senate candidate to criminal defendant in less than three years. The stressors were undeniable: in addition to going through the investigations, she filed for divorce and faced the possible loss of her law license and freedom.

Kane devolved into someone refusing to accept responsibility for her actions, being blind to her own shortcomings, blaming others for her mistakes and turning on those close to her, in my opinion. When facing trouble, she repeatedly lied according to a statewide grand jury and the criminal charges. She had no political allies to speak of. She hired and fired people as if their lives did not matter and surrounded herself with sycophants. Some of the traits were there before, those who had been close to her say. But from my outside view, it just spun out of control.

Who among us could remain rock solid in those circumstances?

But it was mainly stubbornness, anger and vindictiveness toward her perceived enemies that triggered her difficulties. Her seeming vendetta against Fina is exhibit A.

Former Chief Deputy Attorney General Frank Fina, who put serial child predator Jerry Sandusky and ex-legislative leaders Mike Veon, John Perzel, and Bill DeWeese, among others, behind bars is the key to understanding Kane's downfall. He was despised by some defense lawyers and defendants. He was clearly admired by most fellow prosecutors as one of the best in the business. A hard-ass, take-no-prisoners investigator, yet cerebral and soft-spoken in the courtroom.

Sources close to Fina say it was not his intention to antagonize her. He just wanted to be left alone. However, he had enormous contempt for politicians in general, and Kane, given her inexperience and criticism of the successful Sandusky investigation, probably ranked at or near the top. The seizure of his hard drive, I believe, placed Kane fully in his sights.

A brilliant anecdote in the Philadelphia Magazine piece called "The Fall of Kathleen Kane," by Robert Huber conveys their meeting after she first took office. I have heard portions of it before and believe it to be true. I heard some from both sides.

Go back to Jan. 15, 2013. The day after Kane's inauguration, Fina's computer wouldn't work. The following day he got the diagnosis from IT: his hard drive was missing. He went nuts. Remember in the attorney general's office they called him "Sonny" after the fictional hot-headed son of Vito Corleone in the *Godfather*. He had a transition meeting scheduled that morning with Kane and her new team of top aides.

As relayed by Huber, Fina told Kane, "I'm going to do these from memory—I really don't have any choice but to do these from memory. I had prepared a transition memo for you but that was on my hard drive." He immediately went to the grand jury issue. Kane had said during the campaign she would not have used one in the Sandusky case. She said she never used one as a deputy DA in Scranton on child sexual abuse cases.

Fina referred to a grand jury case in Cambria County involving sexual abuse in the Catholic Church.

"Now Madame Attorney General this case is in a grand jury. It . . . (slowing down for effect) seems . . . to . . . me one of the decisions you make is whether you keep it in a grand jury . . . to the extent you want to hear it, there is no way you will ever be able to pursue one of these cases involving the Catholic Church without a grand jury. And if you looked nationally, probably with 27 seconds on Google, you'll see that virtually every case involving the Catholic Church has gone through a grand jury."

"Kane was like a glass. She showed him nothing." Huber reported. I'm sure she was taken back. But she would be a good poker player.

Then he dropped the sting case bombshell.

* * *

As Kane's Fina obsession grew following the March 2014 Inquirer sting story, her mistakes increased and she began to make irrational decisions. Any way to get back at him was worth the risk. It wasn't her entire problem. She was in over her head. And there were Republicans clearly opposed to her 2013 success.

There was a character flaw here, demonstrated long before the sting and Fina's emergence as Kane's Public Enemy No. 1. Anyone she perceived as one-upping her or acting disloyal was at risk of incurring her wrath.

Moreover, Kane's extreme arrogance seemed to have her believing that no matter what she did she could get away with it. She "always demonstrated a haughty sanctimonious manner," said a lawyer who quit Kane's office.

From the perspective of Kane and her political supporters, the "good old boys' network" was out to get her. While she was accused of leaking grand jury information, apparent grand jury leaks about her went largely unaddressed, her supporters argued. She was a tough, working-class girl from Scranton who worked her way through college waiting tables. She was driven not to let Fina get the best of her. In my opinion, she was prepared to do whatever it took to keep fighting, get the best of Fina, and hang onto her office, even if that meant crossing some lines. She believed the Inquirer was out to get her. Whether true or not, she put a target on her own back by taking renowned libel lawyer Richard Sprague to the newspaper's editorial board meeting.

Former Democratic Gov. Ed Rendell publicly backed Kane through the early days of the sting probe. He told Kane on more than one occasion: "You don't have to crush your enemies. You win by doing your job and getting re-elected," the Philly Magazine piece stated. It was sound political advice for anyone in politics. It was clearly practical advice from a pro.

THE KIDDIE PORN FIASCO

In 2014, after Lanny Davis was on board and directing all media, Kane made an appearance on CNN about the porn. She was taking it national! The interviewer was none other than Sara Ganim, who won a Pulitzer Prize for her coverage of the Sandusky case for the Harrisburg Patriot-News. She then moved on to CNN.

So here's Kane on national TV, talking about the porn. Just like her mistake when releasing the Sandusky Report in June 2014, when she claimed there were additional victims, she went too far during the CNN interview.

It's almost like she can't help herself.

As the porn story unraveled in 2014, Kane and her top aides repeatedly said there wasn't any child porn involved.

But Kane told CNN: "When I saw them they literally took my breath away," referring to the emails in general. "They are deplorable, hard-core graphic sometimes violent emails that had a string of videos and pictures, depicting sometimes children, old women. Some of them involved violent sexual acts against women," Kane told Ganim.

Her CNN appearance was aired the day after her grand jury testimony near Norristown. She needed a big lift.

By Wednesday her office was backpedaling from the statement on CNN.

Office spokeswoman Renee Martin said Kane believed the emails depicting children were not pornographic and no crimes were committed in transmitting them.

Ever the spinmeister, Davis said, "I only looked at two photographs and I stopped because of how awful the extreme pornography was among the emails publicly released. My personal reaction was: In the context of the disgusting and extreme pornographic material that I saw in some of these emails, I personally regarded them as inappropriate and borderline pornographic."

They're from a series of photos dubbed, "Men in Training": In one case a male toddler is kissing a girl his own age on the mouth; another shows a boy, maybe 4 or 5, peeking into the girl's underwear. Both kids are wearing no shirts, just underwear; in another a child is seated in a high chair with a beer in front of him.

The Morning Call quoted Northampton District Attorney John Morganelli as saying the photos are not pornography under state law. Morganelli at that time was still supporting Kane.

"I saw some of these emails, I personally regarded them as inappropriate and borderline pornographic," Davis said.

Kane's position took yet another turn.

Martin later stated that "she misspoke" when telling reporters no one would be prosecuted for child pornography.

After that incident, Martin was no longer speaking for Kane. The next month or two was consumed by statewide grand jury issues and Davis moved to the forefront.

Why include the CNN appearance here when the story is about office morale? Because state employees who work for Kane see her go on CNN and make an unsupportable claim, back off of it, then reverse course again. Martin was a Kane loyalist and unlike others whose heads would roll she went back to director of education and outreach with her $95,300 salary.

This wasn't just "news" for the general public. Her employees were watching closely.

It was embarrassing.

* * *

The bodies started piling up even before the sting case jolted her. Prosecutors and managers in the office were fired, or resigned under duress at an increasingly alarming rate. Some were pushed out. Others simply resigned. Through

2014 and into early 2015, the office became a resume mill as many came to believe the state's chief law enforcement officer, their boss, would be charged with crimes. As it turns out the statewide grand jury presentment would only recommend charges and Judge Carpenter would refer them to Ferman.

* * *

C.C. Parker, a former agent, referred to the mounting paranoia. It stemmed largely from Kane and the loyalist aides with whom she surrounded herself, Parker said. But it infiltrated the rank and file, he said. It infected the ranks to the point where employees became distrustful of other employees, Parker said. It was widely believed that desks were searched at night and emails were monitored.

First Deputy King described it this way to the statewide grand jury:

"I walked into this (meeting about the subject of an alleged leak, Mondesire) and quite frankly to be dead honest, I'm listening to this, and I think it is absurd . . . (it) just seems like a complete distraction. It seems to be paranoid. And I am also quickly clueing into the fact that the people she has her (at) her right hand that she appears to be taking advice from, is her driver (Reese) and the person she has just installed as communications director (Martin) who has absolutely no experience, and they are literally sitting here just nodding their heads in agreement with everything that's being said. And my reaction was that this was nuts. I don't want anything to do with it."

In the words of Kane's former Deputy Press Secretary J.J. Abbott: the scene in Kane's office was an "unholy mess." He made the statement in an email obtained under the Right to Know Law when he later worked in the press office of Governor Wolf.

THE ENFORCER

Agents and prosecutors were coming to me as sources. It wasn't my great source development technique. It was Kane primarily and the fact that I'd be balanced and endeavor to peel away layers of the truth. People from her office knew they could call me and remain anonymous. I would then branch out to others.

SHOOTING HOSTAGES

Kane fired James Barker, a chief deputy who headed appeals and statewide grand juries. The problem with firing Barker: he was under a protective order from a Montgomery County judge because he had testified against Kane's interests before the statewide grand jury. Barker was by all accounts an excellent lawyer with considerable prosecutorial experience, previously in the Dauphin County DA's office. Kane loyalists said she had a right as an elected official to run the office without interference. Kane's office said it was part of a reorganization of the criminal division.

Barker told me that the evening he was fired was the first he'd heard of any reorganization. Kane's then-spokeswoman Carolyn Myers was candid when I asked whether Barker did anything wrong. She said he did not.

Beemer, the first deputy, had refused to fire Barker.

Barker later in 2015 filed a federal civil rights lawsuit against Kane. The complaint recited how he had been marched out by two armed agents, who took the keys to his state car. He had to call his wife to pick him up. He returned that night to box up his belongings "to avoid demoralizing the staff," the lawsuit says. "As Barker boxed up his things under armed guard, Ms. Kane sat in her office down the hall," the document says. If he was simply fired in a reorganization, why wouldn't Kane stop by and talk to Barker and tell him it was nothing personal? And what did they think he'd do—pilfer things from other desks?

Kane fired George Moore, an official who worked in Human Resources. Moore recommended to Kane that Acting Chief of Staff Jonathan Duecker be fired for two sexual harassment complaints. That occurred after Duecker was promoted in April 2015. Kane had the complaints against Duecker on her desk for a few days and promoted him anyway from head of the narcotics bureau. Kane's internal affairs unit had not interviewed Duecker, it was reported later. My question: how come?

"It's like they are shooting a hostage every day," a veteran agent told the Philadelphia Inquirer.

An official close to Kane told me no public official in Pennsylvania from the governor to a small-town mayor could get away with promoting someone with at least two sexual harassment complaints. The Inquirer reported there was a third alleged victim. I don't know whether Duecker, a former Navy pilot, did what's alleged. But why would Kane promote him without resolving the matter? I will tell you a woman I interviewed, prosecutor Michele Kluk, was scared to talk about it but she sounded very credible. The long and short of it is she claimed Duecker felt her up in a bar while out of town on a work assignment. The details seemed right. Kluk reported it to her supervisor but didn't come forward with a formal complaint at that time. Only later did the Attorney General's Office of Professional Responsibility come across it. Kluk felt compelled to come forward after Duecker became chief of staff with the ability to hire and fire. She had everything to lose and nothing to gain by going public. Kluk did so at the risk of being fired. Duecker never publicly responded to my inquiries.

The Inquirer reported it was "an office awash in backbiting, anxiety, and fear." Couloumbis and McCoy reported that current and former staffers said it's a workplace where supervisors "go through office phone records to see who is calling whom—and talking for how long."

The chief issue after Duecker became chief was simple: loyalty.

There came a point in August 2015 when Duecker put out a memo about not talking to reporters. I had it minutes later and posted it on the Trib's web site. He had little respect from agents and prosecutors that I interviewed.

An earlier memo showed Duecker, I believe, to be power hungry. In July 2015, Duecker sent an email to staff saying, "ALL personnel issues come through me to the General," the Inquirer reported. The Inquirer's disclosure, I'm told, drove Duecker wild and prompted a mole hunt within the agency.

Duecker drove a Mercedes-Benz SUV as his state vehicle. It had been seized in a drug raid. Taxpayers spent about $6,000 on its repairs, Kane's office said.

A state law restricts use of vehicles seized in drug cases to use in drug investigations, according to the Controlled Substances Forfeiture Act. The repair costs were "actually a savings to taxpayers" compared to leasing a state car, Kane's spokesman Ardo said. Ardo also said Duecker was still at that time actively involved in narcotics investigations so he was qualified to use that car. He retained the title of "Special Agent 6" while effectively running the office. Beemer's salary was higher, $146,661, but he'd been shunted aside.

THE NEGATIVE IMPACT

Kane's trip to Haiti in April 2014 had been a mystery to reporters who looked into it amid rumors that it triggered investigations.

Twice, Kane's office told me—once in a Right to Know law request—that no state money was expended.

Kane made the weeklong trip with her twin, Chief Deputy Attorney General Ellen Granahan, Special Agent in Charge of Investigative Services David Peifer and Daniel Block, a supervisory agent. Kane's spokesman said it was a "charitable trip." Granahan incidentally was hired under Corbett but promoted under Kane with a 19.6 percent pay hike in 2013, Kane's first year in office. Her salary increased from $69,771 to $83,423. By 2015, it was $88,509. King said he made the 2013 decision.

Why the fuss about the Haiti trip if no state money was spent?

It is briefly recounted in a public document filed in Montgomery County in August 2015, without explanation. That made it even more mysterious.

Also, the Legal Intelligencer in August reported that federal authorities made inquiries about the Haiti trip. The FBI's inquiry centered on how the trip was paid for and related details, though it wasn't certain why agents were asking about the trip, the newspaper for the legal community reported.

Numerous law enforcement sources told the Trib Kane's refusal to sign documents before she left—designating a subordinate to sign in her behalf—may have handed defense attorneys a potential issue in challenging criminal cases arising from wiretaps during that week. And apparently there were some. Catherine Smith, Kane's former executive assistant, told county investigators that Kane left without signing a letter to designate someone "to take any necessary action in the attorney general's absence," investigators said. "For this particular trip, Kane wrote a letter designating former First Deputy Adrian King but did not sign it," documents showed.

In fact, issues arose while Kane was gone where law enforcement officials needed a wiretap in a drug case.

King, a partner with the Philadelphia law firm Ballard Spahr, and another former top aide, David Tyler, at the time instructed Smith to sign the letter authorizing King to act in Kane's absence, documents show. It was not clear which case may be tied to the wiretaps.

State law requires the attorney general or a deputy "designated in writing" to sign a wiretap application to the Superior Court.

"If someone in a position which has not been appropriately designated by statute applies for a wiretap, that wiretap is not lawful" and could be argued in court, said John Burkoff, who teaches criminal law at University of Pittsburgh Law School.

Why would Kane do that? She didn't forget, according to Smith.

Kane was on the outs with King by then and didn't want to give him that power out of spite.

ENOUGH IS ENOUGH

Harold Johnson was a western Pennsylvania-based agent who'd finally had enough. Despite Duecker's order, he gave me an on-the-record statement about his feelings about working for the attorney general.

A decorated Navy veteran who served on a destroyer during the Viet Nam War in the early 1970s, Johnson, 62, of Greensburg, spoke out after people told him that they hold the Office of Attorney General in disrepute because of the criminal investigation of Attorney General Kathleen Kane.

His message to the office's estimated 740 employees: "Hold your heads high; you deserve to because you earned it."

Johnson counts 45 years of public service as a career law enforcement officer, a volunteer and his military service.

"I have had several people that I have known for years say that they have lost respect for the Pennsylvania Office of Attorney General," he said. "Do not associate me with the problems at the OAG. I have never been a problem for the people of the Commonwealth."

"I am not pointing my finger at the attorney general specifically," said Johnson, "but all the things bad that have been associated (with the agency) over the years—and not everyone at the OAG is involved. There are good people who do the right thing, and have their entire career. They and I are tired of the association."

Several people I know worried about Johnson being fired after his statement. But he didn't respond to the press as Duecker's order forbade.

He called me.

He survived.

Firing Johnson would have made him a hero within the agency, which he already was to a degree for speaking out.

* * *

To get some idea of the contempt many employees held for Kane consider the parting statement of Deputy Attorney General Clarke Madden when he left to join a Harrisburg law firm in September 2015: In a backhand slap at Kane, Madden said, "It has been a privilege working for the First Deputy (Bruce Beemer) and serving the people of the commonwealth."

"It's bad off," said a prosecutor who stayed. "The agency is going to have to be torn down and be completely rebuilt." The lawyer, speaking anonymously for fear of being fired, said he believed Kane saw an internal conspiracy against her.

The one solidifying force in the days when mania gripped the office was Bruce Beemer, the first deputy in name only. He was technically second in command but had been shunted aside by Kane. He was under a court protective order or he would have been fired. Of course there was always a risk, because it did not help Barker. Prosecutors looked to him as a quiet leader willing to pick his battles and stand up to Kane at key moments.

Kane blamed Beemer for not finding offensive emails of Justice Eakin's. The purpose internally in 2014 primarily had been to look for conflicts between judges and prosecutors on current cases. Beemer didn't even write the report, but he transmitted to Kane. He kept his mouth shut and took the fall so two attorneys under him wouldn't be blamed.

Watching this from afar, Robert P. Strauss, professor of economics and public policy at Carnegie Mellon University, put it this way in an email to me: "It's Kane versus World."

* * *

(Sources: Philadelphia Magazine; numerous Inquirer stories, including the McCoy and Couloumbis May 10, 2015, story on Human Resources and the June 2015 piece on the "hell" the AG's office had become; numerous private interviews with agents and prosecutors; Parker's interviews with me; Johnson's statement to the Trib in August; my Trib story on the first sexual harassment complaint; two of my Trib columns about the paranoia and fear gripping the office; the Legal Intelligencer story about Kane's Haiti trip; my Trib story in August about the trip and her failure to sign the paperwork; criminal complaint filed in Montgomery County Clerk of Court's Office; Morning Call story by Steve Esack, Peter Hall and Scott Krauss on Kane's CNN interview, my Trib story on the same topic Nov. 19, 2015, and a Philadelphia Inquirer story Nov. 21, 2015; my column on Sept. 27, 2015, in the Trib; Madden statement upon departure.)

* * *

Next: Risa Vetri Ferman steps up.

20

RISA

Aug. 6, 2015

It reminded me of the months before Bonusgate. The Capitol in 2008 ran wild virtually every day with rumors about when then-Attorney General Tom Corbett would file the first charges against people with ties to the House Democratic Caucus for campaign work on state time and/or using tax money to reimburse caucus staffers for campaign work. It was insane. A rumor would fly around the Capitol and those spreading it would sound as if what they were saying was fact. The truth is nobody outside of the AG's office really knew. There were snippets here or there about who had testified before a grand jury. But until the night before—and then I wasn't 100 percent certain—the truth about who would be charged remained a mystery. The charges were filed July 10, 2008, against 12 people, ten of whom were eventually convicted.

Starting shortly after Memorial Day 2015, the rumor mill would heat up about once or twice a week—and with increasing intensity through July—on when Montgomery County District Attorney Risa Vetri Ferman would file criminal charges, if that was happening, against Kathleen Kane. I recall one day, July 1, where the rumor was rampant, truly rampant, with reports coming in from Pittsburgh and Philadelphia and many of my usual sources in Harrisburg that Kane would resign at 3 p.m. and turn herself in the following Monday. It was not believable to me, given the repeated statements by Kane that she would not resign. "Rumors should be treated with skepticism and in this case, extreme skepticism," spokesman Ardo told me in a text message. "It's an unfounded rumor."

Given it stemmed from a leak investigation, the last thing Ferman could do was leak information under any circumstances. To my knowledge, not a single word leaked from April 1 through Aug. 6.

It's true that I was able to write the story on Aug. 5 about charges the following day. But it came from no one in the DA's office. It came from numerous layered sources but not Ferman or her assistants.

* * *

I had virtually no doubt that Kane would be charged. Just my opinion and a gut feeling for it based on the players involved and the nature of the case. Ferman's investigation was launched April 1, 2015, after the Pennsylvania Supreme Court rejected Kane's bid to invalidate Montgomery County Judge William Carpenter's appointment of special prosecutor Thomas Carluccio. My feeling was unless the case was really bogus, Ferman had received the high court's blessing that the procedure was sound. Ferman, a Republican, was running for judge in November 2015. But everyone told me she was a straight shooter and would file—or not—based on the facts. And the timing would not affect her. It would be done when it was ready. But most analysts figured the sooner the better before the November General Election. An October surprise would look political even if it wasn't. September was stretching it. That belief among many Capitol observers led to the intense speculation in July that charges would come any day. By the end of July, it was beyond insane.

The rumor mill was like something from another galaxy.

You might wonder why reporters would even pay attention to wild rumors.

The reason: sometimes, every once in a while, they're true.

* * *

Ferman never went to law school with the intention of becoming a prosecutor. It was the last thing she contemplated as a career path while attending Widener University Law School. After graduating from the University of Pennsylvania, she worked as a waitress and then a bartender in the White Dog Café in West Philadelphia and then in a recording studio. She often talked with her father, Sal Vetri, about a business venture and practicing business law after law school. She began at Widener by attending night classes. Sure enough, her life took a sharp turn when a friend told her about a great internship with the U.S. Attorney's office in 1991. Almost as a lark, she applied and got the internship. The idea of being a prosecutor hit her like a lightning bolt. It was an area of the law, she believed, where one could help people who don't have a voice and who have been victimized. After leaving law school, Ferman joined the Montgomery County District Attorney's office in 1993 and she's been there ever since.

She worked her way up through the ranks and was named captain of Sex Crime and Child Abuse. Ferman was meticulous and thorough in her approach to criminal cases, said former colleague, Barbara Ashcroft, a Temple University Law School professor. Ferman has handled cases from domestic violence to homicides. A decade later, Ferman became first assistant district attorney under District Attorney Bruce Castor.

Ferman became the first woman elected district attorney in Montgomery County in 2007.

In July, as her Kane investigation was moving forward, Ferman was elected by her colleagues as the first woman to hold the office of president of the Pennsylvania District Attorney's Association.

By contrast, her mother entered the legal profession when most women were turned away by big law firms. So Barbara Vetri helped found what was then the first woman-run law firm in Pennsylvania. Ferman also saw her mother take on long odds by challenging the Republican Party by running, without the party endorsement, in a Republican primary for county judge. Challenging GOP office holders was verboten anyway in what was then a bedrock Republican county. For a woman to do it made it an even bigger sin. As a teen, Ferman traveled around the county with her mom. She heard the ugly talk about her mother and decided she wanted no part of politics herself.

Her love for being a prosecutor though drew her into running.

By the time Ferman filed criminal charges against Kane, she had been a prosecutor for 22 years. She did it while she and her husband Michael raised three children, the youngest of whom was still at home in 2015. In her "spare time" she wrote children's books, publishing her second in 2015 titled *The Mouse Who Beat the Jungle Bullies*.

Every prosecutor knows by the very nature of criminal law they could wind up with horrific cases. But in her wildest dreams she never would have imagined a case this big being dealt to her.

Exactly how big none of us knew at the time.

* * *

"When someone entrusted with the solemn obligation to uphold the law deliberately violates the same laws she is sworn to uphold, we are all victims of this breach of the public trust," Ferman said.

"When an elected official betrays the confidence and trust placed in her by the public, we must do everything in our power to hold her accountable. The laws of our Commonwealth protect all her citizens and as citizens we can expect those who have the obligation to enforce the laws to abide by their mandates. This investigation and the charges filed today show, beyond all doubt, that no one is above the law; not even the Chief Law Enforcement Officer of the Commonwealth."

Thus Ferman began the criminal case against Kathleen Granahan Kane and her driver and bodyguard Patrick Rocco Reese, who was so powerful he was described as the go-between for staff and Kane and was sometimes called the "chief of staff."

"THIS IS WAR"

The day had arrived. It was Aug. 6, 2015. Some of us from Harrisburg arrived at the county detectives' office, across from the courthouse, an hour to two hours early. We took seats in an anteroom, outside the relatively tiny room where Ferman holds her news conferences. After an hour, I had to make a bathroom stop before the press conference kicked off. I was surprised at the turnout, a blend of Philly, Montgomery County and Harrisburg reporters, lined up along both sides of a narrow hallway, maybe 30 deep on each side.

Getting there early didn't get us in the door sooner or secure a better seat. The DA's office allowed "local press" in first taking care of the home crowd. I get that but didn't like it.

I wondered how everyone was going to fit into the room. They did, just barely, though some were hanging at the entrance.

You know the basic allegation by now: angered by the sting story and blaming Fina, Kane set the Mondesire leak in motion to attack and discredit Fina. J. Whyatt Mondesire was a former Philadelphia Inquirer reporter who later served as head of the Philadelphia NAACP. The attorney general's office investigated financial irregularities in the Philadelphia NAACP in 2009 but never brought charges against Mondesire. Fina was then the chief deputy attorney general in charge of the investigation. Prosecutors later claimed Kane concocted the notion of leaking documents on the Mondesire investigation to show Fina had dodged the filing of charges against an African-American leader. Kane was convinced Fina was behind the leak of the sting information to the Inquirer about black elected officials who were not charged by her office. Using the Mondesire case was allegedly a way for Kane to get back at Fina, a grand jury claimed. Mondesire was never charged with a crime. The fact he had been under criminal investigation was leaked by Kane's office to the Philadelphia Daily News, a grand jury report said. Mondesire told me in two brief phone interviews he considered publication of that 2014 story by the Daily News devastating to his reputation. When charges were filed against Kane for the leak, Mondesire told me he read the grand jury presentment with disbelief. He said in a Tribune-Review story published in April 2015 he found it "stunning to see the attorney general was completely oblivious to what impact her leak would have." Mondesire was publisher of the Philadelphia Sun newspaper when he died in October 2015.

Ferman's investigation took the skeleton of the statewide grand jury report and put flesh on it. Her affidavit of probable cause filed by Detective Paul Michael Bradbury was rich with anecdotes and added substantially more evidence than the statewide grand jury case.

In a March 16, 2014, email exchange with an unidentified media consultant about the Philadelphia Inquirer article, Kane wrote, that "I will not allow them to discredit me or our office." She concluded by writing: "This is war."

The complaint painted a picture of a dysfunctional office in which Kane intimidated and threatened to fire underlings to get them to do her bidding, undercut her top deputy and later tried to blame King for her legal difficulties. The office was marked by intrigue with Kane confidants allegedly prying into confidential files to see which employees were cooperating with a grand jury investigating their boss.

"If I get taken out of here in handcuffs, what do you think my last act will be?" investigators said Kane told First Deputy Beemer and three other top aides, implying they'd be fired if they did not challenge protective orders Carpenter issued for witnesses from her office.

The Inquirer in its coverage of the Kane charges said the complaint portrayed her as a "Nixonian figure." It was apt based on the allegations.

Kane gave her top two deputies, including bodyguard Reese and David Peifer, an agent in charge of special investigations, authority to go through employee emails, the complaint alleged.

Ferman charged Reese, a former Dunmore police chief, with indirect criminal contempt. Reese was accused of gaining access to the files of the grand jury that was investigating his boss.

Reese used key words to search for emails regarding the grand jury, its supervising Montgomery County Judge William Carpenter, its Special Prosecutor Thomas Carluccio, and even retired Pennsylvania Supreme Court Chief Justice Ronald Castille, who supervised all statewide investigating grand juries, the complaint says.

Castille, a Republican, told the Inquirer, "That's so highly illegal, it's unbelievable."

He told me it was "beyond outrageous."

An audit showed Reese allegedly searched for reporters who wrote critically of Kane and topics such as "subpoenas" and "transcripts." Peifer was not charged and he testified against Kane at a preliminary hearing in Norristown in August 2015, where Kane was held for trial.

THE LEAK

"Kane stood defiant and increasingly isolated after Ferman unveiled new evidence to buttress a grand jury's finding that Kane illegally planted a newspaper story to damage a critic, then perjured herself when questioned about it," the Inquirer's story on Ferman's press conference stated.

Kane was heedless in how she "mistreated Mondesire" by dredging up a 2009 inquiry, prosecutors said. Mondesire was never charged. Mondesire died in 2015 eliminating the likelihood of a libel suit against Kane for the leak. Mondesire had threatened to sue.

It was a pure "act of vengeance," prosecutors charged.

The complaint says it "was done entirely without regard to the collateral damage it would cause to the person who was the subject of a secret investigation."

Kane denied leaking confidential information or breaking any laws.

It is true that Fina and Costanzo got the investigation of her started by going to Judge Carpenter. But they did so after being contacted by the Daily News about the Mondesire case, which they knew was protected by grand jury secrecy laws and therefore a violation by someone in the attorney general's office. It was their duty as lawyers. Still, it was up to Carpenter whether to start that investigation.

After Fina and other former state prosecutors were questioned by Daily News reporter Chris Brennan, they complained to authorities that the reporter had gained access to secret grand jury material. (Brennan is now a reporter for the Inquirer.)

This, in turn, prompted Montgomery County Court Judge William R. Carpenter to appoint lawyer Carluccio to lead a grand jury investigation of the leak.

Fina has repeatedly declined to comment on the record other than saying "I don't respond to criminal defendants."

In her testimony before the secret panel, Kane said she had lawfully authorized her staff to release non-confidential information on the Mondesire case. She said she could not explain how grand jury material reached the media.

Ferman's investigators contended Kane was lying.

Building on evidence compiled by Carluccio, Ferman alleged that Kane, to get back at Fina, broke grand-jury secrecy law.

"It should be noted that, since Kane took office, she has issued hundreds of press releases and conducted numerous press conferences through her press office," the affidavit says.

"However, rather than utilizing these same conventional means, Kane instead chose the cloak-and-dagger technique of leaking the information to the press through a political operative. The fact that Kane caused this information to be released in this secretive manner is evidence that she knew that what she was doing was not lawful."

Kane gave an envelope to First Deputy King to deliver the material to Josh Morrow, a political operative who served as Kane's campaign press secretary, the complaint said. King told the grand jury he didn't know what was in the envelope and thought it was campaign material. King left the 8 ½ x 11-inch envelope at his residence for Morrow to pick up.

The envelope contained a memorandum and a grand jury transcript on the Mondesire case.

"Investigators concluded that Kane was responsible for release of the documents used in the June 6, 2014, Daily News article," the complaint said. "Kane authorized release of the documents in order to retaliate against someone she believed had made her look bad in the press."

Most of us missed this the day of its release. On Page 31 of the 42-page complaint, the complaint says Ferman's investigators found *"no evidence to suggest Fina or Costanzo were the source of the leak of the Ali investigation material that was used in the March 16, 2014, Philadelphia Inquirer article."*

No evidence? All of this on a twisted belief? Spite? Blind venom?

* * *

In her Nov. 17, 2014, grand jury testimony, Kane repeatedly stated that she had not seen the 2009 Memorandum between Fina and former prosecutor William Davis before that day in the grand jury room. Investigators claimed this was false.

"Have you ever seen that (memorandum) before?" Kane was asked. "No," she stated.

Subsequently, she said, "I had never seen this document before today."

Two top aides including Peifer contradicted that testimony.

"Kane lied about her role, falsely claiming that a former top aide, Adrian King, joined her in the leak," the complaint said.

Kane "minimized her role" saying she did not direct how it should be done and that "King took care of that himself."

"Investigators concluded that these were false statements," prosecutors said.

The professional relationship between King and Kane had virtually collapsed after the Inquirer's publication of the sting article and Kane's meeting with the Inquirer's editorial board, multiple witnesses told investigators.

On March 24, 2014, King sent Kane an email "questioning the legality of disseminating (any criminal files) to individuals outside the office of Attorney General," the complaint said. Kane responded that "she would manage requests from her private attorney, and that she was 'well aware of the limitations of disclosing criminal files and the Wiretap Act,'" having been in this business for some time.

Kane did acknowledge before the grand jury that she okayed release of information on Mondesire. "I said to Adrian, you know, we should get it out. We should put it out to the press. People have a right to know." She claimed King agreed, which he denied.

She testified she didn't know anything about the actual documents that went out.

Peifer stated that he saw Kane "flipping through" a transcript with confidential investigative information and secret grand jury information. It had a "blue back and clear face." Morrow told investigators one of the files he received was a transcript with a "blue back and clear face."

Investigators found Kane's claim that King alone orchestrated removal of confidential files from the office, based on telephone records, was "not credible." Moreover, King and Kane's relationship had deteriorated to the point of being "toxic" and she told him she would focus on press while he ran day-to-day operations.

"STAY AT HOME MOM"

Kane and her lawyers developed a "novel" interpretation to the grand jury act that she was a "stay at home mom" in 2009 and therefore wasn't specifically sworn to secrecy for that grand jury. She and her spin doctor Lanny Davis repeatedly made that argument. Criminal defense attorneys and prosecutors I spoke with thought it was bogus.

Of course, as attorney general you're sworn to uphold the Constitution and as a rule, all past grand jury information even before you took office is confidential.

"I didn't release grand jury information from 2009," Kane said in her grand jury testimony file with the Supreme Court. "I was not sworn into the (2009) grand jury, as I could not have since I was home with my kids at the time."

The statewide grand jury investigating Kane heard from Allegheny County District Attorney Stephen A. Zappala Jr. as an expert witness. He's been the DA in the second largest county in the state for 17 years. He testified it would be unlawful for the attorney general to disclose secret grand jury information regardless of whether they signed an oath to that specific grand jury. Grand jury testimony remains secret in perpetuity, he said, unless disclosure is authorized by a judge.

CONCLUSION

"Kane's decision to release confidential investigative information and secret grand jury information through political back channels, her demands that Beemer cease from cooperating with the grand jury investigation, her threats to terminate employees for not following orders to challenge the grand jury's investigation and her baseless explanations to legitimize her actions are all examples of her guilty conscience," the complaint alleges.

KATHLEEN KANE'S STATEMENT

(Delivered in the Capitol Media Center on Aug. 12, 2015, six days after the charges against her were filed. She took no questions afterward.)

> Let me first repeat what my lawyers said upon my indictment so you can hear it clearly from me: I am

innocent of any wrongdoing. I neither conspired with anyone nor did I ask or direct anyone to do anything improper or unlawful," Kane said.

My defense will not be that I am the victim of some 'old boys' network' it will be that I broke no laws of the Commonwealth. Period.

Until now, only a portion of the story has been told. Both in press accounts and in the presentment of charges the story begins with the publication of two newspaper articles in the Spring of 2014. That story centers around a personal conflict between me and a former prosecutor in the Attorney General's Office. That story is as incomplete as it is inaccurate," Kane stated.

Today I intend to begin to reveal the *whole* story but before I do let me say this: I know that some of you came here today expecting a freewheeling give-and-take press conference. Under advice of counsel, and for reasons that will become quite clear a few minutes from now, I cannot. But stick around. I think the story I am about to tell will raise some very troubling questions of its own. For it's not a story about sting investigations, personal vendettas or press leaks. It is a story that begins with pornography, racial insensitivity, and religious bigotry; more specifically, a story that begins and ends with the circulation of pornographic, racial and religiously offensive emails both within and outside of the Corbett Attorney General's Office.

The chain of events that led to charges being filed against me did not begin with the printing of newspaper stories in the Spring of 2014. It did not even begin when I was sworn in as Attorney General of the Commonwealth of Pennsylvania.

No, the chain of events that led to this moment began long before that and it began with a group of state prosecutors and judges passing pornographic, racially offensive, and religiously offensive emails among each other. Email traffic sent and received on government computers and on government time.

From the moment this email traffic became discoverable—from the moment I announced that the

Moulton investigation had the technology in hand to track down every email in the Corbett Attorney General's Office—some involved in this filthy email chain have tried desperately to insure that these emails, and more importantly their attachment to it, never see the light of day. Literally within days of the Moulton announcement, newspaper stories appeared questioning my decision on a case which was thought to embarrass and intimidate me. Then they moved to the empaneling of investigative grand juries and the abuse of grand jury secrecy laws, all in an attempt to conceal their involvement in a chain of pornographic and racially or religiously offensive emails swirling around the Corbett Attorney General's Office and distributed beyond that office to lawyers and judges around the Commonwealth.

At each step on this trail of concealment, they have been assisted, wittingly or unwittingly, by judges and prosecutors and, in particular one, Judge William Carpenter, who to this day prevents the complete public dissemination of these emails under a tortured interpretation of our state's grand jury secrecy law. It is this same use of these secrecy laws that prevents me today from answering the questions you want answered. You may be asking why individuals would go to such lengths to conceal their involvement in this email chain. But make no mistake: the stakes for these individuals, whose participation in this email chain has remained concealed behind the cloak of grand jury secrecy, could not be higher. Porngate, as it has been called, has led to the termination of six, the resignation of two, and the reprimanding of 23 employees of the Attorney General's Office. It has caused the forced resignation of our state Secretary of Environmental Protection, his top attorney, and a gubernatorial appointee to the State Board of Probation or Parole. And as you know, the same emails led to the suspension and resignation of a Supreme Court Justice.

I am sure that, at this moment, as I stand under indictment and fighting for everything I believe in and have stood for all my life, these individuals believe that they are on the precipice of their ultimate goal—the burial of this email chain and their involvement in it forever. For only a grand jury protective order stands in the way of my releasing their names and their emails to the public. And should I be removed from office, either by conviction or through the suspension of my license by the state's Disciplinary Board, the one person who would challenge that order would no longer have standing to do so. That was their plan all along. What this means to Pennsylvania voters is that politicians will now choose their next Attorney General for them and in essence take away the 3.125 million voters who wanted an independent AG. As a matter of fact, we heard even before the charges were announced against me that this grand plan was in the works. This process is now the new stealth political weapon that has not popped up on the media's radar screen, yet.

I cannot, I will not let that happen.

Today I call upon Judge William Carpenter to once and for all authorize the immediate release of all pornographic, racially offensive, and religiously offensive emails currently in the possession of my office. I do not do (so) as part of some vendetta. I do so to begin to tell the whole story; a story that is critical to my defense against the charges I face. Let me be clear: Today I am calling for the whole story to come out. Today I seek the following:

- An order signed by Judge Carpenter authorizing the Attorney General to release to the public all pornographic, racially offensive, and/or religiously offensive emails that were housed in Attorney General files on Commonwealth of Pennsylvania servers;
- Language in this order stating that the release of these emails by the Attorney General pursuant to this order shall in no way subject the Attorney General to any civil and/or criminal penalty including specifically any penalty for intimidation, retaliation, or humiliation of a grand jury witness or individual named in a grand jury proceeding.

- Judge Carpenter's contemporaneous release of all transcripts, emails, and supporting documents related to the issuance of the protective order under which I am currently prevented from releasing these emails.
- The Pennsylvania Judicial Disciplinary Board to suspend any activity it is contemplating or currently engaged unless and until Judge Carpenter takes the above-referenced actions.

The moment Judge Carpenter takes these steps I will schedule a press conference at which time I will stand before you with my lawyers and answer all of your questions. In the absence of Judge Carpenter taking these steps, I must take every precaution to insure that I am not subject to any further allegations of violating grand jury secrecy laws.

I would like to now address those who have called for my resignation in light of the charges brought against me last week. It has been 9 months between that grand jury presentment and last week's charges being brought against me. Nine months since some politicians and editorial boards called for my resignation.

In those 9 months . . . my office has announced 135 Child Predator Arrests, 645 Drug Arrests and a 3rd settlement with electric generation suppliers to give back $2.4 million to consumers in addition to their previous payout of $4.1 million.

It has been 15 months since the first news stories cited in the charges against me and the criminal charges. Again, 15 months since the first calls for my resignation. In those 15 months, my office has announced 247 Child Predator Arrests and 1,174 Drug Arrests. Since I have taken office, there has been an 800% increase in child predator arrests and 30% increase in drug arrests. As you can see, and as any mother of two young boys can you tell you, we are experts at multitasking.

Finally, to my boys: As you know, on the playground, sometimes you pick the fights and sometimes the fight picks you. I am as much to blame as anyone for bringing this fight to my doorstep. But, as you also know, the moment the fight is at hand, it is far more important to figure out how to deal with it than why it got there in the first place. At that moment, you will be forced to decide whether to stand and fight or leave the field and live to fight another day. Neither choice is inherently more noble than the other. At times your decision will simply be grounded in how you assess your odds of victory. But there are times when the fight is worth waging no matter the odds; for your mother, this is one of those times. Only the Lord knows how this will turn out but regardless of the outcome know that, at all times, I tried to stay true to the promise I made to the people of Pennsylvania on the day I swore my oath of office—a day that now seems so long ago: The promise of an Attorney General's office that was open and transparent in its administration of justice across our Commonwealth. And this promise I still believe is one worth fighting for.

* * *

Author's note: It should be noted Judge Carpenter wanted and asked that he be able to release the emails. The Supreme Court in an order reminded Kane of its December order telling her she could release the emails—they were not grand jury material. One week after that order, when Kane failed to act, the high court in August 2015 released 398 pages that contained many pornographic emails. The pages had been attached to a filing of Kane's.

(Sources: My Aug. 6, 2015, story on filing of charges; Couloumbis and McCoy's Inquirer story on the charges; Aug. 6, 2015, criminal complaint filed by Risa Ferman against Kane and Reese; Supreme Court order giving Kane the green light on porn release; Kane's Aug. 12, 2015, statement delivered in Capitol Media Center.)

* * *

Next: Were Mexican Cartels after Kane?

21

THE CARTELS

Aug. 8, 2015

NORRISTOWN—When her full-size black Chevrolet Suburban, the standard protection vehicle often favored by the Secret Service and the state police, arrived at One Montgomery Plaza, we knew it would be just a few minutes or less before Kathleen Kane would step out on the street for a short walk to a concrete stairway, the cut-off line for the press.

The Suburban pulled up behind a white Cadillac Escalade, used by two advance attorney general's agents. The Escalade was a vehicle seized from drug dealers. How wise it was to have it on every TV station across Pennsylvania if it was ever to be used undercover again was a question beyond my pay grade. Two agents were there an hour early to do the advance work.

When the Suburban rolled in, three agents hopped out. They were big guys, and one of them, an African American agent, appeared to be the size of an NFL defensive lineman. I received several texts from sources asking if Kane had private security for the event. Chuck Ardo, her spokesman, would later inform me, these were in fact the attorney general's agents.

Former Attorney General Tom Corbett rarely had more than a lone agent. Kane normally had two, but one was charged with her in an extensive criminal complaint filed just the week before by the Montgomery County district attorney's office.

Kane wasn't handcuffed like most public corruption defendants during Corbett's era as attorney general. Some would say that's a good thing. Joshua Lock, one of the defense attorneys for a Republican legislative leader, called cuffing white-collar defendants for a perp walk a "Medieval" practice.

Many legislative employees and lawmakers who were handcuffed for a perp walk might think Kane's treatment was unfair. In the least, it was inconsistent.

Kane had about a 15-yard walk before she hit the stairs and was free of the reporters. It was a mini-perp walk sans cuffs. She was so heavily guarded by her phalanx of agents that it was often difficult to see her, even though she stood out in flashes through the crowd in her white dress. Kane was "confident and upbeat" for the arraignment, her attorney Ross Kramer said.

Reporters' questions were shouted: "Can you comment on the charges?" "Kathleen Kane, do you think you are getting preferential treatment?" "What do you say to the voters?" "How do you feel about getting fingerprinted and photographed like other alleged criminals?"

Behind me came forceful shouting and it threw me off balance. "Good luck, Ms. Kane. Good luck, Ms. Kane." I had no idea who he was. Not a reporter.

"The Lord be with you," the man said. "Good luck, Ms. Kane."

I can't explain it. It seemed like the guy was gone in a flash.

* * *

For almost two hours before her arrival, reporters and TV crews baked in the broiling August sun across from the Montgomery County Courthouse. Heat seemed to waft up from the concrete. There was virtually no shade. At one point a blonde TV reporter shot across the street as if she'd spotted something. Soon a woman with long brown hair emerged around the corner and headed toward the courthouse. Was it her? I started to move in that direction and immediately realized it couldn't really be *her* since the brunette was moving on foot and since there was already a parking space reserved for her black SUV in front of the steps of One Montgomery Plaza.

It was a false Kathleen Kane sighting.

A well-dressed gentleman was in the crowd, earlier talking about a book, *The Midnight Ride of Jonathan Luna* by William Keisling. I told him I have the book and know Keisling.

Bill Keisling is a friend. Every once in a while he hits the epicenter. Other times, he misses by several miles, critics say. He's a conspiracy theorist. He's referenced earlier in Chapter 3 of this book where he is quoted as a turnpike analyst, a topic on which he commands expertise.

Luna, an assistant federal prosecutor, disappeared and was found dead in a Lancaster County Creek in 2003, stabbed 36 times with his own pen knife.

It is a true-life mystery so I won't ruin it for you, except to say Luna was prosecuting two drug kingpins.

In any case, this man at Kane's event told me, "Well, that's what's happening to Kane!"

"What on earth do you mean?" I asked him. He said big drug dealers are trying to take out Kane through this prosecution.

Oh . . . OK then.

That would mean Montgomery County judges, Philly prosecutors, a grand jury, Ferman, key members of Ferman's staff, and many others, were involved in a highly improbable, ludicrous conspiracy.

But still I asked Chuck Ardo why such heavy security and did Kane believe it had anything to do with her prosecution of drug traffickers from the cartels?

C.C. Parker, a former agent, told me his network of agents within the agency told him that was exactly what she believed. "That is oversimplifying it," Ardo said.

The heavy security was in part to grant her safe travel in and out of the building with the mob of reporters attending to make sure she didn't get jostled, he said.

"All attorney generals get threats because their offices deal with very bad and dangerous people," Ardo said. "The attorney general's administration is operating in an era when cartels are expanding their reach into the Northeast."

When I said cartels may kill cops in Mexico but I've never heard of an attorney general in the U.S. hit by the traffickers, Ardo said her office is making sure she doesn't become the victim of an organized cartel.

As some cynical agents of hers suggested she was putting on a show for the courts, in the event she is convicted, to show that she can't go to prison where she'd be bait for the cartels and their operatives. I am not sure Kane thinks that far ahead. She tends to react.

But it was plausible she and her Acting Chief of Staff Jonathan Duecker believed the cartel threat was real.

* * *

Parker, the retired agent, said the suggestion Kane was targeted by Mexican cartels "brought laughter and snickering amongst the rank and file" and the same with some managers. "First of all Kane herself and Duecker have never to our knowledge arrested anyone," Parker said. "It is the brave men and women (of the agency) who investigated and arrested violators.

"It seemed during the time Kane and Duecker were in office paranoia was mounting.

"We never heard one piece of credible evidence relayed back to the troops that cartels were in fact targeting anyone in Pennsylvania, nor do we believe that any true interruption of cartel activity was occurring" said Parker. "It was instead Duecker who brought this information up at a staff meeting of managers where he instructed them to watch their backs."

* * *

Kane attempted to justify more funding for her office in 2013 by suggesting Mexican cartels were a huge threat to Pennsylvania that kept her awake at night worrying. "Mexican drug cartels. They are in Pennsylvania—they are taking over our neighborhoods," Kane was quoted by KYW Radio as saying.

Senators on the Appropriations Committee seemed to eat it up. Most of them seemed to want to curry favor. After all, she was the Democratic Party's star and a legitimate "friend of Bill" as in Bill Clinton, who endorsed her and appeared at one of her events during the primary.

But Tony Romeo, KYW's Capitol reporter, noted a week later that then-State Police Commissioner Frank Noonan told the Senate Appropriations Committee he knew of no place in

Pennsylvania where cartels were taking over neighborhoods. "As far as, like, Mexican cartels coming into Pennsylvania and taking over drug distribution—we don't see that. What we do see is Mexican cartels—they're the source of drugs," Noonan said.

So the cartel chatter wasn't new. And they may indeed be a growing threat in non-border states. Still, it was a flimsy excuse for Kane's security retinue fitting for a head of state.

Take Times-Leader columnist Steve Corbett, looking back to the Fourth of July celebration in Scranton's Courthouse Square:

"Surrounded by statues signifying glory in battle, Pennsylvania's embattled attorney general stood her ground in her hometown, seemingly immune to persecution and prosecution.

"If she has truly been targeted by Mexican drug cartel gunmen—or gunwomen—as her press spokesman says she is—evidence seemed slim and none that she is in the cross hairs of the banditos . . .

"Other than her dour-looking co-worker and twin sister, Ellen, Kane's only other backup was a young woman who smiled and stood to the side—maybe a cop, maybe not a cop. But even if she hid a Glock somewhere beneath her summer outfit, and even if Kathleen and Ellen were packing as well, they would have been no match for grim cartel assassins," Corbett wrote.

LA SANTA MUERTE

Mike Argento, the acerbic columnist for the York Daily Record, picked up on the cartel fixation in August 2013.

"When the state attorney general's office busted an alleged cocaine ring in York County, police said they found a shrine to La Santa Muerte in the home of one of the suspects, evidence, allegedly, of ties to Mexican drug cartels that believe the saint is their patron."

Argento wrote that the "attorney general's office made a big deal out of it, releasing a photo of the shrine and mentioning in a news release that it had seized several statues of La Santa Muerte from the home of one suspect." The saint, the attorney general's office reported, "has become a 'narco patron saint' within the Mexican drug community. Drug cartels allegedly believe this saint will protect them from law enforcement and from other drug cartel members. The shrines typically include money, lines of cocaine, or blood that are given as sacrifices to the saint."

CREDIBLE VOICE

Parker, who spent 28 years as an agent in the Attorney General's Office, sought me out shortly before his retirement and said he wanted to talk. Parker had some valuable stories to tell, he said. He was very concerned by what he saw and heard about the office.

I was wary.

I never heard of him. There were plenty of rumors about Duecker "plants" acting on his behalf to gather information. Duecker's background was in counter-intelligence.

So I asked around. Agents told me Parker was the real deal. It was clear he was the last guy who would be a Duecker "plant."

Parker, 50, of the Erie area, joined the office at 22 under the first elected attorney general, Leroy Zimmerman. At age 29, he was shot four times by a drug dealer. Parker worked under every elected attorney general. He retired in June 2015.

Parker was not anti-Kane. In fact, he voted for her and saw her taking office in 2013 as a "hopeful time" among those fighting the "drug war." The hope was that equipment, training and attitudes would change, Parker said. "Unfortunately it did not," he said.

* * *

(Sources: Tribune-Review story on Kane's preliminary arraignment; Romeo's KYW story on Noonan story following the appropriations meeting 2013; Mike Argento's column as cited; Steve Corbett's column also cited; numerous phone and email interviews with Parker; Keisling's book, *The Midnight Ride of Jonathan Luna*.)

* * *

Next: The Supremes take action.

22

SUPREMES

Sept. 28, 2015

James Koval, director of communications for the Administrative Office of Pennsylvania Courts, sent the email at 12:49 p.m. on Sept. 21, 2015. The Harrisburg rumor mill had it right this time. The Pennsylvania Supreme Court suspended the law license of embattled Attorney General Kathleen Kane, dealing a crippling but not necessarily fatal blow to the chief law enforcement officer trying to remain in office as an accused felon.

John Burkoff, a University of Pittsburgh Law School professor called it "an incredible and almost unthinkable development."

Most of what the attorney general does is supervisory, Burkoff said. "But the dramatic psychological, emotional, and political impact of this order on the office and the AG herself has to be enormous," he said in an email for a Tribune-Review story.

It was a unanimous decision by the court comprised at that time of three Republicans and two Democrats. The order said while she was "temporarily suspended" under an emergency rule used for "egregious conduct"—typically used to stop thieving lawyers from dipping further into client trust funds—Kane would remain in office. That averted any type of constitutional issue some had imagined if the judicial branch removed a statewide elected official even though the high court wields complete and total control over the practice of law. The state Constitution requires only that the attorney general be a member of the "bar." A suspended lawyer is still a lawyer and a member of the bar,

Bruce Ledewitz, a Duquesne University Law School professor, had explained to me. That lawyer just cannot practice law. Only if "disbarred," would the person no longer be a lawyer, Ledewitz said.

It was huge news and sent a high-voltage jolt through the Capitol Newsroom and the Harrisburg political community.

"There are few things like listening to the sounds of a newsroom when a big story breaks," Angela Couloumbis wrote that night on Facebook. "The ringing phones; the questions being fired out; the irreverent debate; the buzz. This job may not give up a lot of things—money, or spare time, or uninterrupted vacations—but it's a hell of a ride."

The suspension was not about Kane's criminal case. It was about her alleged conduct as a lawyer, particularly the leak.

Only the next day would we find out that Kane would continue being able to practice law for 30 days. A lawyer in Kane's office told me only lawyers would allow other lawyers to continue practicing for a month after being suspended for a month. Can you imagine a heart surgeon continuing to operate for 30 days after being suspended for misconduct? A surgeon with a wild scalpel can inflict life-threatening damage.

But Kane was capable of inflicting damage on the reputation of the legal profession, former Chief Justice Ronald D. Castille said before her suspension. He told me in a telephone interview if the court suspends Kane's law license before her criminal case is resolved, it would be "unprecedented, but her actions are unprecedented."

The situation is unique because Kane "is flouting court orders, and she allegedly violated grand jury secrecy," said Castille, 70, a Philadelphia Republican. His last day was Dec. 31, 2014, under the mandatory retirement law for state judges. He didn't like it a bit and wanted legislators to change the law. In my opinion, it is an idiotic state law. I saw U.S. District Judge Sylvia Rambo preside at age 79 on the federal bench and she was sharp.

One week after Kane's suspension, Chief Justice Thomas G. Saylor, who replaced Castille as chief, addressed the Pennsylvania Press Club. Over a lunch of meatballs, pasta, salad and baked vegetables, PR-types, lobbyists and reporters got what might have been their first glimpse of the state's top jurist on Sept. 28, 2015. He is clearly one of the five most powerful elected officials in the Capitol. I thought Saylor would come armed with "no comments" for the inevitable Kane questions. The soft-spoken judge is several steps ahead of most people. He answered virtually every question. He was direct like Castille but without the hyperbolic comments or the edge.

Saylor said Kane could remain the state's top law enforcement official even with a suspended law license. He confirmed the license suspension "is in no way constitutionally disabling" because she remains a member of the bar in Pennsylvania—a requirement, under the state constitution to be attorney general. An attorney who is the attorney general, and is suspended, is still a member of the bar of the Supreme Court, because the suspension is just temporary, Saylor said.

Kane's suspension set up the potential for an unprecedented Senate vote to remove her from office. Impeachment, which takes place in the House first with a later Senate trial, was also another constitutional mechanism for removal. The latter seemed less likely because the House with 203 members is unwieldy and impeachment historically has been reserved for convictions.

The Senate, however, can vote by a two-thirds super majority to remove a public official for reasonable cause either on an action launched by the governor or on its own, according to Senate Republican General Counsel Andrew Crompton. Wolf has called for Kane to resign.

But the suspension by the high court came in the midst of a contentious budget impasse that spilled over to the fall of 2015.

Crompton said he's confident the Senate could proceed with removal without the governor initiating it. But that did not mean it would happen.

One change after the suspension: Kane for the first time stated she would likely be unable to seek re-election in 2016. It seemed a ludicrous prospect anyway with Kane facing criminal charges.

"While I am disappointed in the court's action, I am grateful that the court recognized my constitutional rights both as a democratically elected official and as a citizen of the commonwealth," Kane said in a statement. "The court, in specifically recognizing my continuing authority as Attorney General of the commonwealth, today allows me to continue the good works of this office: work which has transformed our war on sex crimes and fraud; work which will also root out the culture of misogyny and racially/religiously offensive behavior that has permeated law enforcement and members of the judiciary in this commonwealth for years."

In an amended statement, she added in light of a Commonwealth Court hearing the week before on Right to Know law requests, "I've instructed my office to engage in a comprehensive review of all emails sitting on (attorney general) servers to fully comply with the RTK (requests). Our preliminary review has generated emails of government officials, including law enforcement officials and judges, heretofore unknown to us. These emails will be fully released either as public documents defined by the Commonwealth Court, or at my discretion."

Again, Kane issued the porn threat when facing trouble.

MORE CHARGES FILED

Once the suspension took effect Kane could not appear in court on a legal matter or sign legal pleadings, but she could perform administrative duties, former Acting Attorney General Walter Cohen told me.

Questions were being asked by Republicans whether she should still collect her $158,700 salary since she would not be performing the entirety of the job she was elected to do.

Kane was an accused felon presiding over the state's chief law enforcement agency.

Trouble came Kane's way again as Hurricane Joaquin was on its northern path.

Ferman announced Kane would face an additional perjury charge and more counts of obstruction and false statements. It wasn't so much the additional charges but the nature of the new perjury charge that was potentially problematic.

"The guillotine blade hanging over AG Kane's head just dropped another few inches," Burkoff, the Pitt law professor said. "These new charges were not unexpected, but they make it even more unlikely that AG Kane can possibly hang in there and ride this storm out. Certainly it will come as no surprise to anyone if some sort of plea agreement is reached in the near future, resolving all the charges against her and giving her some way to save face by not having to admit her culpability for everything with which she is now charged."

The new charges stemmed from the third search warrant served on Kane's office in September 2015.

Four Montgomery County detectives seized signed documents and a notary's log book.

They show Attorney General Kathleen Kane lied to a grand jury, the state Supreme Court and the public when she claimed she wasn't sworn to secrecy for grand juries that happened before she took office, prosecutors said.

Kane still said she did not commit any crimes. "Absolutely she maintains her innocence," said Kane's lawyer Gerald Shargel, a partner at Winston & Strawn in Manhattan, on his way to her preliminary arraignment. "She never intended to release grand jury material."

Ferman used the evidence seized by her detectives to charge Kane with an additional count of perjury, swearing and obstruction of justice. Kane showed up at the district justice's office in blue jeans, boots and a leather jacket.

The criminal complaint said Kane and her attorneys insisted during her testimony, in filings to the Supreme Court and in multiple press conferences, that she was never sworn in for grand juries before her tenure.

Testifying to a grand jury investigating her in November 2014, Kane "told these lies knowing she had signed grand jury secrecy oaths for statewide investigating grand juries" dating before her time in office.

"Moreover, the defendant perpetuated her lies about never being sworn to secrecy . . . to the Supreme Court of Pennsylvania and the citizens of this commonwealth" through her attorneys, the complaint alleged.

The search produced a Jan. 17, 2013, document from Kane's second day in office showing she swore "under penalty of contempt" to keep a 2009 grand jury case confidential, as well as other past grand juries.

"Kane will likely say 'I can't remember all the documents I sign,' but the new evidence shows it's not just one thing, and perhaps, she was misleading the grand jury," said Northampton County District Attorney John Morganelli, who was a staunch supporter of Kane's until the first round of charges was filed.

"I don't know what the end game is for Ms. Kane," Morganelli added. "I don't know why she wouldn't get out (of office) and try to save her (law) license," said Morganelli, who ran for the office in 2008 and was contemplating another bid in 2016.

Detectives confiscated 28 signed and notarized documents and notary Wanda Scheib's log book that show Kane and top aides signed "secrecy oaths" for three active grand juries and 32 expired grand juries.

But during sworn testimony to a statewide grand jury in November, Kane "repeatedly claimed that she had never signed a secrecy oath" for the earlier grand jury that investigated former Philadelphia NAACP head Mondesire, who was never charged, Ferman said.

"Any time a defendant will be facing additional charges and the additional charges appear to be 'you absolutely said you did not sign this and here it is' that puts additional pressure on her," said Bruce Antokowiak, a law professor at St. Vincent's College in Latrobe. "But I am not sure the new allegation will change anything. She's contested the essence of this from the outset." Antkowiak said the new charges "are just another manifestation" of the perjury case.

From a public perspective "it's just one thing after another" with Kane, said Jack Treadway, former chairman of the political science department at Kutztown State University. Treadway is unabashedly a Democrat.

"Kane will probably say 'she forgot.' And do you really think people will believe that?"

Yet there remained a segment of the public, which tended to be Democratic women voters, who found her claims of a conspiracy to prevent her from busting a porn ring credible, Treadway said.

Kane's supporters have long said if it goes to trial she needs women on the jury and she only needs to convince one to hold out to get a hung jury. It's one hell of a risk. Even then, prosecutors could try her again.

"It's one more (felony) count," said Bev Cigler, a political science professor at Penn State University's Harrisburg campus, said of the Oct. 1, 2015, charges. "I don't look at it as piling on. I'd like to think it's not political but I have no way of knowing. Everything in terms of perception is very bad, but she has every right to defend herself."

Not only was Ferman on the ballot a month later but Kevin Steele, her first assistant, was running for District Attorney as a Democrat.

The charges, based on documents, appeared substantive.

According to the complaint, Kane had testified, "When I first went into office, there were existing grand juries at the time and we signed those oaths. And then, of course, new grand juries have developed since I've taken office, and we sign those oaths. . . . We don't go back and sign every grand jury from the beginning of time. You just can't do that."

She denied that any senior staff members were sworn into the 2009 grand jury, according to the complaint. "We all knew that we were not sworn into a 2009 grand jury. I was a stay at home mom at the time," Kane testified.

Kane made the same claims in filings before the state Supreme Court when her attorneys attempted to throw out a subpoena compelling her to testify before the grand jury, the complaint says.

"As an attorney, Kane has an obligation to be truthful in any court filings," the complaint says, citing lawyer rules of conduct. "Clearly, Kane's false statements in her filings before the Pennsylvania Supreme Court are in violation of her duty of candor toward the tribunal."

The complaint notes that Kane and her attorneys stated several times publicly that "she was not sworn to secrecy and therefore could not be criminally culpable for leaking any information learned from the 2009 grand jury investigation."

Wes Oliver, who teaches criminal law at Duquesne University Law School, said, "Certainly more charges make it more difficult for her to stay in office."

PORN THREATS

When leaving the district judge's office after new charges were filed, Kane turned to her weapon of choice: threats to release porn passed around by public officials.

They came from a batch of pornographic emails she identified one month before, in September 2015, as "heretofore unknown to us."

Ardo said they were recently discovered emails as a result of reviewing a Right to Know law request.

Kane claimed she turned over 1,500 emails of Justice J. Michael Eakin to the Judicial Conduct Board that included emails Eakin sent and received that contained "racial, misogynistic and pornography."

In fact, there were about 1,000 personal emails and Kane had turned them over to the Supreme Court in the fall of 2014, her spokesman Ardo later explained. Eakin used a private email address, Johnsmith@yahoo.com.

The Supreme Court in 2014 had hired a Pittsburgh lawyer, Robert Byer, to go through them. Byer found them largely unremarkable, mostly about fishing, fantasy football and sports. None of the emails Eakin sent contained pornography, Byer reported. Of 905 sent to Eakin's account, one contained "offensive sexual content" and Eakin did not reply or forward it, Byer reported.

But that was then.

The Philadelphia Daily News in 2015 said it had obtained some of Eakin's emails sent or received that mocked gays, made fun of blacks, and abused women.

The newspaper, for instance, reported Eakin sent an email with "a joke about a woman who complains to her doctor that her husband 'beats me to a pulp' when he comes home drunk. The doctor advises her to swish sweet tea in her mouth and not to swallow until her husband is asleep. The punch line from the doctor: 'You see how much keeping your mouth shut helps?'"

Eakin also received an email portraying a photoshopped Jerry Sandusky sneaking up on Macaulay Calkin, the child star of *Home Alone*, the Daily News reported.

Not those but other Eakin emails that had been reviewed by the Judicial Conduct Board were released by Kane the day after her law license suspension took effect in October 2015. The timing seemed more than coincidental. The Eakin emails became the story in some newspapers.

Kane claimed to be holding emails of federal prosecutors, public defenders, private lawyers and some to or from Pennsylvania State Police addresses and Montgomery County government addresses. What they had in common was at some point traveling through OAG servers.

Again, it was not illegal.

But her scorched earth policy clearly was underway.

Whatever the outcome, people who sent porn to or from government computers "should be convicted of stupidity," Treadway said.

The broader issue was the appearance of coziness between prosecutors, judges and some police and defense lawyers. To what extent that was true had not been fully examined by October 2015 because Kane had not released all the emails in her possession.

The Supreme Court in 2015 hired the Pittsburgh law firm of former Superior Court President Judge Joseph Del Sole to review the emails Kane sent to the Judicial Conduct Board. Hiring Del Sole was a brilliant move. Del Sole had represented Kane before the Supreme Court on her unsuccessful arguments to throw out the statewide grand jury investigation. How could she ever claim the law firm she had hired was part of a conspiracy against her? In 2015, Eakin said he withheld comment while that new review played out. Eakin also apologized.

In October 2015, the Pennsylvania Supreme Court said that it found news accounts of the emails attributed to Justice Michael Eakin disturbing, and that the Attorney General's Office had not previously provided some of those emails to a judicial ethics board or Byer, the court's special counsel.

The court "aspires to maintain the highest ethical standards and the trust and confidence of the public at large," it said in a statement.

The Judicial Conduct Board, which was conducting a separate review, "has confirmed that a number of the emails on discs were not made available" when former Chief Justice Ronald Castille in 2014 requested any emails involving jurists that the Office of Attorney General had, the court said.

Kane's spokesman Chuck Ardo first said the emails she sent to the conduct board were "recently discovered." That was the first line of defense. But he then said the office had turned over everything available. "We are very confident everything was provided. The only question is why the board didn't look at them," Ardo said.

Asked to explain, Ardo said he had referred earlier to recently discovered content.

Notable was the lack of outrage about Eakin compared to McCaffery, though there was more to the McCaffery allegations than porn emails. A key difference, fundamental as it seems and contrary as it would appear to legal precepts, Eakin was well-liked on the court and McCaffery was not. It also appeared Kane might have some 'splaining to do, as Ricky Ricardo might have told Lucile Ball, if she held back any of the porn emails. Ardo denied Kane had done so.

REAL TROUBLE BREWING

The most immediate problem for Kane emerged in October 2015. She might have to wage a battle on another front to retain her office. Senate Republican leaders, with Senate Democratic leaders in agreement, launched a special committee to look at whether she could still perform the duties of attorney general without a law license. Despite her claims that legal work is only two percent of the job, lawyers in and outside the office thought that portion absurd.

Her claim, in fact, prompted jokes: a government lawyer told me there should be a name change for the office: Pennsylvania General (taking attorney out of the title).

Another attorney still employed by Kane said "attorney" is "50 percent of the title but only 2 percent of the work."

But what the Senate was embarking on was "a very grave, serious and unprecedented action" that could lead to Kane's removal from office, said Senate President Pro Tempore Joe Scarnati, a Jefferson County Republican. The committee, evenly divided between Democrats and Republicans, had 30 days to report to the Senate. The next phase would be deciding whether removal was warranted. Notice would be given and Kane would have a hearing.

Senate GOP leaders were relying on an obscure section of the Pennsylvania Constitution that allowed removal of a statewide row officer like attorney general by a super majority that would require Democratic votes.

Senate Minority Leader Jay Costa, D-Forest Hills, told the Tribune-Review the committee's review of Kane's ability to perform the work was not about her criminal case. But he thought the initial review was "entirely appropriate."

Ardo, Kane's press operative, stepped in it while talking to reporters about her license suspension. Kane told top staff at a meeting that 98 percent of the job is administrative and there would be little change. Ardo told reporters there were no objections raised by senior staff. A few hours later, he had to backtrack and say some senior staffers had expressed doubt at the meeting.

The problems in staying on as AG were myriad. Every deputy attorney general derives their authority from the attorney general. That means any deputy prosecuting a criminal case would likely face challenges from defense lawyers contending the prosecution was invalid. Ardo acknowledged the office had already been notified of such a challenge.

While Scarnatti stressed there was no "predetermined outcome" insiders speculated that the Senate would not have moved forward without the votes to go through with Kane's removal. Any hearing with Kane addressing the Senate would be a first-class spectacle and worth the price of admission.

The provision, Article 6 Section 7 of the Constitution reads as follows:

"All civil officers elected by the people, except the governor, the lieutenant governor, members of the General Assembly, and judges of the courts of record, shall be removed by the governor for reasonable cause, after due notice and full hearing, on the address of two-thirds of the Senate."

If the Senate moved forward to oust her, the governor clearly would have a say, said G. Terry Madonna, a political science professor at Franklin & Marshall College. The Constitution states the officer "shall be removed by the governor for reasonable cause" following a Senate vote. Wolf had called for Kane to resign and he reiterated that on the fateful day the Senate launched the removal action: Oct. 23, 2015. Wolf's lawyers and Senate Republican legal staff had talked behind the scenes before the committee was launched.

Kane at any point could initiate a legal challenge. It was a battle that would likely end up again before the state Supreme Court.

Much of the legal and political war ahead for Kane was clouded in uncertainity while she still maintained her innocence. Ardo, on Kane's behalf, said any attempt to remove her before the criminal charges were resolved, was premature.

And the sad saga of Kathleen Kane continued.

* * *

(Sources: My Tribune-Review article on Kane's suspension in September; Couloumbis and McCoy, Philadelphia Inquirer piece on the suspension; my coverage and Couloumbis story on Saylor's speech to the press club; my phone and email interviews with Ledewitz, Burkoff, Oliver, Treadway, Crompton and Morganelli; Tribune-Review on Kane's threatened porn releases; Inquirer story on porn release threats in October 2015 statements; Inquirer story by Couloumbis and McCoy in October 2015 on the Judicial Conduct Board's statement; Associated Press story on the conduct board's statement; Steve Esack's piece on the conduct board and the Supreme Court; several interviews with Ardo; statement provided by the Supreme Court; my Trib story on the skirmish over Eakin's emails; Senate news release by Senate Republican leadership; phone conference with Senator Scarnati; comments on the process by Senate Republican General Counsel Drew Crompton; and comments by Kane's office through Ardo.)

* * *

Next: Kane appoints porn prosecutor. Really.

23

PORN WARFARE

Dec. 16, 2015

In the fall of 2015, Kathleen Kane strapped on the political equivalent of a suicide vest.

With the criminal charges filed in August, the loss of her law license in October, and a removal petition launched in the Senate the next day, Kane's days in Harrisburg appeared to be numbered.

Kane was taking people out with her.

It was consistent with her tough-fisted Scranton attitude about political scrapes. If you are going down, you go down swinging.

Kane had in her possession more porn and offensive email of Eakin's obtained from OAG servers. And there were tens of thousands of emails from others still to examine.

Kathleen Kane said in 2012 she was going after the "old boys' network." She deserves credit for at least keeping that campaign pledge. The way she did it though was despicable and hypocritical. She targeted perceived political enemies. She can claim she exposed porn that had been exchanged on state computers. But she did so only when it suited her political purposes.

Through 2014 and 2015, she formally opposed general release.

By December 2015, Seth Wiliams was on his heels defending Fina, Costanzo and Blessington. They were transferred to a civil appeals unit within the DA's office, a major waste of talent, but the political price DA Williams had to pay. Critics such as the National Organization for Women and Philadelphia council members continued to demand their firing (over emails exchanged or received under a *prior employer*). A fledgling group called "Citizens 4 Kane" displayed Fina "wanted posters" on the capitol steps at a news conference. Even if Fina survived in the DA's office, he may be hamstrung in future cases involving women's issues, racism and porn. Serving as a prosecutor was his life's work. It was noteworthy these critics never made a stink or called for the resignation of Duecker, who had been recommended for termination internally because of unresolved sexual harassment complaints.

Fina was more culpable because he sent or forwarded some porn, while Costanzo and Blessington merely received it, Philadelphia Magazine concluded, in a story that begged to know why Fina hadn't resigned. The article spoke of Fina's "Porngate public humiliation." Blessington appeared to be collateral damage.

Fina was severely wounded. At that Kane had to be smiling. His last laugh, however, might come in his federal defamation lawsuit, if it progressed in court.

Kane, meanwhile, was headed toward becoming a significant footnote in history.

Her porn jihad was moving ahead at a rapid clip.

But by mid-July 2016, it was not clear that Gansler would be prosecuting anyone—or if or when his report come out. Kane's new Solicitor General Bruce Castor, a former Montgomery County District Attorney, in May 2016, made clear Gansler would have no prosecutorial powers. He later established some limitations on what would be required for releasing the report. Castor, hired by Kane in March, helped stabilize the office. Some employees believed he was a micromanager. But he was effectively the acting attorney general in part because Kane did not have an active law license. Castor had his critics, but he was a skilled prosecutor.

It wasn't Gansler's first rodeo either. But it appeared to me that Castor was calling the shots.

Castor postponed a June 2016 news conference for release of a preliminary report on Gansler's investigation because he stated the report was incomplete. Gansler maintained throughout that the advantage of using an out-of-state ex-prosecutor was independence, but here was Castor directing timing and content. Castor later massaged the wording about the postponement in a public statement, but it was clear internal disagreements were affecting how and when the report would be released. At the time that was occurring, Kane was still scheduled for trial in August 2016. Pennlive's Wallace McKelvey reported in a thorough July 2016 analysis that the Gansler report, which at that point cost taxpayers $160,000, might never see the light of day. McKelvey tied it to House investigators working on Kane's impeachment investigation.

Rep. Todd Stephens, R-Montgomery County, who was spearheading the possible impeachment effort, previously told me he wanted to obtain court orders protecting witnesses who cooperated with the impeachment investigation. If such an order were obtained, it "could prevent Kane from the wholesale naming of names she promised" in December 2015, "when she hired a team of prosecutors to investigate the so-called 'Porngate' scandal,'" Pennlive's McKelvey reported. Castor told McKelvey he needed to "get the report into a condition that can be released." Castor also said "then I'll decide if the release would be violative of any court orders." The cost of the House using outside counsel to obtain protective orders still wasn't resolved in July 2016.

It was just not clear what *would* be released. But it was crystal clear this material was vital to Kane's criminal defense should she go to trial.

Impeachment by the House seemed unlikely, given the short tenure remaining for Kane through January 2017 and a General Election looming for lawmakers in November 2016. If the House approved Articles of Impeachment, a Senate trial would be required to sustain any of the noncriminal charges against her. It was not out of the question, Stephens said, that impeachment could still be pursued after Kane was out of office.

Former Supreme Court Justice Rolf Larsen was convicted of one count of the impeachment articles in 1994 for improperly meeting with an attorney who had cases before the high court. It came after his criminal conviction earlier in 1994 for having his physician write prescriptions for antidepressants for his own use in the names of court employees to hide his use of medications. A judge removed him from the bench after his criminal conviction. The Senate conviction of one impeachment count barred Larsen from holding public office in the future. Larsen's supporters claimed he was railroaded. "He was bitter–with good reason," Larsen's attorney William C. Costopoulos told the Tribune-Review in an August 2014 article about Larsen's death.

THE PORNGATE "SPECIAL PROSECUTOR"

There are plenty of folks I know who believe exposing porn exchanged on government computers was cathartic and a positive step. I am almost 100 percent for disclosure. But some events gave me pause.

On Dec. 1, 2015, Kane announced the hiring of former Maryland Attorney General Douglas Gansler to further investigate porn in the attorney general's office and other branches of government. Gansler said he and his Washington D.C. law firm would do the job for less than the $2 million limit established under Pennsylvania's expired special prosecutor law.

Kane could have saved $2 million and simply released all the porn and offensive emails to the media in one stroke. Trust me, any public official transmitting hardcore porn would be at least outed. She didn't need to spend scarce agency resources on a porn prosecutor.

Gansler spoke of charging people with crimes. Would he do that even if the chance of winning under some novel legal theory was minimal at best? Apparently so, based on his track record. He was sanctioned by Maryland's highest court in 2003 when he worked as a state's attorney in part for implying he would prosecute cases he couldn't win and for talking out of school to the media in high profile cases.

"Among the statements for which he was sanctioned was a pledge that he would prosecute cases he couldn't win," Dennis Roddy wrote.

> After a judge tossed out charges against a high schooler accused of phoning in a bomb threat, explaining that the prosecution offered no proof they had the right person, Gansler said this:
>
> > We try hard cases. . . . Juveniles who phone in bomb threats will be prosecuted. It's more

> important to prosecute someone and have them acquitted than let them commit crimes with impunity.
>
> In short: forget proof, we'll punish you by prosecuting. This fits perfectly with his new post," Roddy wrote.

The price of exposure is steep. More careers would be ruined for emails sent as long as seven to eight years ago.

It had the feel of an expensive taxpayer-financed witch-hunt. Looking at thousands of people's emails, who perhaps sent no more than a joke or two, or in some cases no offensive emails or porn? The thousands still unreleased were personal emails, not necessarily porn. Gansler said he would have subpoena and grand jury power. His advantage was independence, he argued: he knew none of these agency staffers and OAG personalities and politics were irrelevant. He was a pro and definitely experienced.

He first had to get a Pennsylvania law license. Like Kane, he could not legally practice in this state. But *pro hac vice* motions allowing out-of-state lawyers to practice here in one case or two is a fairly routine practice in the legal profession. He said he would not need one unless he would eventually appear in Pennsylvania court. Several members of his firm were licensed in Pennsylvania.

Roughly one million emails were turned over to Gansler's law firm in December 2015. Agency insiders say the document dump likely contained confidential files, such as letters to law enforcement, informants' names, case strategies, and potentially secret grand jury information. Top brass called on him to return the hard drive. Gansler refused. Clearly he was working for Kane.

Kane, who had been scorched by Senate hearings investigating her removal, seemed to be on a whole new level of seeking retribution and revenge. Wearing a white dress, Kane took the stage at the National Constitution Center in Philadelphia on Dec. 1, 2015. After an introductory showing of racy images and insulting racial jokes on a large screen, Kane unleashed her most stinging comments yet in announcing Gansler's hiring.

She was playing to her core support: women, minorities and hardcore Democrats.

"To the few who challenge it, including some members of my own staff," Kane said, "I pose a simple, three-pronged question: Are you a white male? Are you or one of your buddies in this email network? Are you trying to get my job without the benefit of having to run for it and being chosen by the people of Pennsylvania?"

Heads were turning in the newsroom as we watched a web stream of the event in Harrisburg: *"Are you a white male?"*

Say what?

Only white males watch porn? Other races don't engage in racism? Granted white males made up the "old boys' network" Kane so detested. Feudale, the former jurist, had even admitted there is one. But Gansler, her white knight, was a man. When in trouble she turned to other men: Sprague, Shargel and Patrick Reese—her bodyguard and driver.

This was gender politics, pure and simple. There was also a widespread belief that Kane would try to find years-old porn on Senate Republicans and staffers to try to force the Senate to back off.

"TITTY DEFICIT"

Eakin's case—reignited by Kane—was pending before the Judicial Conduct Board as she spoke at the constitution center. My general sense after looking at the emails the justice sent and received was that—unlike the former Corbett prosecutors—he had a bigger problem with so-called jokes than photographs. His banter with Jeffrey Baxter, a deputy attorney general who had worked under Eakin when he served as Cumberland County district attorney included discussions in 2009 emails about strip clubs they'd hit in an upcoming trip to Myrtle Beach and jokes about how they'd like to take along two female members of Eakin's staff and what the sleeping arrangements would be. Baxter was disciplined for the porn. He had been suspended by Kane's office. Maybe he should have been given a raise because his friendship with Eakin and his OAG email address helped Kane bag another big pelt.

Eakin stated that he had $50 in $1 bills for the trip to take care of his "titty deficit." Those presumably would be stuffed into strippers' G-strings.

As a lawyer colleague said to me later, how would you feel about your daughter working as a staffer to Eakin? Even if it was just a joke? But the two women who worked for him, a secretary and office manager, testified at Eakin's Court of Judicial Discipline hearing that they weren't offended. Janey Thrush, the secretary, said she was not bothered by another Baxter email to Eakin telling him to give Janey a pat on the ass. "Will do," Eakin wrote.

Sounds bad, looks bad, but the women knew it was a joke. He never made any advance on females in the office and was respectful and courteous to his employees, they testified.

Was there value in exposing this—with both Eakin and McCaffery? Yes.

Was it worth taking away their careers and jobs? You'll get mixed views at any water cooler.

Again, disclosure is most important. The consequences are unfortunate and troubling when the original source is private email. Sending anything controversial to a government server, however, is a huge mistake and potentially a career-ender.

The more troubling questions: did the cozy relationships between prosecutors, justices, some defense lawyers in porn networks impact what happened in the courtroom? No clear conflicts were discovered by December 2015 on specific cases or motions.

Were these guys reflecting their actual views? Or were they consummate professionals who joked around like frat boys but stuck to the letter of the law in their daily work? Sam Stretton, an expert witness for Eakin who attended law school with him at Dickinson, said he examined every one of Eakin's appellate court opinions and dissents and never detected any bias, racism or discrimination.

WOMEN HATERS?

Kane looked at it in the harshest light.

"No African-American should walk into a courtroom where the judge or prosecutor or defense attorney mocks and ridicules him or her behind a closed network because of the color of his skin," Kane said. "No woman should go to work and be subjected to consistent treatment of disgusting indignity by women-haters because they were born with one less body part, which the last I heard does not contain any extra brain cells."

Here, in my view, she got closer to the truth. Porn is in the eye of the beholder. But some of the offensive "jokes" mocking blacks, gays and battered women, in my view were worse than close-ups of vaginas. As the Judicial Conduct Board would say in its formal complaint against Eakin on Dec. 8, 2015, his emails put the judiciary in "disrepute" and created the appearance of conflict of interest.

In 2015, words, more than pictures or videos, became the issue.

Creating a private email account to send and receive smut showed Eakin's *mens rea* or state of mind that he had the intent to deceive yet still participate in the behavior, the review board claimed.

William C. Costopoulos, Eakin's lawyer, told the conduct court that the review board had cleared Eakin in 2014 and there were only 24 new emails uncovered and sent to the board by Kane. "There's nothing here," he told the court in a session at the Northampton County Courthouse in Easton in December 2015.

The complaint claims that by sending and receiving emails from 2008-14 containing "attempted humor based upon pictures of nude women; sexually suggestive stereotypes, homophobic content; socioeconomic stereotypes; violence toward women; race or ethnicity; and stereotypes of religious groups, Justice Eakin engaged in conduct so extreme that it brought the judicial office in disrepute."

EAKIN: "SORRY BEYOND WORDS"

Eakin, trying to hold back tears on the witness stand, was contrite but defiant. He shot the messenger, repeatedly referring to the media coverage, tabloids and having been "dragged through the mud."

Eakin repeatedly apologized for emails he sent on a private Yahoo account to Baxter in the Attorney General's Office, though some were "a half-dozen years old."

"It is not criminal. It has nothing to do with performance on the job," he told the Court of Judicial Discipline on Dec. 21, 2015. "Don't hold me accountable for what my friends sent. I didn't open half these things."

"What I sent I sent, and I am sorry for that beyond words. The media circus cannot be ignored, but it is not public opinion."

But the justice also said he " had been dragged through the mud without the opportunity to address the misstatements and, in my mind, the total dishonesty in many of the news reports."

Regardless of the final outcome, the formal charges filed against Eakin represented a "win" for Kane. She could count two justices, a Cabinet secretary, a top prosecutor and many others who lost their jobs or had been publicly shamed. All from porn she supposedly stumbled upon in her Sandusky investigation. McCaffery was an unfortunate accident for Kane. His email might not have been exposed if Castille hadn't demanded it and the Morning Call hadn't reported it. McCaffery likely would have been a strong voice for Kane on the court. His brother Dan McCaffery, a Philadelphia Common Pleas county judge, served as master of ceremonies at Kane's swearing in ceremony in January 2013 after briefly running in the Democratic primary for attorney general.

There was an air of political correctness though when the email discussion moved from pictures to words.

Make no mistake, some of the jokes were way out of line and insulting to women and minorities; some were mild, borderline, again depending upon your point of view. They weren't all nasty.

Some were demeaning:

A video called "what have we done" showed a black woman speaking about Barack Obama's election as president, the complaint says. Because of it, she says, black people won't have to pay bills and "they'll have to get jobs."

Others were crude but fairly innocent such as "Why I Failed Fourth Grade." It shows a female elementary teacher teaching "Grammar 101." She asks the students to name an abstract noun "you can think of but can't touch."

"Can you give me two examples?" she says. "Your tits," a boy answers.

Of the emails cited in the complaint against Eakin, he received seven times as many as the 157 he sent or forwarded.

If Eakin sent and received only from other private accounts, no one would have been the wiser.

"There's not a man alive who hasn't viewed pornography or laughed at an off-color joke," Stretton said.

Coming from a different perspective, Duquesne Law School Professor Bruce Ledewitz told the Washington Post: "Some of these things are really disgusting. You get the impression that every white male officer holder in the state is a creep."

The Post in its Dec. 26, 2015, piece said it was hard to tell the "creeps" from the heroes. The "epic mess is a disaster for the state's judicial system," the Post wrote.

For me, the issue was not as much the content. It was the clubby atmosphere with agents, defense attorneys, police officers, prosecutors, even if there was no evidence of abuse. The appearance is sleazy.

It was also an issue of poor judgment by those like Eakin, who either never thought of sending only on private email systems or failed to ask his old buddy Baxter to stop sending to him on OAG servers.

With Kane, the problem was using offensive emails as weapons instead of releasing them all in 2014.

Not to mention her outright duplicity.

THE TWIN'S EMAILS

Kane was holding back racy emails exchanged by her twin sister.

Rumors were rampant for months that Ellen Granahan received and sent some offensive emails during her tenure as a deputy attorney general. Kane's office repeatedly denied it. Ardo said he was told they didn't exist. But after Assistant Philly DA Gilson publicly challenged Kane on her sister's emails, her office released 58 of Granahan's, after first denying once again they existed. They "compare illegal immigrants to lazy sperm, mock Asian accents, toy with the old trope of African Americans as rapists and make light of domestic violence," Pennlive columnist Dennis Roddy wrote. "How I wish I could express the same pious outrage Kane poured out when she unmasked similar emails from the inboxes of her enemies," Roddy, the former press aide to Corbett, added.

Where in the hell were they? On a thumb drive in Kane's desk? At her home? With a trusted top aide? Kane, a Democrat, disciplined about 60 people for pornographic and inappropriate emails last year.

You guessed it. Granahan wasn't one of them.

Kane received one controversial email from OAG servers before she took office, a string of photos that showed a man's genitals poking out of his kilt. The sender was redacted in the email released by her office.

Just one.

The revelation of Granahan's emails was a major blow to Kane's old boys' network theme. Another setback near the end of 2015 was the Philly DA's office successfully repudiating the racial targeting theme in the sting case against Bishop. It seemed to stop Kane's traction and those of her supporters implying racially insensitive emails sent to ex-prosecutors like Fina were evidence of racism in the case. Yet another was the conviction of her confidant, bodyguard and driver, Patrick Reese, in Montgomery County Common Pleas Court. Reese was charged with Kane in August on a single count of indirect criminal contempt. Reese was found guilty in a bench trial before Judge William Carpenter in December. Despite a protective order Carpenter had issued preventing grand jury interference, prosecutors say Reese at Kane's direction searched the office email system for information on witnesses, Carpenter, the special prosecutor, Carluccio, Fina and James Barker, who previously headed the office's grand jury, and numerous others. Kane knew at every turn what the grand jury investigating her was doing.

SHOWTIME IN SENATE

Despite all the allegations about Kathleen Kane, from lying to a grand jury to allegedly violating ethics law by using a state media center for a "press conference" about her criminal case, the Senate was focused on one and only one issue: whether Kane's license suspension prevented her from doing her job as attorney general. A Special Committee on Address held three hearings in November 2015. At one, three district attorneys testified. Bucks County DA David Heckler, a former judge and state senator, said virtually every decision he makes heading a prosecutorial office has a legal foundation.

The "Four Horsemen" as Ardo called them also testified. I liked his name for the top Kane aides. It had an apocalyptic ring. They were Beemer, the first deputy; and the three "ED-AGS," Executive Deputy Attorneys General: Robert Mulle,

Lawrence Cherba and James A. Donahue III. They testified under subpoena. Beemer on Nov. 18, 2015, laid out the "nuclear scenario" feared by top brass: a judge somewhere in the state would grant a motion from defense attorneys to dismiss charges against a defendant because the top prosecutor in the state did not have a law license. Just for example, motions were filed in Allegheny and Armstrong counties. As of December, none had yet prevailed. But if one attorney wins, and the defendant is a violent criminal, the public potentially would be endangered, Beemer said.

If "one of the many hundreds of Common Pleas judges we have in this Commonwealth found that (a) motion was valid and dismissed the case, that person would be released, even if it was in the short term, until we could address that issue. That is what I like to call—I mean, what I would call a sort of nuclear scenario," Beemer said. "We pray that does not happen, but it's one that we have to vigilantly guard against all over the Commonwealth and that we're going to have to deal with, and we recognize that."

The committee found "sufficient basis" for proceeding before the full Senate on the issue of Kane's removal.

* * *

(Sources: Story by Joe Myers, Philadelphia Magazine, Dec. 9, 2015; Karen Langley piece in the Pittsburgh Post-Gazette on Gansler's appointment Dec. 1, 2015; Kevin Zwick, Capitolwire.com also on Gansler's "porn" contract; Bumsted, Tribune-Review, on the appointment; Mark Fazlollah and Craig McCoy, Philadelphia Inquirer on Dec. 6, 2015, on previously undisclosed Eakin emails; Dennis Roddy's column on Pennlive.com Dec. 1, 2015, on Gansler's appointment; Roddy's column on Dec. 20, 2015, on Granahan's emails; memo by Philadelphia DA's Office on Evidence of Racial Targeting Does Not Exist (Commonwealth V. Louise Bishop); my column, Tribune-Review, Dec. 5, 2015, on Gansler; Bumsted, Tribune-Review, on the complaint against Eakin by Judicial Conduct Board also in December 2015; Bumsted, Tribune-Review, on Court of Judicial Discipline hearing for Eakin that same month; Bumsted, Tribune-Review, on Granahan's emails; Natalie Pompilio, Washington Post, Dec. 26, 2015, on Porngate; the Legal Intelligencer, Dec. 23, 2015, by Ben

Seal, Lizzy McLellan, on legality of Kane giving emails with confidential information to out-of-state special prosecutor; Pennlive, Wallace McKelvey, Dec. 10, 2015, on Senate vote to consider ousting Kane; McKelvey's Dec. 29, 2015, story on Ethics Commission investigation of Kane; Special Committee on Senate Address report on Kane, November 2015; testimony of Beemer and Heckler before Senate committee in November 2015.)

* * *

Next: Final political chapter for Kane.

24

CITIZEN KANE?

Feb. 10, 2016

On the eve of the Senate Committee on Address' final hearing in January—the one intended to give Kane due process—Kane threw the committee a sharp breaking curveball with her typical drama and flair. She filed an emergency petition with the newly constituted Pennsylvania Supreme Court to rescind her suspension as a result of Justice Eakin allegedly tainting the panel because he knew she had copies of his offensive emails when he voted to suspend her. Or so her theory went. It prompted speculation that a new Democratic-majority court with three new members might see things her way and lift her law license suspension thus negating the Senate's removal hearings. She filed with the Supreme Court late in the day on Jan. 11, 2016, causing chaos in the press corps. She had never mentioned it to Ardo and he wasn't provided copies. The court closed at 4:30 p.m. but the court system couldn't provide copies on the 11th because it wasn't docketed. Kane told Ardo to tell reporters to call her lawyer, James Mundy, of Scranton. Those who were persistent or lucky got through to him.

Kane's Senate hearing was set for Jan. 12, 2016. She never took the opportunity to testify but sent former Democratic Gov. Ed Rendell and her chief of staff, Jonathan Duecker. Rendell just a few weeks later would endorse Montgomery County Commission Chairman Josh Shapiro in the attorney general's race even though Kane was an unofficial candidate for re-election at that time. Rendell's loyalty only went so far. Rendell advised the committee to hold off any action until the Supreme Court ruled on Kane's suspension. After all, what a mess it would be if the Senate removed her and then the court restored her law license, Rendell said. He advocated impeachment as the correct process for removing an elected official.

Kane was trying to get her suspension lifted but some members of the Senate panel believed she had more violations of the lawyer discipline code since her suspension. If true, that should warrant further discipline such as a suspension for a year or two, or disbarment. According to Sen. John Gordner, R-Berwick, chairman of the special committee, there was no evidence Kane had a lawyer supervisor as required for a "formerly admitted attorney," the legal euphemism for someone suspended or disbarred. Sound like a big deal? Not to us non-lawyers. But it raised the issue whether she felt she was above the rules. John or Jane Doe, as a solo practioner, would be jammed up big time for blowing off the rules under suspension.

Another issue was continuing to use her attorney general letterhead. Gordner said an "individual" on the committee sent that evidence to the lawyer discipline board or the "D board," as it was called.

Activist Gene Stilp, of Dauphin County, who was trained as a lawyer but doesn't practice, filed nine complaints against Kane with the lawyer discipline board for allegedly continuing to practice law during her suspension. He covered the above points—and more. The D board is notoriously slow. The complaints aren't public record at the filing stage.

Turning over almost 1 million emails without the permission of a grand jury judge to Special Deputy Douglas Gansler could also be a D board violation—or worse, a grand jury secrecy violation, the very issue at the heart of her 2015 criminal case. Sen. Lisa Baker, R-Luzerne County, obtained a statement from Beemer, the first deputy, indicating the grand jury judge was taking the appropriate steps to investigate. Those emails, which may have contained grand jury information, also had confidential informants' names, and agents' health histories. They were sent to an out-of-state attorney, Gansler, who did not have a Pennsylvania law license. They were sent without the approval of the grand jury judge, according to Beemer's letter to Baker. Due to time constraints, Baker could not incorporate it into the committee's final report but she made it part of the Senate record.

Kane's eleventh-hour filing put the Senate Committee on Address in a defensive posture. Its Jan. 27, 2016, report showed the committee hedging every recommendation based on what the court might do. The senators really had no choice. The report said in essence the panel would vote on Kane's removal only if the high court cleared the path by keeping her suspension in effect.

The court wasted no time. Nine days after the Senate's report the court issued its order.

It had been pure nonsense to think one of the first acts of a new court would be to overturn Kane's suspension.

The new members of the court, David Wecht, Kevin Dougherty and Christine Donohue, weren't about to do anything other than look at the law. Party affiliation tends to mean little at the appellate court level even though judges and justices are elected. The court would have had to reverse a ruling that three of the justices, who served on the court before, supported. If party does mean anything, two of them are Democrats, Debra Todd and Max Baer. The third was Thomas Saylor, a Republican, who remained chief on the new court due to seniority. For Kane to prevail, at least one of the justices who was on the court last year would have had to switch providing all three new members supported Kane's position.

On Feb. 5, 2016, in a *per curiam* order ("by the court") the justices unanimously rejected Kane's petition for extraordinary relief. Her "claims of bias" were "untimely," the court ruled in an 87-word order. Kane didn't seek relief at the earliest possible time therefore the court couldn't "invalidate a judicial determination," the court said. Kane had waited four months before claiming Eakin was biased against her, Chief Disciplinary Counsel Paul Killion had argued. Further, the court's earlier ruling also had been unanimous. Take Eakin out and instead of 5-0 it would have been 4-0. Kane's lawyer, Mundy, argued that Eakin's suspension in December was the trigger for her filing. Nonetheless, the door was now open for a Senate vote. It could come any day.

"PATRON SAINT OF LOST CAUSES"

Much had changed in late 2015 and early 2016. Risa Vetri Ferman was no longer the Montgomery County District Attorney. A Republican, she was elected to the Montgomery County Court of Common Pleas in November. Kane's criminal prosecution was now in the hands of Kevin Steele, the former first assistant who was elected DA. He was a Democrat. Steele served as the lead prosecutor at Kane's preliminary hearing in August 2015. He was a career prosecutor who previously headed the trials division where he oversaw major crimes, narcotics, sex crimes, domestic violence and insurance fraud. He had been captain of the narcotics unit and earlier worked for the Department of Justice in Wilmington, the U.S. Attorney's Office in Washington and the United States Secret Service.

Steele had the creds but he also had his hands full, deciding in late 2015 to prosecute entertainer Bill Cosby for the sexual assault of a woman 12 years before. It had been a campaign promise of Steele's to re-evaluate the case. His GOP opponent Bruce Castor, who served earlier as DA, had decided not to prosecute Cosby. The charges were based on a woman's allegation that Cosby drugged and sexually assaulted her in 2004.

Cosby maintained his innocence and vowed to fight the charges.

So Steele liked a fight and he would now get one on two fronts, with Kane and Cosby.

Ardo, meanwhile, was trying to survive under a boss who communicated very little with him. When he inquired at reporters' requests whether there would be any additional 11th hour legal filing before the Senate removal vote (there was not), Kane told him it was none if his business. Rendell told Ardo in a text message he was the "Patron Saint of Lost Causes." That fit. Ardo was also trying to represent the office of attorney general and that meant balancing the views of folks like Beemer and Mulle into his statements. It was the classic case of the kids' game of "pickle" and he was "it," smack in the middle.

You may wonder why reporters didn't ask Kane. She was rarely around the Capitol. For that matter, she was rarely in her Strawberry Square office in Harrisburg. She spent most of her time in the Scranton office. Under questioning by Scarnati, Duecker said he didn't see Kane's schedule so he could not say how often she was in Harrisburg or Scranton.

In an age of telecommuting, there's nothing wrong with working off a laptop in say, a Starbucks—unless you are the elected leader of an 800-person office. There's a concept called leadership. Employees needed to see the attorney general regularly and hear from her periodically. That wasn't happening.

Kane was openly talking about a re-election bid but it was not clear even to those close to her in 2012 where she would have any organization to run a statewide campaign. Renee Martin, her former spokeswoman, was gathering signatures for her to get on the ballot. But Kane was vowing not to talk to Pennsylvania reporters, whom she felt were biased against her. She set up some national interviews. Author Keisling had taken up her cause and Kane used his research extensively on Direct Address. It's hard to run for statewide office in Pennsylvania and not talk to state media. Pennsylvania reporters knew the full story and had witnessed the downfall of Kathleen Kane. And it was in fact a downfall, even if she is acquitted of criminal charges.

BE CAREFUL WHAT YOU WISH FOR

As the Senate moved toward a removal vote, the state House, also controlled by Republicans, was using a different section of the Pennsylvania Constitution to consider Kane's removal. The House Judiciary Committee in January 2016, set up a full House vote on launching an impeachment investigation of Kane for "misbehavior in office." It's the route Kane said was appropriate. It was markedly different from the Direct Address removal effort in the Senate:

- There was already a record based on the 1994 impeachment of the late Supreme Court Justice Rolf Larsen, who had been convicted for having his doctor write prescriptions to his court employees so they could pick up anti-anxiety medication for him to hide his depression.

- There was already an experienced hand in the state House who served as a House prosecutor against Larsen: Minority Leader Frank Dermody, a Democrat from Allegheny County, a former assistant district attorney.
- Impeachment required action by two chambers; if the House finds evidence of misconduct it presents articles of impeachment to the Senate, which sits as a jury and renders a verdict.
- If impeached, that ex-official can no longer hold elective office in Pennsylvania. (Under the Senate removal process, Kane if removed could continue to run for re-election and if acquitted of criminal charges, serve as attorney general again. Not so with impeachment.)
- Impeachment is a lengthy process and if the House moved forward it's possible Kane would be close to completing her term in 2016 before impeachment ever came up for a vote.
- Broad bipartisan support existed in the state House for an impeachment investigation and perhaps that stemmed in part from the timing. It was, in a sense, a "freebie" vote. The actual vote to impeach may never occur or it could be put off until after Kane's trial.
- Impeachment "is a joke," an attorney general's agent told me. It was viewed with skepticism because the House didn't start officially until almost six months after Kane had been charged with crimes.
- Democratic Gov. Tom Wolf needed to sign off on Direct Address if the Senate approved it. While Wolf had called for Kane's resignation in August 2015 he avoided saying what he would do if presented with a removal petition. He has no role in impeachment.
- Articles of impeachment can be broad and clearly the author of the House resolution, Rep. Garth Everett, R-Lycoming County, wanted the investigation to look at Kane's entire record not just whether she can serve without a law license.

I certainly shared some of the skepticism about impeachment having much meaning in Kane's case. But it could serve as a "Plan B" and depending how events unfolded with the attorney general there was the potential to move quickly. The representative launching it, Everett, was solid. Everett was a career Air Force guy who obtained his law degree as a 40-something student. I always thought of him as a country western singer because of the first name, Garth, and that other guy—Brooks.

Kane's erratic behavior was "embarrassing for all Pennsylvanians," Everett told me. The House had experienced and capable lawyers from both sides of the aisle in place to handle an impeachment investigation: Republican Rep. Todd Stephens, a former assistant district attorney in Montgomery County and Rep. Tim Briggs, a Montgomery County Democrat and an attorney.

Impeachment is the "most prescribed, recognized method of removing an elected official," Everett said. There he hit on the bothersome aspect of Senate removal. Yes, it was part of the Constitution. But Direct Address hadn't been used since the late 1800s. Even Rendell acknowledged the Senate probably had the authority to remove Kane from office. But the Constitution didn't specifically refer to attorney general as an officeholder who could be removed for "reasonable cause." It referred to "civil officers" and exempted the governor, lieutenant governor and legislators. The attorney general had been appointed not elected when this provision of the Constitution was adopted. But just because it was "silent" on attorney general didn't mean the Senate was precluded from using it to remove an attorney general, Senate lawyers argued.

If removed, Kane planned an appeal. She contended it was unconstitutional and a violation of due process, considering the criminal charges against her. Sen. Art Haywood, D-Philadelphia, a member of the special committee, said Kane was being "railroaded" by the Senate. She's primarily a "CEO" and didn't need a law license to fulfill her duties, Haywood stated.

The evidence showed otherwise, several GOP senators said.

Kane herself contended impeachment was the proper course of action to remove her. But once the House effort got underway she called it "unwarranted and ill-timed." Removing her "runs contrary to the well-established norms that are the foundation of our legal system and sets a troubling precedent for the future," Kane stated.

As the Senate removal vote became imminent, it also became apparent the House effort and Rendell provided political cover for Senate Democrats, who said impeachment was the better course of action. That's not to say House Republicans wanted it to work that way. It just happened.

CAMPAIGN FUNDS PAY FOR HER LEGAL DEFENSE

As the vote approached, Kane filed her statement of campaign expenses with the Pennsylvania Department of State. She had actually "announced" her intention to run for re-election a year ago in December 2014 at the Pennsylvania Society in New York. That was before the statewide grand jury report was issued and she wavered at least twice after that on whether she would run.

Run, really? While facing criminal charges? Pennsylvania candidates have done it before successfully, ex-House Speaker Bill DeWeese, D-Waynesburg, not to mention former Senate Majority Whip Jane Orie, R-McCandless. Both of them won their seats while facing criminal charges. But those elections were confined to small geographical areas and limited media scrutiny. A statewide race for the post of Pennsylvania's top law enforcement officer was a whole lot different.

Kane spent the bulk of her campaign money, $310,000, on legal and public relations fees related to her criminal defense. It also showed she owed $1.5 million from the 2012 campaign to her estranged husband Chris, whom she was divorcing. She didn't raise a cent.

Incredibly, using campaign money for one's defense appears to be legal in Pennsylvania. Robert Mellow, the former Senate Democratic leader, hit his campaign fund for $738,000 in legal fees, ex-Senate power broker Vincent Fumo used $1.1 million in campaign money, and Orie used $110,000 from her campaign. That means contributors unknowingly donated to Kane without any awareness they'd be paying Manhattan defense attorney Shargel, and Washington D.C. spinmeister Lanny Davis, who left Kane's employ in the spring of 2015. Still, it wasn't much money. The

$150,000 to Shargel might be enough to have coffee with him at a midtown Manhattan eatery, maybe a little more. Where was Kane getting the rest of the money for her legal defense? Reporters and political observers often asked that question.

THE VOTE ON REMOVING KANE

The Senate vote on removal was announced around 6 p.m. on Feb. 8, 2016, the night before Wolf's budget address to the General Assembly. The vote was scheduled for Wednesday, Feb. 10. I was on my way to do a PCN call in show with John Baer (read the Forword to this book) when I saw an email and got dinged a few times on texts. I had planned to grab something small to eat anyway so I stopped at a Giant food store next to the PCN studio off of Trindle Road in Camp Hill. I dictated a story into a text message and sent it to my email. I cleaned it up on my phone while gulping down a prepackaged salad and sent it to Pittsburgh. An editor added some background on the Senate hearings and process. So it was set for Wednesday, I was assured. As much as anything is ever solidly scheduled in the General Assembly, that is.

"After considerable discussion with members of the Senate it has been determined that a vote on the removal of the Attorney General will take place on Wednesday, February 10, 2016," Senate President Joe Scarnati, R-Jefferson County, said in a statement. "A Senate Resolution will be introduced during session, which will be voted upon by the full Senate. Once again, I commend the Special Committee on Senate Address for their thorough examination of this matter. Prior to the vote, I strongly encourage my Senate colleagues to review all documents provided by the Committee."

Here was the part I didn't fully get. It sounded like Senate Republicans planned to push ahead with a vote, regardless. I kept hearing from sources there were not enough Democratic votes to hit the high water mark of 33 votes (two-thirds) needed for removal. So why would they run it? Was this purely a political vote to let the Democrats buy into supporting Kane?

Apparently there had been some Democratic support but it withered away.

The part of me that's a historian recognizes that events rarely, if ever, happen for single reasons. Human beings often act on multiple layers of reasons. And there were many layers of motivation on the Kane vote.

The debate went on more than two hours. Only one Democrat spoke in favor of ousting her.

The vote to remove Kane failed 29-19. That means 29 senators voted to remove her—a clear majority. But it fell short of the standard required under the Constitution. One Republican Senator, Stewart Greenleaf, of Montgomery County, voted against removal. A sole Democrat voted with Republicans for removal: Sen. Rob Teplitz, of Dauphin County. Another GOP senator was missing due to a death in the family.

Senate Republicans held a news conference outside the Senate chamber immediately after the vote. Scarnati and Senate Majority Leader Jake Corman, R-Centre County, said it was not a political vote and was up to each member. The quick response of the new Democratic Supreme Court sustaining Kane's suspension was a factor in scheduling it quickly, Scarnati said.

But he added, "We weren't counting votes.

"The Senate had a duty to make a vote," Scarnati said. It was a matter of taking a stand against "corruption," Scarnati said, though he quickly noted he meant the loss of a law license not Kane's criminal case.

"This was the right thing to do," Scarnati added.

"It's clearly become a circus (on the attorney general's office) in my view and the view of many Pennsylvanians," said Scarnati.

But then the political fallout factor was certainly noted: "Clearly those who made their votes will have to defend their votes," Scarnati said.

Some cynics believed many Republicans wanted to leave Kane dangling through the 2016 election year as an albatross, perhaps, on Democratic candidates and to poison the AG's race for Dems.

I believe Scarnati, Gordner and other GOP senators did want to remove her. But they could not lose, politically, either way. If they voted her out it was a win politically. If the Democrats failed to support it, they would wear it.

A RELUCTANT YES

In perhaps the best and clearest oratory, Sen. Rob Teplitz, D-Harrisburg, showed at the same time why Democrats were wary of voting for removal but also why he thought she had to go. Teplitz, an attorney, has a reputation as a reformer. He is also in a district where he's potentially vulnerable. But he had the guts to break ranks with Democrats. Here is an excerpt of his floor speech:

> "Let me start by making clear what this vote is not about.
>
> "This is not a vote about whether Kathleen Kane is competent or incompetent in the performance of her duties.
>
> "This is not a vote as to whether Kathleen Kane is a victim of the legal or political process or whether she has violated the law herself.
>
> "This is not a vote as to whether Kathleen Kane should run for election, should be re-nominated by her party, or should ultimately win re-election.
>
> "And, significantly, this is not a vote about whether this body should have the power to remove a public official from her elected position under a specific, unique, and rarely used procedure.
>
> "That power already exists, whether we like it or not. I don't.
>
> "The exercise of that power is being considered today, whether we like it or not. I don't. And I really don't like the idea that three dozen people could overturn the will of three million voters.
>
> "I would also note that this vote today is not about whether or not Kathleen Kane meets the state constitutional requirement for eligibility to serve as Attorney General.
>
> "Our constitution requires that the Attorney General be 'a member of the bar.'
>
> "Based on court orders, rules, and case law, it is clear that an attorney is still a 'member of the bar,' despite the temporary suspension of her law license.

"If 'temporary suspension' meant 'disbarment,' we would all be required to vote for removal because Kathleen Kane would be constitutionally ineligible to serve as Attorney General. That would be an easy decision.

"But that is not the decision we must make today.

"Rather, what we have before us is a much narrower—some might say much more creative or even more ingenious —question. And that is this: whether an Attorney General whose license has been temporarily suspended can still perform the duties of that office and, if not, whether that person should be removed from office by this body.

"That is the question before us, and each of us must decide how to answer it. And let's be absolutely clear—the answer has nothing to do with job performance or political vendettas or porn e-mails.

"On this question, reasonable people can disagree, and none of us can be 100 percent certain that we know how to navigate these unchartered waters.

"There is a school of thought that an Attorney General without a law license can still perform the many administrative duties involved in running any large government agency, such as overseeing the personnel office, the comptroller's office, the purchasing office, the press office, and even the legislative office, and that an unlicensed Attorney General can be walled off from the legal decisions that need to be made and the actions that only a licensed lawyer can take.

"There was certainly testimony before the Special Committee to support that position.

"But that is a very narrow view of the job of Attorney General. It's not consistent with other testimony or with the expectations of the families and taxpayers of Pennsylvania, who—let's not forget—are the clients of the Attorney General.

"I have given this matter a tremendous amount of thought and attention, and I am informed in part by my own experience as a practicing lawyer in Pennsylvania for over 20 years, including eight years as the top lawyer for a large state government agency.

"I cannot escape the conclusion that, when people vote for an Attorney General, they are not voting for someone to merely oversee the administrative offices of that agency.

"They are voting for someone to use her legal experience, judgment, and skills and then act to pursue the mission of the agency in the best interest of the public, and to do so for the entirety of a four-year term.

"Quite simply, the position is 'Attorney General,' not 'Attorney and/or General.'

"Try as I might, I cannot separate the two. The public deserves more than just a 'General.' It deserves a licensed, practicing 'Attorney.'

"I feel no joy in reaching this conclusion, and I'm extremely concerned about the precedent we are setting today. My preference, which I stated publicly last summer under different circumstances, was for Kathleen Kane to resign voluntarily. That, obviously, has not occurred.

"Yet there is another process—impeachment—which has clear rules, standards, and burdens of proof, and which is viewed as much more credible than removal.

"The impeachment process is already beginning in the House of Representatives, and there is no urgency that requires us to use the removal process today. That would be my strong preference and would serve the interests of all parties involved in this unfortunate drama.

"There are some who feel that the Attorney General is being railroaded by this removal process, and I have more than a little sympathy for that view.

"But while I did not choose to get on this train, I feel compelled—for the reasons already stated—not to pull the emergency brake.

"Whether we like it or not, this question has been brought before us today. And I reluctantly vote yes."

* * *

It was a win for Kane, no question, if you consider a majority of the Senate voting to oust you a good thing. But it failed. Republicans filed for reconsideration meaning they can bring it up again if circumstances change. So there's no denying she dodged a bullet. Keisling left the Senate GOP news conference shouting about all the "sad faces" in the media—his way of saying the press was out to do her in.

"Today is a good day for all those who share my desire to restore confidence in our judges and prosecutors and integrity to our system of justice," Kane said in a statement. "Special prosecutor Gansler will press on, leaving no hate-filled email unread and no ex-parte communication uncovered, in our effort to deliver to all Pennsylvanians the system of justice we deserve, rather than the one we have now."

ROAD TRIP

The following week on the night of Feb. 15, 2016, an intriguing text popped up on my phone from Chuck Ardo, Kane's spokesman: "FOR PLANNING PURPOSES ONLY: The Attorney General is planning on making some remarks about the office in Scranton tomorrow afternoon. Specifics in media advisory in the A.M.

"That's all I know. Please no phone calls." It had been sent to a group of reporters who covered Kane.

So I called him. How could I not? He told me he didn't know what it was about.

The next morning, on Feb. 17, 2016, the advisory came from her office: "Attorney General Kane to remark on the future of the Office of Attorney General." It was listed as a "media availability" with Kane at 1:30 p.m. in the Cait Center, 417 Lackawanna Ave., which is also where Kane's Scranton office is located.

The future of the office of attorney general? WTF?

I called Ardo that morning. He knew no more, he said. I asked what time he was leaving. He offered to give me a ride. Sure, I told him. The rain wasn't letting up. There had been ice that morning. But by 9:45 when we left it had turned into a blinding rain. Sheets of rain. We shot up I-81 in his recently purchased black Ford Escape—a great ride. At times, I wondered as we passed trucks how he could see anything. It was like driving through a wave.

Reporters were calling and Chuck was trying to field the calls on the Ford's built-in phone on the dash. He fumbled with the incoming calls and texts. He admitted his technology skills were lagging, as were mine. Each time, he disclosed to reporters that I was in the car. He had to do that. Every reporter asked the same question, essentially. What was this about?

Her paid media consultant and spokesman didn't know.

At one point, he told a reporter he believed she was going to announce she was joining the astronaut corps.

Ardo was like that and everyone who had dealt with him knew to take his quips in stride. You can't blame him for breaking the boredom. He later counted 38 calls and 20 texts about the Scranton news conference.

We cruised toward Scranton, with requisite stops at Turkey Hill convenience stores for bathroom breaks and coffee. I considered the journalistic ethics of the situation. Was I taking a gift from a state-paid consultant by accepting the ride? I broached that with him. He said he'd forgo claiming mileage for the trip if need be. Nice offer, but that's nuts, I thought. If I wasn't with him, he would submit for mileage. I didn't want to stand in the way of him getting reimbursed for driving from Harrisburg to Scranton, about 120 miles one way. It wasn't costing the state more with me in the passenger seat. I decided I could even the score a bit by buying him lunch when we got to Scranton. He agreed.

Sometimes, the ethical questions journalists face border on the ridiculous. But they are worth pondering.

Still, here I was with the guy everyone else was trying to reach. He didn't know what Kane was doing, but he might find out. So it was the most advantageous place I could be that morning. Besides, I had a long professional relationship with Ardo going back to Rendell's first term. I first met him on Rendell's campaign bus in 2000. In the end it would only cost the Trib $28.73 total for two salads, coffees, and a tip at a deli across from the Scranton Times-Tribune office.

I started pre-writing the story in the car. I could imagine one outcome coming on the day nominating petitions were due with the Department of State to get on the ballot in the April 2016 primary: she would not run. My iPad was bouncing around on my lap as Ardo hit the gas and we shared stories about the Rendell days.

He was really getting fed up with Kane not keeping him informed.

More than anything it was the secrecy. Ardo never knew her schedule and she failed to communicate with him on several key events over the past few months.

MUSHROOM FARM

Ardo seriously detested Richard Nixon. So for him to describe the atmosphere under Kane as "Nixonian" said a lot. It was not an unfair appraisal: paranoia, breaking the rules to get an edge and payback to political enemies. Start with Kane allegedly ordering loyal staffers to spy on employees, and then directing the head of her security detail to conduct office computer searches for information on the grand jury investigating her. The aide, Patrick Reese, also searched for emails of the grand jury judge and special prosecutor—even Inquirer reporters McCoy and Couloumbus. Judge William Carpenter said he and his wife believe they were followed. Agents and deputy attorneys general told me they believed their desks were searched. Reese, the former Dunmore police chief and a Kane confidant, was convicted of indirect criminal contempt for defying a grand jury protective order by meddling with the computer system for grand jury information to help Kane.

Ardo did not dislike Kane. He actually thought she was a nice woman. Something though was wrong with her. Whether that existed all along or manifested itself later wasn't clear. But by mid-February 2016, he was close to turning in his ID card, phone, and bidding the office good bye. It was just nuts working there. Duecker, the chief of staff, sat in an office on one end of the room. Beemer, the first deputy, sat on the other. They didn't speak. The animus was palpable even among their secretaries. Beemer was the scapegoat, supposedly behind every slight or criticism of Kane, despite the fact he was the leader people in the office trusted.

Kane threw Ardo under the bus on a couple of occasions publicly blaming him for her own mistakes or shortcomings.

Kane's use of Ken Smukler made it untenable. She was obviously using him to write or advise on statements that Ardo never saw. It was not clear whether he was working for Kane personally or her campaign. It developed into a system of "parallel communication" with Smukler inserting himself into some issues with reporters. It should be noted Kane's fortunes were on the upswing with positive media stories–including some national press–with Smukler on board. But Ardo was representing OAG, the government, not Kane personally.

As of this writing, Ardo was still there. He liked most of the top staffers and attorneys he worked for including Beemer, Mulle and Cherba. He wanted to stay and help them through the transition but it seemed his time there had just about run out.

Even saints have their limits.

THE REMAINING QUESTION: KANE'S FINAL EXIT

There was pathos in watching the proud woman and former rising star of Pennsylvania politics announce she would not seek re-election. She said it was because she needed to be with her two sons, then aged 14 and 15. Her father, one of her sons and a niece stood by her at the press event. Her political operative Smukler was there. She gave a nine minute speech, pivoted and exited the room without answering questions. The reason she wasn't running was simple. She never mentioned it but she no longer had the organization to gather the 1,000 signatures needed in five counties to get on the ballot. "In a strange way this gives her more of a graceful exit, rather than suffering a humiliating defeat" in the April primary, said Jack Treadway, former chairman of the political science department at Kutztown State University. A Muhlenberg College poll, the week before her press event, showed her with an abysmally low 16 percent "re-elect" number—meaning that was the percentage of registered voters who said they would vote to re-elect her.

By Feb. 23, 2016, the House held its first hearing into the impeachment investigation of Kane. Dermody, the Democratic leader, told reporters later Kane's decision not to run "took the wind out of the sails" of impeachment for many Democrats because she'd be gone by the end of the year. But Rep. Todd Stephens, R-Montgomery County, the judiciary subcommittee chairman running the impeachment investigation, vowed to press ahead.

It defies credulity to think all will end well for her. The woman who came in to shake up the state's political system certainly did that. She would have been be a hero to the public if she had released all the porn and "offensive" emails *at once* in 2014, rather than parsing them out for her political and personal purposes, *and* if she had turned her shoulder and ignored Frank Fina.

"While her legal fate is unknown, her political fate is now sealed," G. Terry Madonna and Michael Young wrote in their column, Politically Uncorrected, distributed to newspapers across the state. "This one is over, the tale has been told and the full-sized lady is singing." As to what happened: "In the end, Kane's political demise was more a suicide than a homicide. Still, it's hard to see how her story might have turned out differently. Lack of experience, made worse by bad judgment, a temperament ill-suited for state politics and the tendency to make enemies doomed her," the political analysts wrote.

As of this writing, Kane is innocent of any crime. But she is guilty of staining the reputation and stature of the once proud Pennsylvania Office of Attorney General.

POSTSCRIPT

- On March 1, 2016, Rep. Marc Gergely, a McKeesport Democrat, was charged with using his political influence to help a family friend get video poker machines into bars and clubs. He maintains his innocence.
- On March 3, 2016, Patrick Reese, Kane's former head of security, was sentenced to three to six months in jail for contempt of court. Reese was allowed to stay free on bail while he appeals. Incredibly, Kane kept him on the state payroll as an investigator for about $100,000 per year despite his criminal conviction.
- On March 16, 2016, Justice Michael Eakin resigned amid the controversy over his racy and lewd emails.
- On March, 21, 2016, former Montgomery County District Attorney Bruce Castor, a Republican, became Solicitor General of the Office of Attorney General. Kane appointed him after creating the new position with a $150,000 annual salary pro-rated for the remainder

of her term. Castor became second in a command, a clear slap at Bruce Beemer, the first deputy. The move gave Kane an experienced prosecutor to help carry out legal decisions she clearly should not make. Beemer left the office in July, 2016 to become Inspector General for Gov. Tom Wolf.

- On March 24, 2016, the Court of Judicial Discipline in an order blasted Eakin's conduct and fined him $50,000. But he was allowed to keep his state pension (an estimated $140,000 maximum annual pension calculated by the Tribune-Review based on state figures). It includes his paycheck contributions from 21 years on the Supreme and Superior Courts.
- On March 28, 2016, Tyron Ali, the undercover informant in the sting case, made his first public appearance, testifying in court that he was never told to target blacks or exclude Republicans in the bribery investigation he helped conduct for the attorney general's office. Wearing a dark pinstripe suit, crisp white shirt and red tie, Ali testified at a hearing for Rep. Vanessa Brown, D-Philadelphia, the lone holdout in the sting case, who alleged racial targeting and entrapment through her attorney Patrick Casey. Brown continued to maintain her innocence.
- On April 21, 2016, the Associated Press reported Kane sent or received nearly 4,000 emails on AOL and Yahoo accounts dealing with attorney general-related business since she took office in Jane 2013 (through August 2015). Kane's office released about two-thirds of those emails under the state's Right to Know Law but deemed the remainder to be exempt. Kane transmitted confidential information and other emails that provided identities of undercover agents, the AP story reported. A policy established in 2009 makes doing so a fireable offense. Ardo told the AP since Kane sets office policy she had the authority to exempt herself.
- On July 19, 2016, a U.S. District judge dismissed the defamation suit Fina, Pennsylvania State Police Commissioner Noonan, and three others filed against Kane in November 2015. Judge Harvey Bartle III said

Kane's comments were "mere speech" and the plaintiffs did not suffer concrete economic damages.

- Also on July 19, 2016, Castor revealed he had approved a settlement to a gender discrimination complaint filed by Kane's twin Ellen Granahan, a deputy prosecutor heading the Internet predator unit. Granahan filed the complaint against the agency at the Equal Opportunity Employment Commission. Castor approved a 20 percent pay hike and $80,000 for back pay, legal fees and emotional distress. Castor said he found no evidence of gender discrimination but that Granahan had been discriminated against because she's Kane's sister. Granahan had been hired by former Republican Attorney General Tom Corbett.
- Castor, hired in March to the new post of solicitor general in July 2016, became first deputy, after Beemer departed, to become inspector general with the Wolf administration.
- Former state Treasurer Barbara Hafer was indicted on July 21, 2016, by a federal grand jury for allegedly concealing $500,000 in consulting fee payments in 2005 after she left the Department of Treasury. Hafer, 72, of Indiana, Pa., served two terms as auditor general, the state's fiscal watchdog, from 1989-1997 and two terms as treasurer, the state chief fiscal custodian and investment overseer from 1997 to 2005. U.S. Attorney Peter Smith said Hafer was charged with two counts of making false statements to federal agents when she was interviewed last May. "It's part of an ongoing "pay to play" investigation in state government by the FBI and IRS," authorities said.

Here's the bottom line. Despite her huge margin of victory in 2012, we still don't really know Kathleen Kane. Taking over an office controlled by Republicans since its inception in 1981, Kane had a long line of critics and, perhaps, people trying to trip her and definitely some wanting to see her fail. She wasn't carefully vetted in 2012. She was in over her head. Through her own ego-driven actions, driven by an obsession for revenge and virtual paranoia over any perceived disloyalty, she made serious mistakes. Whether those actions rise to the level of crimes—whether they can be proven beyond a reasonable doubt—remains to be seen. But the Office of Attorney General was tarnished and it will take years to recover its reputation as a top law enforcement agency.

* * *

(Sources: Bumsted, Tribune-Review article in February 2016 on the failed Senate vote; Bumsted, Tribune-Review in January 2016 on Rendell's testimony before the Senate panel; Bumsted, Tribune-Review in February 2016 on the House impeachment effort; Kane statement released after the Senate vote; copy of Senate Resolution No. 284; Supreme Court order in February 2016 on Kane's licensing; Bumsted, Tribune-Review, January 2016, on disciplinary counsel arguments on license; interview with James Mundy, Kane's attorney; Final Committee Report on Special Senate Committee on Address; Aaron Aupperlee's Tribune-Review story on Kane's campaign finance in February 2016. Couloumbis and McCoy's story on the Kane removal vote in the Philadelphia Inquirer; the Inquirer piece on the Supreme Court ruling on Kane's license; Bumsted, 2016 Tribune-Review on the Senate removal vote and Kane's announcement that she would not run; story on Scranton press event by Philadelphia Inquirer, Couloumbus and McCoy; Montgomery County criminal complaints against Kane and Reese, 2015; testimony at Reese's trial; Chris Palmer, Inquirer story on Oct. 30, 2015, tracking release of the porn emails; my 2016 column on Kane's Scranton press conference announcing she would not run; July 20, 2016 Philadelphia Inquirer story by Craig McCoy on Fina's suit; and July 19, 2016 stories by the Morning Call and Tribune-Review on Castor settling Granahan's complaint and Castor's new position.)

* * *

Next: Scandal erupts at Liquor Control Board.

25

LCB'S "DON'T ASK DON'T TELL" CULTURE

Sept. 15, 2015

It was probably decades ago that I last attended a Liquor Control Board meeting. I covered the state agency sporadically in the past but usually from the broader perspective of privatization. Suffice to say, the meeting I attended on July 15, 2015, at which the three-member board would consider a "bottle fee" for new items reminded me of my early days as a reporter covering township and borough meetings in Franklin County in the early 1970s for the Chambersburg Public Opinion. The liquor board members ripped through the agenda with very little discussion and with unanimous votes on all issues. Any concerns members might have had were obviously worked out in advance. An industry representative in the audience who I was told might explain opposition to the fee proposal said very little.

Everything on the agenda was rubber-stamped.

Changing Pennsylvania's state-owned and operated system of selling liquor and wine was a priority for prior Republican governors Dick Thornburgh, Tom Ridge and Tom Corbett. Democratic Gov. Milton Shapp, looking at it from a businessman's perspective, favored selling the state stores but never made it a huge priority.

Needless to say, they failed.

Regular meetings of the three-member board overseeing Pennsylvania's 600-plus Wine & Spirits stores were not high on my must-do list through the years.

In 2012, the Tribune-Review assigned the agency to Kari Andren, who previously worked for the Patriot-News and had twice been an intern with the Pennsylvania Legislative

Correspondents Association. She knew her way around the Capitol. She was based in Greensburg but it gave her a chance to specialize. Kari made periodic trips to the capital.

In July 2015, she couldn't attend an LCB meeting and asked me to go because one of the agenda items could be newsworthy.

BEHIND CLOSED DOORS

I walked over to the drab-looking Northwest Office Building on Forester Street, looking forward (sort of) to an agency meeting of a board I'd never seen, and on an issue—a "handling fee"—that I knew nothing about. That's not uncommon for reporters at any level. You sometimes go to government meetings or write about issues "cold."

I only knew of one, the chairman, by reputation. Tim Holden was a former Central Pennsylvania congressman who'd been a sheriff and "Blue Dog" or conservative Democrat and ex-Schuylkill County sheriff. He served in Congress from 1993-2012 and was appointed to the board by Governor Wolf. Holden lost the 2012 primary, a casualty of new congressional boundaries drawn by a Republican state House and Senate. Joseph E. "Skip" Brion, of Chester County, was an appointee of former Republican Governor Corbett. So was Michael Negra, of Centre County.

The board meets twice a month. Brion and Negra are paid $74,494 annually. Holden makes $77,548 (as of 2015).

My instincts about how they operate—largely behind closed doors—proved correct at least historically. Turns out in November 2012, Andren wrote a story saying that a Trib analysis of three years' worth of the board's meeting showed most lasted 15-20 minutes with little or no public discussion. It was crucial, at that time, after the board had decided to issue eight of its own brands of wine and liquor.

Andren reported that while the brands such as Table Leaf, Hayes Valley and Zita, LA MERIKA, were approved at public meetings, the agendas and minutes didn't reflect that members were voting on the private labels. Critics said the state-issued brands were part of an agency effort at self-preservation as a Republican legislature was actively considering privatization.

If they are saying nothing in public that means, in most cases, things have been worked out in advance.

In other words, it's greased.

The board's business is a bit more open these days, with thick agendas posted two days before meetings and a larger more "open" room.

But operating for years out of the sunlight and with very little scrutiny breeds the kind of arrogance displayed with the secret approval of their own brands of liquor and wine and with what would later be called a "don't ask don't tell" culture of gift taking from booze vendors.

TEE TIME

When Marketing Director James H. Short went to golf outings sponsored by liquor and wine vendors—with drinks, dinner, hotel, swag bags and airfare on some occasions—he typically treated them as ordinary workdays. So did his superiors. He was paid his state salary of $55 an hour (2010) and he typically charged the state for mileage.

Sometimes the outings were close to home like the Alliance Golf Open at the West Shore Country Club in Camp Hill. Other industry-paid trips included a 2011 Alliance Golf Open in Phoenixville with 18 holes, a "19th hole" at 5 p.m. for cocktails then dinner at the Parc Bistro in Skippack. The Alliance open events were held in different cities each year to let vendors have "face time with PLCB officials."

Short would venture much farther from home. He twice received all-expense paid golf trips to Naples, Florida, and another industry-sponsored outing to Pebble Beach, California. The Pebble Beach trip was courtesy of W.J. Deutsch and Sons, a distributor with products including Yellow Tail wines.

He traveled to California as part of the LCB's Chairman's Select program. Capital Wine and Spirits and Majestic covered the tab, records show. Capital Wine and Spirits, Bacardi USA, Brown Forman and Remy Cointreau paid for his Pennsylvania outings.

Short was following the lead of his bosses, CEO Joe Conti and Board Chairman Patrick Stapleton, in attending such events. The three were required to repay a combined $23,232 for the value of gifts they received from 2008-2012, according to a March 2014 Ethics Commission report. An array of liquor and wine companies paid for trips, gifts and pricey bottles of wine and in one case, an engraved bottle of top shelf scotch.

The three former LCB officials were also required to amend their financial disclosure statements.

They didn't report the freebies as required by state law.

Why would liquor companies go to this trouble? Pennsylvania's LCB is the largest purchaser of wine and spirits in the U.S. These were the top guys at an agency with more than $2 billion in sales. Getting good shelf space in Pennsylvania's 600-plus stores translated into big bucks for liquor and wine companies.

Paying for trips and golf outings provides access to top officials—and good will.

Short accounted for $13,582 of the money repaid. Stapleton's total was $7,258 and Conti's was $2,388.

Conti told the Inquirer he considered the investigation fair. Stapleton admitted he might have been "sloppy in how I addressed some of these interactions." But Stapleton said the dealings "served a true business purpose."

THE GOOD LIFE

Conti received a bottle of Johnny Walker Blue from a Diageo representative with the engraving "super CEO."

While Short was on vacation in Hilton Head, he was delivered six bottles of wine and a bottle of Woodford Reserve bourbon, Pennlive reported. He received more than $1,700 in gift cards and a shirt and cuff links valued at $418 from Neiman Marcus.

Diageo gave Short a golf flag autographed by Arnold Palmer. Another vendor gave him an iPad2 worth $500.

The "bright line" rule adopted by the former LCB's director of administration didn't apply to the marketing staff, the employees helping to decide inventory and product.

Still, state law makes it a felony for LCB employees or their families to accept gifts from vendors. The Ethics Commission didn't forward the case for criminal prosecution.

Attorney General Kathleen Kane had a conflict with her family ties to Kane Is Able, which held a $12.4 million warehouse and trucking contract from the LCB. Her then-husband Chris still sat on the board. But Andren reported in October 2014, a federal grand jury was looking at improper relationships between wine and spirits vendors and the agency.

STRIP CLUBS

Former LCB Product Manager Timothy Fringer was dinged by the Ethics Commission more than a year later. He "routinely" accepted meals, tickets to pro sports events, hotel stays and gifts. He was wined and dined and entertained by vendors in strip clubs.

His freebies included Eagles and Steelers games; a promotional event at Savannah's on Hanna, a Harrisburg strip club, and entertainment at Delilah's, a Philly strip club; tickets to Kid Rock Concerts in Hershey, Virginia Beach and Las Vegas; tickets to Dave Matthews concerts in Philadelphia and New York with his wife; and a third-base-line ticket to a 2009 World Series game in Philadelphia valued at $687.

The amount he was required to pay in restitution was $7,180.

Fringer told the Ethics Commission he was doing what his boss, Short, told him to do.

Short told him to take the gifts and as long as no one complained "it's like it never happened." Fringer left his $58,563 a year job and went to work for Constellation Brands, which provided him with $1,600 in hospitality.

On their birthdays and Christmas, LCB employees received gift cards from vendors and on other occasions received sample bottles of wine and spirits, Fringer told investigators.

"The general atmosphere related to vendors providing gifts, hospitality, etc. to PLCB employees was 'don't ask don't tell,'" the Ethics Commission order said.

Holden, who wasn't in office during the gift spree, said he was working "diligently" to inform employees on the law regarding vendor interactions. Under Wolf's gift ban, even accepting a pen or T-shirt would be prohibited. Then again, it was already a felony to take gifts from vendors.

DAY OF RECKONING

On Sept. 15, 2015, in U.S. District Court in Harrisburg Short had to fess up. It was almost anti-climatic. Short, who had been wined and dined by vendors, was humble and contrite as he appeared before U.S. District Judge Sylvia Rambo. The once powerful director of marketing and merchandising answered the court in short, crisp phrases.

"Yes, your honor," he told Rambo, when she asked if it was his desire to plead guilty to mail fraud. The plea was for taking kickbacks—cash, travel, booze, hotel fare and golf outings from a vendor in 2010 and 2011. But by pleading guilty, he admitted to approximately 10 years of receiving benefits from an alcohol distributor and manufacturer, prosecutors said.

Wearing a navy suit, white shirt and gray-blend tie, Short, 50, stood before Rambo while his wife, Denise Dunbar, his father-in-law and pastor watched from the rear of the courtroom.

Short, of Harrisburg, faced a maximum 20 years in prison and a $250,000 fine. His unreported trips at vendors' expense helped put or keep their products on the LCB's shelves.

The U.S. attorney's office said Short was charged "with accepting things of value from the (vendors) with the intent to be influenced in decisions he made to recommend new products and remove others from Pennsylvania liquor stores."

The practice was unseemly and against the law.

* * *

(Sources: Ethics Commission order on Short; Andren's June 2015 Tribune-Review story on Fringer; a Pennlive story and sidebar by Jeff Frantz on the Ethics Commission ruling on Conti, Stapleton and Short in March 2014; the Philadelphia Inquirer's story on those three LCB executives by Chris Palmer and Tricia L. Nadolny also from March 2014; Andren's November 2012 Tribune-Review story on LCB's failure to meet spirit of open meetings law; Trib story I did with Andren on the bottle "handling" fee in July 2015; Andren's October 2014 story on federal grand jury; my coverage of Short's plea in federal court in September 2015; press release from U.S. attorney from Middle District of Pennsylvania.)

* * *

Next: The Federal Sting.

26

THE FEDERAL STING

When he was at the top of his game in 2003, John H. Estey directed one of the most aggressive legislative agendas in decades: Gov. Ed Rendell's Plan for a New Pennsylvania. It included legalizing casinos that would provide revenue for property tax cuts, a stimulus plan fueled by borrowing that would boost the economy, and closing a budget deficit and boosting education spending by increasing the income tax, as well as other taxes. The plan was to get this done while working with a Republican legislature.

Estey, a Philadelphia lawyer, was driving the bus.

Rendell got most of it, though the property tax cuts would be panned as minimal and heightened spending under Rendell would become an increasingly attractive target for the GOP. Still, the plan was bold and ambitious.

It took two years to get most of Rendell's plan through the legislature. Casinos became the crowning achievement in 2004.

Twelve years later, Estey hit bottom when he walked into a federal courtroom with his lawyer Ronald Levine. On May 10, 2016, Estey pleaded guilty to wire fraud. The case was a shocker to the political establishment when it broke a little more than a week before at the end of April.

It's not just that Estey, a respected figure at the Capitol as a former Ballard Spahr law firm partner, was admitting to in effect stealing $13,000 from an undercover FBI agent. What gripped the Capitol crowd was the fact that the feds flipped Estey as far back as 2011 and he wore a wire for the federal government. It was not known at the time of his plea how long he did so. But the idea that John Estey was recording conversations for the feds to make criminal cases was huge.

The day of his plea, Estey walked into court wearing a navy blue suit, light blue shirt and blue tie. His appearance was a bit of a surprise. His close-cropped hair had turned from brown to white. Admittedly it was probably nine years since I'd seen him. But he was 53 years old and he'd lost weight. He'd really aged. The stress of a criminal case, plus acting as an undercover operative for the FBI, could be daunting. Still, his right hand was steady as he was sworn in. His voice didn't quake or waver as he told U.S. District Judge John E. Jones III on the ninth floor of the federal building in Harrisburg that he understood the rights he was waving by pleading guilty.

Estey left Rendell's staff in 2007.

What a mess he'd gotten himself into. From 2009 through 2011 Estey represented a fake company created by the FBI—Textbook Bio Solutions LLC. The company wanted legislation approved to purchase surplus textbooks for developing countries and recycle unusable books into "pellets" to provide alternative fuel for underdeveloped nations. Someone at the FBI certainly knew the political mind quite well. The fake concept supposedly kept piles of text books out of trash dumps, helped poor countries, and appealed to the environmentally sensitive legislator. In the early going, Estey obviously didn't know the company was phony or the representatives he was dealing with were FBI agents. If he had, he never would have kept $13,000 of $20,000 they gave him for campaign contributions to lawmakers. That was another FAQ about this case: Why would a guy who would go on to make $735,919 in compensation at Hershey Trust need to pocket $13,000?

Also why would the FBI let a carefully-cultivated operative go to Hershey Trust to work out a consent decree with the attorney general's office? Was he working that for the feds then? Estey was hired by the Hershey Trust as acting general counsel. By 2013, he became a top executive at the trust. The position seemed "too cozy for some observers," according to *The Chocolate Trust* by Bob Fernandez, considering Adrian King's position as first deputy of Kane's office, which was investigating the trust. They were after all, brothers-in-law. But King had recused himself and had "no involvement whatsoever in the matter," a spokeswoman for Kane's office was quoted as saying.

I didn't know Estey that well when he worked for Rendell but I talked with him or emailed him on occasion. I saw him in the hallways. I thought he was a decent guy. He wasn't arrogant like some of the Philadelphians Rendell brought into Harrisburg, who thought it was outrageous there was no Starbucks in the state cafeteria. (In no time at all, a Starbucks mini-station became a new addition to the Capitol.)

The timing is often an oddity in federal cases. The feds had Estey in their pocket since 2011. That's five years before they charged him. Federal cases seemingly take forever. There is typically no political pressure to get the cases done.

If this was an expansive sting, my first thought was 'it was about time.' But as of this writing (May 2016), there was no way to tell for sure whether we would see an explosion. Talk swirled that some top political figures might go down.

But maybe Estey's plea was the end. Experts thought otherwise.

"You could not conclude it's the end of it," Bruce Antkowiak, a former federal prosecutor, told the Tribune-Review. "The possibility exists the federal government is looking at charges against other people."

"It's not likely a situation where they tried and didn't get anybody," added Antkowiak, a law professor at Saint Vincent College in Latrobe. "These things are done with a considerable degree of investment by the federal government."

It certainly seemed unlikely that Estey, an ex-chief of staff, had been a prime target. He was an important player in state government but not a big fish.

Had the feds been after his boss, Rendell? Was it about Hershey Trust? The legislature? Or was the lobbying community in Harrisburg about to take a direct hit?

Rendell was the most obvious answer for people looking at it. There was no evidence he or anyone at Hershey Trust had done anything wrong. "Ed Rendell doesn't have a criminal bone in his body," said Ardo, his former spokesman. "Some of his bones may have been fractured and badly reassembled, but they aren't criminal." People at the Capitol typically said of Rendell, a former district attorney, that he knew where the line was, sometimes inched right up to it, but he wouldn't cross it. The Hershey Trust came up in the gossip mill only because Estey worked there.

Estey struck me as a straight arrow, a buttoned-down lawyer from a mega Philly firm. He had been a deputy mayor of Philadelphia when Rendell served as mayor.

It's just not clear what led Estey off course.

JITTERY LOBBYISTS

The thought that federal agents were recording their conversations left some lobbyists at the Capitol more than a bit nervous. They had to wonder whether a colleague or state official they were about to talk to was wearing a wire and might be a federal undercover informant.

The jokes about it were only *half* in jest, one lobbyist told me.

The safest place to cut a deal in Harrisburg was the YMCA's steam room.

Another lobbyist told me he was going through his client list to make sure all the companies were real.

WEB OF RECORDINGS

There were more reasons than just the Estey revelations for legislators, current and former state officials, to suspect the FBI might have been listening:

-- Former State Treasurer Rob McCord pleaded guilty to extortion for shaking down state contractors for campaign money when he ran for governor in 2014. His phone was tapped, court documents suggest. It was later reported McCord also wore a wire.

There is a link between Estey and McCord's 2014 campaign. The Trib reported Estey was co-owner of a Political Action Committee, the Enterprise Fund, which mysteriously gave $125,000 to McCord *after* he lost the governor's race. You wouldn't know on the surface Estey was involved. His name was in the PAC registration statement.

-- McCord's former chief of staff, John Lesko, received notice from the feds his phone conversations were tapped for a month in 2014, the Trib also reported. Lesko was not accused of wrongdoing.

-- Mike Fleck, former political aide to Allentown Mayor Ed Pawlowski, wore a wire for the FBI, the Morning Call reported, and the mayor once patted him down in an elevator. Pawlowski is at the center of a pay to play investigation. He denies wrongdoing. Fleck worked briefly for McCord when Pawlowski dropped out of the governor's race. McCord finished third.

--Estey and a John Miles (really an FBI agent), of Textbook Bio Solutions, sprinkled campaign contributions to lawmakers recommended by Estey. In 2010, twenty senators signed onto a bill to authorize the "company" to launch its textbook recycling plan. It was sponsored by Sen. Ray Musto, D-Pittston, shortly before Musto would be charged in a separate federal corruption case. Among other things, he was accused of bribery. The charges were dismissed in 2014 before he died. He was leaving office anyway in 2010, and passage of the Textbook Bio Solutions bill was viewed as a final salute to Musto.

The fact that a bill for the phony company passed the Senate unanimously, was "absolutely jaw-dropping," said Christopher Borick, a political science professor at Muhlenberg College. It died in the House, though it would be reintroduced the next year by Musto's successor, Sen. John Yudichak, D-Luzerne County.

Yudichak and many other senators I contacted said they had no idea it was a fake company or an FBI front. Estey, as a former Ballard Spahr partner and Rendell's top guy, had credibility with lawmakers. Lobbyists depend on accuracy for their reputations. Think about it. Would you believe a prominent member of the bar would ask you to cast a vote for a company that didn't exist?

YET ONE MORE INDICTMENT

An odd thing happened on the day Estey pleaded guilty. Later that day, the Department of Justice in Washington issued a press release saying a state senator was indicted for a bribery, vote-buying, and fraud scheme. Sen. Lawrence Farnese, D-Philadelphia, 47, allegedly paid $6,000 to a college study-abroad program for an Eighth Ward Democratic Committee woman's daughter as he attempted to become the Eighth Ward chairman. The woman, Ellen Chapman, 62, was also charged. Farnese made the payments in 2011 from his campaign fund. Farnese falsely listed it as a "donation" on his campaign finance report. They maintained their innocence.

It was an unusual case, and some thought it was a bit bogus given it was for a political office not public office. But the timing was interesting. The same day as Estey pleads guilty? A coincidence? It also concerned Farnese's actions in 2011 when Estey began cooperating.

Trying to read the tea leaves of federal prosecutors though is a pointless prospect.

The most common phrase heard after Estey's plea was "who knows?"

(Sources: Joint Statement of Facts, Information, Plea Agreement, in United States of America v. John H. Estey, defendant, filed April 29, 2016, in U.S. District Court; press release from U.S. attorney's office, Middle District of Pennsylvania, on Estey being charged; Department of Justice, Washington D.C., on May 10, 2016, on indictment of Farnese; legislative history of Senate Bill 1379 on Pennsylvania General Assembly's web site; May 8, 2016, story by Craig McCoy, Angela Couloumbis and Mark Fazlollah, Philadelphia Inquirer, on Estey wearing a wire; Pittsburgh Tribune-Review story by Tom Fontaine on Estey being charged, April 29, 2016; May 2, 2016, story by Fontaine on Estey being fired; Story by Fazlollah, McCoy and Couloumbis detailing the sting; Estey's guilty plea May 20, 2016, by Bumsted, Tribune-Review; Lesko's phone was tapped, Bumsted, Tribune-Review, October 2015; Morning Call story on Pawlowski's consultant wearing a wire, July 2015; also as noted above, *The Chocolate Trust,* Camino Books, 2015, by Bob Fernandez; Bumsted, Tribune-Review, May 9, 2016, on Estey's expected guilty plea; Bumsted on May 10, 2016, Tribune-Review, "Estey plea may not be the end of sting"; Bumsted column, May 15, 2016, portions of which are incorporated into this chapter.)

* * *

Next: In the Final Analysis.

27

IN THE FINAL ANALYSIS

As a transplanted Californian, Laurel Brandstetter knew next to nothing about Pennsylvania politics. The first time she was asked about Mike Veon, the former House Democratic Whip, she had to google his name. So she came at the corruption cases like the Beaver Initiative for Growth, turnpike and a gaming board investigation from what she calls an "outsider's perspective" while serving as a prosecutor in the attorney general's office.

So much later, when asked about the root of Pennsylvania corruption she had answers—gut level answers—that jive with decades of political science literature and corruption experts.

Just why the state produces so much public corruption isn't due to any single cause. It ranked fifth in a study by the University of Hong Kong and Indiana University, Bloomington from 1976 through 2008. That study is skewed because it is only based on federal prosecutions. State corruption convictions in Pennsylvania have gone through the roof.

Brandstetter, of Pittsburgh's Stanton Heights neighborhood, believes corruption continued because the legislature didn't enact major reforms following scandals that rocked House Democrats—and later Republicans—for using public resources for campaigns. The grand jury that recommended criminal charges against Democratic staffers and lawmakers, for taxpayer-paid bonuses for campaign work, had urged sweeping changes. There were some minimal changes enacted by legislative rules.

It was called the "mad as hell" grand jury by former Grand Jury Judge Barry Feudale because that is how jurors felt after the Bonusgate corruption case and testimony from a Rutgers University expert on legislatures. Duplication of services, high levels of partisanship, a bloated staff, all geared to incumbency protection and partisan edge in the next election mark in Pennsylvania's system. Yeah, I know, prosecutors can get grand juries to do whatever they choose. But Jerry Sterner, foreman of that grand jury, told me they were an independent bunch and no stooges for the prosecutors. The report called for term limits, staff reductions—essentially returning to a part-time legislature. But I doubt the grand jurors wrote it.

Ex-speaker John Perzel, a convicted felon, explained the scrambling for every campaign edge that led to his conviction. If yours is not the party in power you have nothing. The controlling party picks the committee chairmen, decides which bills to vote and what policy to enact. It is a winner takes all system, he testified in 2012. It's the motive behind the mad scramble for campaign cash.

It is driven by the partisanship and the taxpayer-fueled caucuses that the grand jury called for eliminating. It stood no chance because it was against lawmakers' self-interest of getting re-elected with partially-taxpayer funded campaigns and continuing to reap benefits like lifetime health care, per diems ($163) for reporting to work and salaries always among the top tier in the nation ($85,338 in 2015) with automatic increases virtually every year based on inflation.

When a report like the ground-shaking Bonusgate grand jury presentment is shelved, "that sends a huge message," Brandstetter said.

"There's an old-school quality to Pennsylvania (politics)," she said. "I don't know that Pennsylvania has seen the structural changes that other states have. You have old-time politicians ruling the roost."

Mark D. Schwartz, a Bryn Mawr lawyer and former Democratic House staffer for the late Speaker Leroy Irvis, said too much money is available.

"There are too many ways to siphon money out of the system," he said, citing state funds, campaign money and nonprofits founded or influenced by lawmakers.

"I blame the professionalization of the legislature" that began under former Speaker Herbert Fineman, himself a convicted felon. The move to a professional "full-time" legislature has meant "more corruption," he said.

None other than corruption expert James Wedick, a retired 35-year FBI agent, validates what Brandstetter and Schwartz are saying. He was one of the agents on the Abscam sting operation on Congress and New Jersey officials, which began in the 1970s and is portrayed in the movie *American Hustle,* in which members of Congress were videotaped taking would-be bribes from a phony sheik.

Now a consultant in Sacramento, Wedick in a 2014 interview did not hesitate when asked to explain what might foster the "culture of corruption" that analysts identify in Pennsylvania's General Assembly, marked by the arrest of a state senator that week as the 15th current or former lawmaker accused of corruption since 2007. Ironically, the Pennsylvania sting case run by Fina was about to explode the day the Wedick interview was published in the Trib.

"It's money," said Wedick. "There's a lot of money to go around in professional (full-time) legislatures," such as those in Pennsylvania, California, New York and Michigan. "It's a way for (legislators) to bleed assets from the state without anyone really knowing."

The Pennsylvania General Assembly is the second largest in the nation with 253 members. Only New Hampshire's citizen legislature is larger and it is part-time. Then again so is Pennsylvania's behemoth. It is clearly not a full-time body as members pretend. Members are in session 70 to 80 days year. They are gone two to three months every summer and they take weeks to campaign.

The full-time status is a sham.

Only overwhelming citizen demands would change it. It would take a charismatic populist governor with huge voter approval ratings and a commitment to serve only one term to lead the charge.

And then it still might not happen.

Legislative leaders take the long view. They'd wait the governor out—unless their constituents were angry enough.

New in the reform arena, at least in Pennsylvania, is a proposal to clean up lobbying in Harrisburg. The idea comes from a lobbyist, Stan Rapp, partner in one of the largest and most prominent firms in the capital city. He contends lawyers who lobby should have to register and not "hide behind the Supreme Court" rulings that their work on Capitol Hill is protected by attorney-client privilege, firms should disclose specific amounts spent to entertain legislators and lobbyists shouldn't be able to lobby on issues a lawmaker is involved in and also help run their campaigns. Rapp argues it will happen eventually so lawmakers should get ahead of the issue. After he raised it, the issue fell like a deflated balloon.

* * *

What about the executive branch? In recent decades Pennsylvania governors have not faced legal troubles for misusing their office. However, state officeholders have—from former Auditor General Al Benedict, to ex-Treasurer Budd Dwyer, Ernie Preate, the former attorney general, former Treasurer Rob McCord, and Attorney General Kathleen Kane, faced criminal charges.

Campaign finance abuse runs as a thread through most of those cases. I've never been a fan of limiting campaign contributions, but maximum donation levels by individuals and Political Action Committees like those for federal candidates might curb some of the madness. But politicians always find ways around it.

Now Super PACs can accept unlimited contributions from individuals, corporations and unions to make "independent" expenditures. They can't coordinate with campaigns or parties, but there's no legal limit on donation size.

We now see out-of-state PACs for national Republican and Democratic governor's associations and attorney general's associations pump big money into the contested state races.

Barry Kauffman, executive director of Common Cause, has long advocated campaign donation limits and public financing of governor's races. Using tax money for political campaigns in my view uses scarce resources that might otherwise pay for education, law enforcement and key social services.

What about self-financing? Donating way beyond those limits for oneself?

I personally don't mind Tom Wolf spending $10 million of his own money to get elected. He forgoes a state salary and pays for his own security detail and office in Mt. Wolf.

His critics say he more than makes up for it in terms of giveaways to unions and educators. Others call it buying an election.

But voters, many of whom may be ill-informed on issues and too few of whom actually vote, are nonetheless discriminating. Remember Ross Perot?

Wolf's moves may be symbolic, but they are an example of ethics at the top. Combined with a gift ban, those moves may help steer state employees in the right direction.

You run the risk rich leaders will be out of touch. But they are far less susceptible to financial corruption. They don't need it and wouldn't risk it. Wealthy ketchup heir John Heinz, the late Republican U.S. senator, is a good example. He was clean with never a hint of scandal.

Kauffman would also like to see an independent prosecutor law re-established to avoid some of the legal "mess" that occurred in the Kane case with questions and legal challenges over the appointment of a special prosecutor to investigate her. The state's independent counsel law expired in 2003. To avoid continuing questions, Rep. Mike Vereb, R-Montgomery County, was pushing legislation "so the process is very clear about who can bring a case against the attorney general in the future."

"We want to restore the public's trust in the attorney general's office," Vereb said. "We need to establish in law an independent process for reviewing the legality of actions taken by the Commonwealth's top prosecutor." His bill calls for the creation of an independent, three-member panel of judges to oversee the appointment of an independent prosecutor.

Under the heading of transparency, what's sorely needed is a user-friendly state elections bureau web site. Now it's useless, a joke.

It is likely that way on purpose: to shield elected state officials, Kauffman said.

The Wolf administration at this writing had a team working on the web site with hope of revamping it for greater public access.

Pennwatch, the state web site where salaries and other data can be accessed, is virtually useless. It's for micro searches not macro data gathering. It's good for looking up a single salary but you can't download salaries of say, an entire agency. I had high hopes for Pennwatch when it was created by the legislature a few years ago. It's better than where we were 10 years ago but not nearly where we need to be today for real transparency—that buzz word pols use so frequently but seldom adhere to with any real commitment.

Again, it is no doubt intentional to keep the prying public and bothersome journalists less informed.

Matthew Brouillette, president and CEO of the Commonwealth Foundation, a free market think tank, advocates moving the inspector general out of the governor's office and creating an independent agency with the same powers and staff. The inspector general charged with rooting out fraud is beholden to the governor who is the appointing authority, he says. Sen. Ryan Aument, R-Lancaster, has a bill to do just that and create six-year terms for the inspector general. The nominees for inspector would require Senate confirmation by a two-thirds vote under Aument's bill.

That would provide some scrutiny for the person holding the post. Who can name the state inspector general, who usually wears proverbial green eyeshades and works out of the limelight?

Wolf's choice was Grayling Williams, a 30-year-law enforcement official with experience at the federal Drug Enforcement Agency, Homeland Security, Baltimore Police Department and state attorney general's office. He headed internal affairs in the Baltimore PD.

"When was the last time you heard the OIG (Office of Inspector General) announce significant cases of 'fraud, waste, abuse and misconduct in any agency?' Brouillette said. 'Is it because there isn't any? Or is it, more likely, that an IG serving at the Governor's pleasure is not about to publically and dramatically expose illegal or unethical behavior by the Governor's employees?'"

Most of the agency's work is detecting and preventing welfare fraud but it also does special investigations. Michael Sprow, a former corruption prosecutor who previously worked for Corbett in the attorney general's office, was the previous inspector general. In 2012, investigators uncovered the gifts and trips paid for by liquor vendors to LCB officials. The report itself wasn't public but the results were leaked to the Inquirer. It led to the ethics case and the federal investigation.

It's been frustrating that most of the agency's work has been shrouded in secrecy unless criminal cases are filed. Wolf moved to make summaries public record.

Moving the office out of the governor's office would achieve more independence. But Eugene DePasquale, the state's auditor general, is already an independently elected statewide fiscal watchdog with jurisdiction in the governor's office and executive branch agencies. He says Ament's proposal is worth considering but redundant.

The real scandal in Pennsylvania politics over decades is the fact that the auditor general cannot audit the legislature, said G. Terry Madonna, a political science professor at Franklin & Marshall College who by training is a historian.

Former Auditor General Barbara Hafer, a Republican who later became a Democrat, tried to audit WAMs (Walking Around Money), the funds divvied up among the caucuses—tucked into executive branch budgets such as the Department of Community and Economic Development—and doled out by leaders for lawmakers' pet projects. They were used to reward loyalty among the rank and file. They were also a "cudgel" leaders could use to garner votes and keep the rank and file in line, ex-Speaker DeWeese said in his heyday.

If Hafer had auditing authority over the legislature and WAMs, that would likely have saved taxpayers hundreds of millions of dollars and prevented much corruption, said DePasquale, a Democrat elected in 2012. Former Sen. Vincent Fumo's non-profit that he abused was funded with WAMs. So was former House Democratic Whip Mike Veon's non-profit, BIG (Beaver Initative for Growth). Both were convicted for misusing non-profits.

Opponents say it violates separation of powers principles, but DePasquale, an attorney, isn't convinced it would.

DePasquale incidentally is the only one of three statewide row office officials elected that year to remain unscathed by scandal or corruption. McCord has resigned and Kane self-imploded. Entering 2013 at their swearing in, I believed both Kane and DePasquale would provide a check and balance on former Governor Corbett, a Republican.

* * *

Footnote: This book barely touched on Pennsylvania corruption since 2013. There's been no chance in this sequel to delve into the 499 criminal charges Kane originally filed against former Harrisburg Mayor Steven Reed—great background for which can be accessed in the book *Capital Murder* by Chris Pabst (Sunbury Press)—or the blossoming federal investigation into potential city hall corruption in Allentown and Reading, both spinoffs of the McCord case, with other offshoots still in the wind. The investigation netted six guilty pleas in Allentown and Reading as of January 2016. It appeared to be ongoing. Meanwhile Reed's lawyer, Henry Hockeimer Jr., a prominent white-collar criminal defense attorney with the Ballard Spahr law firm, as of this writing had already moved for the vast majority of charges to be dismissed because they exceeded the statute of limitations (filed too late, based on the law, for the crimes alleged). Reed maintains his innocence. The Reed charges were filed just a few weeks before Kane herself became an accused felon. Rumors at that time were swirling wildly about when Ferman would announce her criminal complaint. Schwartz and some others viewed the timing as political and an effort to distract attention from Kane's own problems).

* * *

(Sources: Interviews in 2015 with DePasquale, Brouillette, Aument, Kauffman, Schwartz, Brandstetter, Rapp and Wedick in 2014; contemporary coverage of Hafer's efforts on WAMs and numerous interviews and conversations with Madonna over many years; discussions with Vereb and news release on his web page; Philadelphia Inquirer and Morning Call stories on first plea in municipal corruption probe in Allentown and Reading; *Capital Murder* by Chris Pabst; Hockeimer's motion to dismiss 388 charges against Reed.)

* * *

Next: Epilogue.

EPILOGUE

By Robert B. Swift

Readers of Brad Bumsted's first book *Keystone Corruption* could be forgiven if they assumed that Pennsylvania had reached its quota of political corruption scandals.

Keystone Corruption explored a century of scandals from the 1906 Capitol graft scandal to Bonusgate's illegal use of taxpayer dollars for political work.

Surely Bumsted's depiction of a century's worth of crimes, bribes and fallen politicians should have sent a sobering message to the political class. Yet in 2013 as *Keystone Corruption* was published, a new wave of Pennsylvania scandals started to shake the political landscape. They have yet to run their course.

Bumsted's second book *Keystone Corruption Continues: Cash Payoffs, Porngate and the Downfall of Kathleen Kane* picks up where the first one left off.

What a parade we've witnessed during the past two years:

- The Turnpike Commission's pay to play case.
- Philadelphia Senator LeAnna Washington's plea deal for using taxpayer resources for political work.
- Philadelphia Rep. J.P. Miranda's guilty pleas in a ghost employee case.
- The abrupt departure of Treasurer Rob McCord in advance of a guilty plea to extortion charges.
- The Abscam-style sting operation that has ensnared six Philadelphia officials in criminal charges. Three legislators plus a former judge had entered guilty pleas as of this writing.
- The influence peddling scandal enveloping the state Liquor Control Board.

- The criminal charges against Attorney General Kathleen Kane for leaking secret grand jury information to a reporter to hurt a perceived foe.
- The porn email scandal that ousted a Supreme Court justice and top Corbett administration officials.

It's all covered here.

While Bonusgate was a legislative branch scandal, the new wave of scandals is more ecumenical reaching into the recesses of the executive branch, judiciary, state row offices and the chief law enforcement agency as well.

One thread links the old and new scandals. That is the reluctance of the state's elected officials to pass tough new anti-corruption laws as a deterrent to would-be lawbreakers.

The response to a generation of legislative leaders going to prison as a result of Bonusgate-related convictions was anemic. A new public open records law, creation of a state website to post information about spending and self-enforcing rules in the Senate and House to ban political activity on legislative time. That's it.

The revelations that Philadelphia lawmakers caught in the "Ali" sting took cash payments led to the chambers again passing self-enforcing rules to ban cash gifts.

But there's been no serious effort to give the cash ban some teeth by putting it into law with stiff penalties for violators.

More comprehensive legislation to ban gifts for public officials is stuck in the legislative whirlpool.

Pennsylvania's campaign and ethics disclosure laws remain weak due to the lack of spending limits and high monetary thresholds for reporting outside income.

Reform proposals outlined in *Keystone Corruption* to provide for outside audits of the Legislature and provide dedicated funding to oversight agencies like the state Ethics Commission and Office of Open Records continue to get short shrift.

New proposals emerge to make the state Inspector General an independent office and create a public integrity commission, but have trouble getting traction.

The bottom line is that reform takes a back seat in Pennsylvania while the scandals continue.

* * *

Swift is the Capitol bureau chief for Times-Shamrock Communication, which includes the Scranton Times-Tribune. He is the author of *Mid-Appalachian Frontier: A Guide to Historic Sites of the French and Indian War.*

* * *

REFLECTIONS

By Franklin Kury

(Author's Note: No one in my time at the Pennsylvania Capitol better earned the reputation of "Mr. Clean" more than former state Senator Franklin Kury, a Sunbury Democrat. People on both sides of the aisle respected him. He was a reformer before reform was cool. He was The Real Deal.

I asked Franklin to provide his thoughts on corruption that's ricocheted through the halls of the Capitol from 2008 through 2016. He served in the House from 1967-72 and in the Senate from 1973-80.

Franklin wrote Article 1, Section 27 of the Pennsylvania Constitution, popularly known as the Environmental Rights Amendment: "The people have a right to clean air, pure water, and to the preservation of the natural, scenic, historic, and esthetic values of the environment." For the uninitiated, changing the state Constitution is a daunting task.

More than four decades after he penned those words, the Pennsylvania Supreme Court would cite the language as part of its reasoning for overturning pre-emption of local zoning in Act 13, of 2012, the landmark legislation that dealt with regulation of natural gas drilling in the Marcellus Shale industry. Few legislators in a lifetime have as much impact as Franklin did with those 25 words. He is the author of *Clean Politics, Clean Streams* by Lehigh University Press, and *Why Are You Here?* by University Press of America—a treatise asking state legislators in every state to re-examine their purpose.)

By Franklin Kury

Brad Bumsted's comprehensive reporting of the criminal and ethical scandals that have afflicted Pennsylvania government from time to time is a stark reminder of the challenge that continues to mar public confidence in government.

Like people in every walk of life, legislators are subject to the temptations of power and position. Sadly, some are not able to resist it.

Wall Street financial houses, churches, West Point cadets, lawyers, doctors, and state universities have been visited by episodes of greed and dishonesty that have discredited them. Legislators and other public officials, as Bumsted has so crisply reported, are no exception.

The test for all of these institutions is how quickly and effectively they deal with a scandal when they become aware of it.

There is no way to know beforehand how any particular person will respond when confronted with the temptations or pressures of power. I served in the legislature with a number of colleagues who I found to be like the others, until a prosecutor and the courts showed otherwise. Most of them resigned before legislative discipline could be administered. The one exception was Senator Frank Mazzei, found guilty of taking bribes for state leases. Even after he was sentenced by the judge, Mazzei claimed he was entitled to stay in office until his appeal was completed. The Senate did not agree and expelled him 49-0 in 1975.

Cases like Mazzei's are clear—a criminal statute was violated and a judicial conviction followed. There are other scandals not so unambiguous, cases of ethics and moral judgment.

Confronting and preventing these issues rests with the legislature itself, an independent branch of government.

The leadership of all four caucuses must make clear the standards of conduct they expect and then set the example in following those standards.

Legislatures are not seminaries. They are not schools to teach right and wrong. Those who serve in public office bring with them the moral values learned at home. The state Capitol can be a tough testing place for those values.

In my experience as a legislator, and later as a lobbyist, the overwhelming majority of legislators bring solid personal conduct codes with them and act honorably within them.

Brad Bumsted's reporting forcefully tells of the few who acted otherwise. There can never be complacency by the public or the legislators themselves in eliminating the stain of scandal from the legislature. Brad Bumsted has made it clear that this challenge will always be with us.